ON HIGH
STEEL

ON HIGH STEEL

STEEL

The Education of
an Ironworker

MIKE CHERRY

Quadrangle / The New York Times Book Co.

BOOK DESIGN: VINCENT TORRE

LIBRARY OF CONGRESS CATALOGING IN PUBLICATION DATA

Cherry, Mike, 1934–
    On high steel.

    1. Structural steel workers—United States—
Personal narratives. I. Title.
HD8039.B82U63   331.7′69′3710924 [B]   74–77935
ISBN 0-8129-0470-2

for Joanne

*Give them great meals of beef
and iron and steel, they will eat
like wolves and fight like devils.*

—Henry V

ACT III, SCENE VII

Contents

A Note To The Reader

THE people in this book are ironworkers. They are the men you see clambering up the columns and walking along the beams that form the skeletons of most tall buildings. They belong to a union called The International Association of Bridge, Structural, and Ornamental Ironworkers. The columns and beams are steel, but the men are called ironworkers. They are *not* called steelworkers. Steelworking is another trade altogether.

I have chosen the things that happen here from a journal that I keep, so they are told pretty much as they actually happened, and the people to whom they happen are real people, although in a couple of places, for fear of lawsuits or sudden blows to the head, I have changed their names.

The final third of this book centers upon the erection of a single building on Sixth Avenue, in New York City. It was "topped out" in the spring of 1971, and was designed to yield an appropriate profit to its builders by virtue of standing long enough to repay the loans floated to finance its construction. If you walked down Sixth from Rockefeller Center to Bryant Park you would pass in its shadow, but you'd be unlikely to pay it any special attention: it's no taller than its neighbors, it has no visible architectural peculiarities, it is not an odd color, and though a good friend of mine fell from its forty-fourth floor to the street, there is no plaque to mark the spot.

First

A foreword, it seems to me, is a device by which an author attempts to protect himself. It provides a platform for apologies, excuses, and confessions of inadequacy. This is mine.

What I've attempted in this book is to make something of the work, life-styles, attitudes, and aims of one trade—ironworking—in some measure more accessible to the general public. There are 175,000 ironworkers in this country, which is about eight-tenths of one percent of the population, and apart from our silhouettes ant-size atop a new bridge or skyscraper, we are pretty much invisible. Generally our friends are others like us, and by and large we don't write books. Most of us scarcely use words at all, tending to make our needs known to each other through inflection, gesture, and yelling. At work we signal each other with arm and hand motions, with bells, and by banging on the iron with wrenches, because the noisiness of a construction site precludes ordinary speech, and most of us, after spending a few years alongside air compressors, jack hammers, unmuffled donkey engines, and welding machines, are deaf anyway. Noise, however, is not the only source of our difficulty with words: We come from a variety of cultures and have a variety of tongues and accents. I'm a white transplanted Southerner. My regular partner is first generation Scotch-Irish. The others in our gang include a Newfoundlander, two American Indians, and an Estonian Jew. Where words might confuse, signals are universal, and if my partner and I have finished connecting a piece of iron, we can communicate this to our operator with a hand signal, even if he's a Transylvanian mute.

Few of us have much education, though I know several ironworkers with some college, and a few with degrees. Our most common recreations are gin mills, movies, and sports, though I know a couple of opera buffs and one balletomane (who tries to keep it a secret). The Newfies are often hockey freaks, and the Indians (most of whom go home to Canada every weekend) are big on snowmobiles.

We get sort of clubby when we drink, tending to collapse back into ethnic groups: Irish in this bar, Newfies in that, Indians in the other, and so on. Like all generalizations, however, this one is a bit leaky. I've spent evenings drinking with Indians (most of my attention focused on trying to figure out what was going on, since when they form a majority they speak Indian), and evenings with the Fish (a not wholly complimentary term for men from Newfoundland, of whom there are in New York a whole bunch), trying to decipher a language which although nominally English is so heavily accented that it can sound, especially after a few shots, as much like Zambesi as anything else, and evenings with White Anglo-Saxon Protestants and White Anglo-Saxon Catholics. But in none of these situations does Language as Word play a central part. Most of us simply don't know a lot of words. It doesn't really matter: I have a Newfie friend who can say "Laird sufferin' Jayesus" in so many ways that it provides specific judgment on everything from a collapsing derrick to a pretty girl at lunchtime. And I stayed on top of the Knights of Columbus building one afternoon after the workday was over, watching the tankers in New Haven Harbor turn slowly into black bugs as the sun went down behind Fisher's Island, while the man beside me, previously known to me only as a loquacious idiot, stood for half an hour stock-still with his mouth shut.

All of which is by way of apologizing to my friends. And to my enemies, too, for that matter. This is mostly a book of praise. Some of it's left-handed, but it's still praise. Those of them who read this will recognize this incident or that, and will probably come for me with spud wrenches to explain to me gently on the top of my head that I haven't got it quite right. But I don't know how to record the set of a man's jaw as he tries to shove a twelve-ton column into place, or the sound of his breathing after he's climbed 135 feet of derrick mast, without some use of words, so if I've gotten an inaccurate inflection here or too long a word there, I can only beg his pardon.

My buddy Patrick and I were drinking one night when he suddenly turned to me and said, "You ever do a wrecking job?" I said yes, and he said that I should avoid them. I nodded. "Don't do wrecking jobs," he added, and lapsed into silence. I said nothing, because Patrick's speeches always begin in the middle, and there is no point in interrupting him. About ten minutes later he said, "Tearing things down is a drag. I like to watch things grow." I didn't answer, and another several minutes passed before he elected to continue. When he did, it was to say this: "A derrick is a great big bird building a steel nest."

Now, the trouble with that is that if you were to ask him if he said it, he'd deny it.

Hey, Patrick! And you, Coley, and Larry, and Louie, and I'll-Drink-To-That: shove it up your nose. I've done the best I could.

ON HIGH
STEEL

Long Before

THE street corner was full of shouting men in yellow hard hats, screaming at drivers to get their cars out of the way. A couple of blocks down Seventh Avenue a police siren was shrieking helplessly, unable to get through the spillback-blocked intersection. One man, with a long steel bar in his hand, told a cab driver that if he didn't get his taxi out of the way, he was going to rip it to pieces and throw it out by hand. From the top of the skeletal building a giant latticework boom was tilting slowly outward. The sun was behind it, and every time I tried to look up at it I sneezed. From the end of the boom there hung a cable ending in an open box about six feet square. A man was standing in it, holding the cable with one hand, making rapid circular motions with his free arm as the box descended. By the time it reached nearly to the street, like a gargantuan spider dropping a single forty-story web, a landing space had been cleared. Men grabbed at the box, steering it this way and that. One man, who had been hauling in the slack on a rope that ran from the box to the street, and who was standing in a 500-foot-long pile of line and completely soaked in sweat, dropped to his knees and clutched his stomach a moment before he was able to get up to help his fellows. Patrolmen arrived and began ordering spectators out of the way. The police car and an ambulance arrived together. As the box hit the ground, the man standing in it reached down and began to gather up a bundle that was now visible on the floor of the box. The others reached in to help, while the ambulance drivers brought a stretcher. It wasn't until I could see a leg sticking out of the pile of jackets in which he was wrapped that I was sure the bundle was a man. His head was so bloody that it was impossible to tell which way it faced.

The injured man was put in the ambulance, and the man who had ridden down in the box with him jumped in beside the stretcher. The doors shut, and the car started away. It went no more than ten yards before skidding to a halt as the rear doors swung open. The man who had jumped in came leaping out, screaming, "The arm! For Jesus' sake, gimme the fuckin' arm!" The men in hard hats began running confusedly in all directions. One man leaned into the box and grabbed a rolled-up jacket. He ran to the ambulance shouting, "I got it! I got it!" He handed over the jacket, and the car sped off again, led down the way by the police.

Most of the spectators resumed their previous paths, though there were scattered calls of inquiry. None of the men in hard hats answered. They stood without talking, taking a few steps in any direction, then returning. One man stood in the street, facing the vanished ambulance, forcing cars to detour around him. There was blood on the dirt, on the sidewalk, and a great puddle of it in the street where the stretcher had banged against the rear of the ambulance as it was being loaded. I caught myself looking at it, wondered why, then turned up Seventh Avenue until I saw a sign that read White Rose Cafe, and went inside.

The bar smelled of roach killer. The three bartenders were identically clad: white shirts with the sleeves rolled up above the elbows, ties pushed inside their shirts above the third button, fresh white aprons tied tightly at the waist. A sign behind the bar warned them not to smoke while on duty. The one who brought my beer, a disinfected Irishman with a faceful of destroyed capillaries, asked what had happened on the corner. I pushed a dollar at him.

"Man hurt on that construction job," I said.

"Bad?" he asked.

"Bad enough, I guess."

"He go off the top?" The man's eyes had a peculiar translucent quality, and I shook my head and turned away from him, hoping he would disappear. He turned, however, toward the center bartender, saying, "Hey, Charlie! Fellow here saw it all." The middle man trotted down to me, asking what had happened. I told him I really

4

didn't know, that I only saw them take the man off in an ambulance.

"Well, who was he?" he persisted. "You know any of those guys?"

"No, I don't know any of those guys."

"Well, then, *what* was he? I mean, was he a white man, or an Indian, Guinea, or what?"

"I don't know."

"A nigger?"

"I don't know. Whatever he is, or was, as you put it, he's missing about a half-gallon of blood. And a face, and an arm. And I didn't come in here to talk about it."

The bartenders looked shruggingly at each other as though I were some kind of nut, and left me alone.

Before

WHEN my wife divorced me I went up to Elmira, because I didn't know anyone there, and rented a room. July and half of August passed without my noticing them. I took out a library card, using it a couple of times a week to check out great heaps of garbage: science fiction, mysteries, fantasy. There was a pizza shop two blocks from my room, and I stopped there periodically, buying three or four whole pies at once. They were stacked in my room and eaten over several days, washed down with warm quarts of beer. I had no refrigerator, nor cared whether the beer was warm or the pizza cold.

By the middle of August I realized I wasn't going back to my job, and spent two days writing a letter of resignation to the school. The first draft said, "You can take school teaching in general, and math in particular, and shove it up your goddam nose." The final version was an utter tissue and employed no profanities, but it accomplished the same end: I was shut of a job I had held for nine years.

At the end of September I was about broke, and began looking for work. It felt strange, at first, being out on the street again, seeing other people, being forced to talk to them. But I began to get used to it, even stopping in from time to time at a bar in the neighborhood. The owner told me that there was a wire mill a few miles down the road that was always short-handed, and I went there to apply. I told the personnel manager pretty much the truth, but he hired me anyway. It was, like all the jobs in the mill, a piece-work operation, which meant that the more wire I drew, the more money I got. The base pay rate was $2.525 an hour. A man willing to break his butt ten or twelve hours a day—he could work as many hours as he wanted—could take home a net of perhaps $120 a week. This was in the late sixties and was enough to get by on if he had no family, children, or desire to own anything.

A majority of the 300 or so men who worked there were from Maine—onetime farmers who had fled their rock-infested fields to follow their cousins and brothers to the riches of the industrial Empire State. Many of them lived in little trailers, overgrown with the weeds of ten or fifteen years of immobility. They were content in their frustration and returned once a year in their battered cars to Maine, where they could visit and despise such of their relatives as had not yet had the sense to leave the rocks and blight.

In February I bought a new car, which caused considerable amazement. "Ai-yup," one would say, sniffing mucus back through one nostril with a knuckle in the other, then making "tssksing" noises as he sucked his teeth into place before going on, "mighty costly, I reckon."

"It's a little car," I said.

"Still," said another, "I'd guess even a little car takes a fair amount a'cash."

"Cash? How the hell would I get cash, working for these wages? I signed a three-year note." This statement produced a whole chorus of disapproving sighs.

"Ought not," said a third, his hands stuffed into the bib of his overalls, "buy things you can't pay cash for, young fella."

"I'm not particularly young, Charlie," I replied, "I'm thirty-five, and I want that car now, before that goddam machine I operate over there sneaks up on me and rips off my head."

"Still," said number two, who could begin a sentence no other way, "man pays a lot more when he don't pay cash." All nodded heads in agreement, and we folded up our lunch pails and started back to our machines. For some days afterward, whenever a man walked past me at my machine, he would shake his head at my foolishness.

That machine was the heaviest in the plant. It was called the "bull block." (The word "bull" shows up a lot in industrial applications, as you'll see. It refers not to hot air, but to heavy labor.) The machine was made up of two parts: a die in front and a three-foot-diameter powered drum behind. I fed the sharpened ends of 1200-pound spools of crude wire, five-eighths of an inch in diameter, through the die, wrapped it around the drum, which drew it on through, yielding finished wire just under a half-inch thick. This I cut into bundles of 400 pounds, bound them in steel straps, and dropped them onto carts. Overhead lifts on rails took most of the weight, but everything still required pushing and pulling, and no part of the device functioned without coaxing, prayer, cursing, and frequent hammer blows. I hated it, and had been sure from the beginning that, sooner or later, it would get me.

I have never known a feeling like that to be wrong: Machines, even simple unpowered hand tools, have explicit and deliberate personalities, and the range of relationships between a man and his machines closely mimics marriage. I have, for example, three twelve-inch crescent wrenches, all made by the same manufacturer and all visibly identical. Only one is a decent tool. It is impossible to say what is wrong with the others; they just don't feel right. I had a Firebird not long ago which with a blower and a four-barrel carburetor would go so fast that I wouldn't want to be specific for fear of retroactive arrest—but it was a neurotic, hostile device, and I had to get rid of it.

I worked in the mill at night, usually, starting anywhere from seven to nine in the evening, quitting anywhere from seven to nine in the morning. To make any money at that job it was necessary to work nonstop. I soon found that eating in snatches while running the machine was (in terms of earnings) worth the stomach bubbles thus produced. Often the machine would break down three or four times in a night, destroying any chance of making money beyond the minimum scale. But, when things were going well, I found myself unable to resist trying to run it faster and faster. This had little, actually, to do with the money: it was the pleasure of seeing completed work pile up, of being able to turn the machine over to the day man, knowing that he would be unable to match what I had done.

And one good night, when the machine had been responsive to my alternate caresses and beatings, when it and I had been running flat out for seven or eight hours, I let my vigilance slide for an instant and it got me. I had been running heavy high-tensile wire. The rack which held the raw spool was some thirty feet from the drum. I was standing beside the drum, baling the previous coil, when the bitter end ran off the rack. It acted like a gigantic spring (the coils were about five feet in diameter), and came flying at the drum, the very tip end hitting me right between the eyes. The force of the blow drove me into the drum itself, which, since it had been running for hours, was just short of red hot. Charlie had been drinking coffee not far away, and I was told afterward that it was he who dragged me off the machine. When I came to, the drum was the first thing I saw, but my first response was nausea at the smell of the blood sizzling on its sides.

The foreman took me to the hospital in his car, and the interns there did a pretty fair job of pulling my nose back out of my skull and suturing my forehead. The skin was split from the hairline to the middle of the nose, so that for some weeks I looked like nothing so much as the House of Usher. The drum had produced second degree burns on one side of my neck and both forearms. The burns healed rapidly, but I still have to have the frames of my reading glasses specially fitted, because of the peculiar shape of the bridge of my nose.

I went to the mill just once after that, to pick up my last check. Because of recurring dizziness I couldn't get a medical clearance to return to work, and at that moment didn't much care if I ever got one.

There was now some money in the bank, since my only standing expenses were $11 a week for the room and a $104 a month for the car. The headaches lasted for about three months. During this time I couldn't read much, nor enjoy a movie, because of them. Drinking seemed to diminish them, and I became, because of this and the gradual reawakening of my ability to pass time with others, a regular in the bar run by the man who had first suggested that I go to work in the wire mill.

There was a small coin-operated pool table in the back of the place, and a blackboard behind the bar carried the name of whoever currently held the table. If you wanted to play, you asked the bartender to put your name up, and thereby eventually challenged the holder of the table. The usual game was snooker, on which I had wasted a large part of my adolescence, so that between headaches I was usually the resident champion. It was through the pool-playing that I became friendly with the next-best player, a young fellow named Patrick. He was about twenty-eight, and insufferably cheerful.

He came in every afternoon about a quarter to five, carrying his hard hat and tool belt with him. He would burst through the door, stalk to the coat stand to hang up his hat and belt, leap astride a stool near the front and holler, "Injun whiskey! And quick, for God's sake!" The bartender would bring him two glasses: one filled with tequila, the other with ginger ale. One glass of ginger ale was enough to wash down six or eight glasses of tequila. His pool game held up fairly well through the first half-dozen glasses, but when it began to slide, he would put away his cue and act out both voices of an old Southern dialogue: "Quittin' time!" he'd shout. Then, immediately jumping a couple of feet to one side, glaring back at the place he had just vacated: "Who dat say 'Quittin' time'? I'se de boss; I tells yawl when's quittin' time!" Half-second pause, then, "Hey, dah, QUITTIN' TIME!" Then he would leap back to his initial place, hunkering over like an ancient cotton-picker, mumbling, "Yassah, yassah," as he put on his hat. He would then throw his tool belt over a shoulder, clap the back of everyone he knew on his way down the bar, and disappear.

One Wednesday night I found, upon returning to my room, a letter which opened up doors I had been trying to keep closed, and I went back out drinking. The next morning I felt pretty bad, and went to the bar at nine o'clock. It was raining.

At a little after ten, Patrick and some of his friends came in, not as noisily as usual. We were nodding to each other as Patrick said, "Be glad you don't work for a son of a bitch like Gill, by the Good Lord."

"Who's Gill?" I asked.

"He's the swine we work for, and a smaller-minded, meaner man was never spawned."

One of the others said, "S'truth, so help me," and another banged his already empty shot glass on the bar and said, "I'll drink to that."

I was introduced around, and in an effort to be friendly, agreed with each man as he took his turn at explaining to me in great detail the causes and effects of the evil Gill's swinishness, or his stupidity, or his "miserability." ("Got more *miserability* t'an any ot'er boss I ever saw," said the last man in his turn.)

Some of what was going on eventually came clear: Patrick and his friends were ironworkers, employed for the moment in erecting the skeleton of a high-rise apartment down the road. They worked in all seasons, hot or cold, but not in rain. According to the rules of the union, the workers must be paid two hours' time for showing up, even though the weather might preclude work. Gill, as the super of the job, must see that they are credited with this time, but has the option of making them wait until ten o'clock for that credit, in case the weather should break. The complaint was that any fool could see it wasn't going to stop raining, and that Gill knew that as well as anyone, and kept them there out of sheer orneriness. One man had told Gill that anybody with half an eye could see that it was going to rain all day, and that he'd be damned if he'd hang around on a fool's notion, and Gill had fired him. This, however, produced no great amount of concern:

"Hell, Bernie, Maxie was just waitin' for an excuse to quit, anyway."

"I'll drink to that," said the man who had said the same thing before, and practically nothing else since.

There was general agreement that Maxie had pretty much been looking for a reason to tell Gill off and get out, and that, after all, why not? Things were good since the strike was settled, the general construction picture was good, and in times like these why in hell should Maxie, or anyone, work for a prick like the evil Gill?

After a little more of this sort of thing the rancor at Gill seemed to blow itself out, and deprived of a focus, the conversation fell away into shapelessness. By noon, only Patrick and I'll-Drink-To-That were left. Patrick and I sat on adjacent stools, but the other man stood, and he never stood still. He would put his weight on his right foot and drink with his left hand, then stand on his left foot and drink with his right hand. He didn't smoke. He was about five feet five and wore a salt-and-pepper goatee. Around midafternoon he suddenly saluted us with his empty glass and slapped me on the back. "Nice to meet you. Patrick, you'll pick me up?" Patrick nodded. It was, I realized, the longest speech the man had made all day. "S'long," he said, and bounced to the door. I waved, turned back to the bar, and hunched over my drink. The hangover was finally fading.

"What're you laughin' at?" asked Patrick.

"How old is that man?"

"Oh," said Patrick, "yes. Some piece of work, he is. About fifty, maybe fifty-one. I saw him climb a two-story column upside down, once. Not that long ago, either." I told him I didn't know enough to know if that was impressive, and he said that in eleven years in the business he'd never met anybody else who could do it at all, not that there was much point to it.

Patrick got drunker than usual that day. He went through his Quittin' Time speech as always, but he pulled the coat tree down trying to get his tool belt, and was unconscious as it lay atop him. The owner called a cab, and I managed to wake him long enough to pry from him the address of his rooming house. I threw him on his bed, pulled off his shoes, and took the cab back to the bar, where I blew myself to one more drink (in reward of my samaritanism) before going home.

We gradually became pretty regular drinking partners, and I found that when the smallness of my room began to work on me, or when demanding letters from my ex-wife's lawyer rankled me, Patrick's windy cheerfulness was a help. Sometimes we played pool; sometimes we just sat swapping lies. New acquaintances are good for altering one's past.

We were bar-hopping one night, knocking back one drink in each place, trying to see if we could hit every gin mill in the area, when a cop flagged us down. We were in Patrick's car, and I leaned over to his side to read the speedometer. "I don't think we're going too fast," I said. Patrick said nothing, but began easing the car over to the side of the road. "Maybe we were weaving too much," I added.

"Maybe so," said Patrick as he got out of the car, "but hide the shotgun, will you?" I looked under all the sweatshirts and overalls that littered the back seat before realizing that there wasn't any shotgun. Then, since I could see the cop and Patrick making agitated gestures at each other, I got out, too. The cop grabbed me by the shoulder and pointed at Patrick. "You know this guy?" he asked. It was such an idiotic question that it was a while before I could answer.

"I never saw him before in my life," I said.

"Then how come you're in his car?"

"What makes you think I'm in his car? I'm standing on the road right here beside you. What makes you think it's his car, anyway? It might be my car."

13

"Well, if it's your car, then you were in it, weren't you?"

"Not necessarily. If it's not my car, my car might be in my garage, in which case I wouldn't be in that one either, would I?"

"My God," said the cop, "you're as crazy as he is." He led me by the arm to the front of the car, and pointed. "Do you know what that thing is?" He was pointing to the end of the hood. From where the hood ornament had once been mounted there was now protruding a horizontal iron bar about a foot long. From the forward end of the bar there hung a wire six inches long, from the bottom end of which there dangled a one-gallon can. I went over and smelled it.

"It's gasoline," I announced.

"Yes," agreed the cop, "it's gasoline."

"Well, if you knew what it was," I asked, "why did you ask me what it was?"

"Never mind that shit," shouted the cop, "what is it *for?*"

"I already told him," interrupted Patrick in tones of pontifical patience, "that it does the same thing for the car that a banana does for a donkey."

"But," I asked, addressing myself to Patrick alone by turning my back on the policeman, "doesn't that make the car want to go straight ahead? How do you steer?"

"Well, it's difficult at the moment, I'll admit," he said, also turning to exclude the cop. "But next week I'm goin' to put a pivot here, at the base of the rod, and run lines back to the steerin' column, and then I think it ought to work better."

I got down beside the front fender and began looking up under the car. "Yes, I see," I said. "There's enough room through here, and, oh! This is fine! There's a giant hole in the firewall next to the clutch pedal. If we welded a pulley here for a fairlead we could run it—"

"Screw you people!" hollered the cop, and started for his car. "You see that bend in the road?" We nodded. "That's the county line." He hitched up his pants before getting in the car. "Cross it!" His wheels showered us with gravel as he drove off. Patrick and I got in the car and dutifully crossed the county line. Neither of us ever mentioned the incident again, but I did wonder how long that thing had been on his car, and how long Patrick would have waited for someone to notice it. And why I hadn't seen it.

At the next gin mill there were a number of ironworkers whom Patrick knew. We stood at the front with three or four, listening to their stories about their jobs, but Patrick kept glancing at a group of men in the back. I went to take a leak, and he came in behind me.

"You want a job?" he asked.

"Doing what?" I said.

"Ironworking."

"I don't know anything about it."

"So what? You can learn, can't you?"

"Yeah, sure. I guess so . . . but I thought you practically had to be God's nephew to get a book in your union."

"You won't get a book. You'll work on permit. Go back and have another beer. I'll talk to you later." He dashed out, and I returned to listen to more stories. Patrick closeted himself with one of the men from the group in the rear. They talked for several minutes, Patrick smiling broadly and nodding his head vigorously every so often. Eventually they went to sit at a table, and Patrick motioned me over.

The other man's name was Jack. He seemed around forty, had gray curly hair, and no patience with small talk. "Are you a drunk?" he asked.

"No."

"Show up regular?"

"Yes."

"You know anything about the work?"

"No, but I learn. . . ." He waved me off.

"You can follow orders?"

"Yes."

"Keep yourself safe?"

"Sure."

"Sure? Don't hand me any of that 'sure' shit. Safe is a matter of workin' at it all the time." He stood up, and Patrick and I followed suit. "I'll put you on because Patrick asked me to and I trust his judgment, so that means you owe him. You understand that, of course." It was a statement, and I nodded assent. "Be at the Nicholson shanty at the Frederick Building at 7:30 Tuesday. Nice to meet you." He didn't offer to shake hands. We all nodded at each

15

other briefly, and the man left. Patrick went to the bar for new drinks while I just stood there, trying to figure the whole thing out.

When Patrick came back with his tequila and my beer, I asked him to give me some idea of what the hell I was supposed to do.

"How much did you make at the wire mill?" he asked, instead of answering.

"Well, the base rate was just over $2.50," I said, "but I was pretty good at it and usually could get it up to near $4, anyway."

"You are now earning $7.63 an hour," said Patrick.

"But, how?"

"Just do what you're told. Keep yourself safe, like Jack said. You won't have any trouble; the building's all up, anyway. I'm not goin' to tell you anything about what to do, because at this point you don't even know the right questions to ask." He was looking at his watch as I tried to question him further. I was still in midquery when he sang out, "Quittin' time!" From the front of the bar someone stole the other part of his dialogue:

"Who dat say 'Quittin' time?'" Patrick ran to the front and grabbed the man by the throat.

"*I'se* de boss! *I* tells you when's quittin' time." Then he turned to face the whole bar and bellowed, "QUITTIN' TIME!" ran laughing to his car, and drove off.

It was a $6.00 cab ride back to my room.

PART 1

LOCATIONS

Three things are to be looked to in a building: that it stand in the right spot; that it be securely founded; that it be successfully executed.

—GOETHE

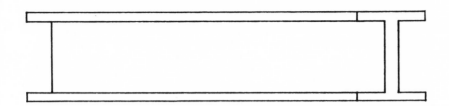

N the twenty-third floor of the Frederick Building there was a small Chicago boom rigged, and my first job as an ironworker was to go out on the sunshade to push it around.

A Chicago boom is simply a pole that sticks out of the side of a building, rather like a fishing pole. It has a line dropping from its end, like a fishing pole, with a hook on the end of the line, like a fishing pole, and it is used to raise things from beneath it, like a fishing pole.

Its base is both pivoted and hinged, so that it can be swung from side to side and tilted from the vertical to nearly horizontal. At its top is a sheave (pulley) or set of sheaves, through which is passed a cable. The inside end of this cable leads to an engine; the other terminates in a weight ball and the hook, to which is attached the material to be lifted or lowered. A second cable runs from another drum on the engine to the top of the boom and is used to change the boom's vertical angle, which is called "booming up" or "booming down." Lateral movement of the boom is controlled either by hauling on a pipe shoved horizontally through the boom near its base or by pulling on ropes leading from about midboom to the building on either side. Or sometimes by a hybrid combination: pole for one direction, rope for the other. The load being handled can thus be placed anywhere within the horizontal arc of the boom: Booming up or down moves the load closer or farther to or from the building; swinging the boom sideways moves the load to the left or right. The engine takes care of moving the boom up or down, and of raising or lowering the load, but swinging the load is done manually. The man who does this takes his title from the system in which a horizontal pipe is attached to the

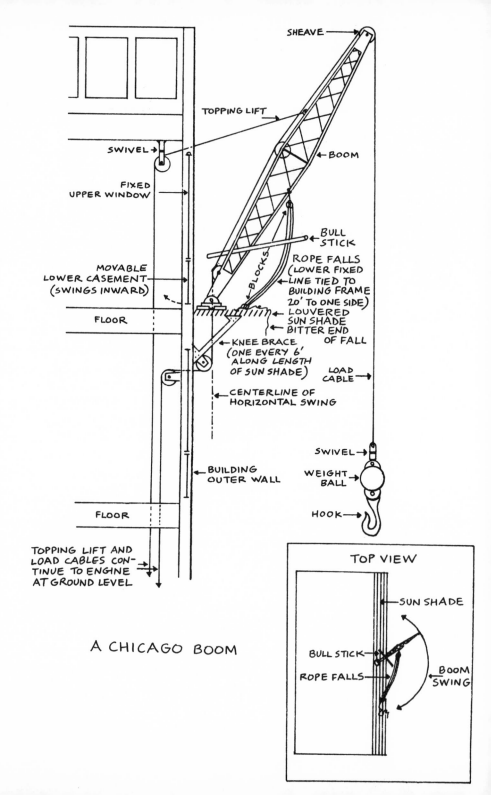

SHEAVE

TOPPING LIFT

SWIVEL

BOOM

FIXED
UPPER WINDOW

BULL
STICK

MOVABLE
LOWER CASEMENT
(SWINGS INWARD)

ROPE FALLS
(LOWER FIXED
LINE TIED TO
BUILDING FRAME
20' TO ONE SIDE)

BLOCKS

FLOOR

LOUVERED
SUN SHADE
BITTER END
OF FALL

KNEE BRACE
(ONE EVERY 6'
ALONG LENGTH
OF SUN SHADE)

LOAD
CABLE

CENTERLINE OF
HORIZONTAL SWING

SWIVEL

WEIGHT
BALL

BUILDING
OUTER WALL

HOOK

FLOOR

TOPPING LIFT AND
LOAD CABLES CON-
TINUE TO ENGINE
AT GROUND LEVEL

A CHICAGO BOOM

TOP VIEW

SUN SHADE

BULL STICK

ROPE FALLS

BOOM
SWING

boom: He is the "bullstick" man. The "stick" part is self-explanatory; the "bull" part becomes so the moment you try to push. Old hands never tire of telling new men that the only two prerequisites of the ironworking trade are a size eighteen shirt and a size three hat.

I hadn't given much thought to working at heights when I started toward the job that morning. Jack hadn't asked if heights bothered me, and besides, Patrick wouldn't just throw me to the wolves. There probably wasn't any open work, anyway; the building was structurally complete, and most of what remained was "finishing" work: inside alterations, the installation of window frames and steel door bucks, cutting and tacking the steel sheets that were to serve as weather-facing on the tops of the towers. It is the kind of end-of-the-job messing around that is called "tit work." The opposite of "tit work," of course, is "bull work."

The super (big boss) introduced me to the pusher (little boss) and told him to put me on the bullstick. On the elevator I thought better of asking him what a bullstick was. He hadn't seemed overjoyed to get me in his gang. The elevator stopped at twenty-one, and we used stairs to get to twenty-three. On the climb he asked me if it was my first job, and I nodded that it was. He made a face that would have gone nicely with the discovery that his girlfriend had syphilis, but said nothing. I wondered what had made him ask the question, not knowing then that new men and old hands don't even walk the same way.

We picked our way through giant heaps of machinery. In a larger building—over, say, thirty stories—it would not have been quite so crowded. As a rough rule, every fifteenth floor of the large building is a "machine floor." It takes a tremendous amount of machinery to make a large structure functional: elevator motors and controls, air conditioning machinery and literally miles of ducts, heating boilers and pipes, giant transformers and their connections to the electrical systems, telephone relays, water reservoirs, plumbing stacks . . . In the World Trade Center there is enough air conditioning equipment to cool every industrial, business, and residential structure in the entire city of Mount Vernon, New York.*

* Mount Vernon is a town of some 75,000 people. Numbers are funny things and don't have to be very large before the mind boggles. The World Trade Center is a god-awful large structure, but does it mean anything to point out that it contains over

21

But in this building, large for upstate but still only twenty-three floors, all support systems had been put in one place. And it looked like everybody in the county was working there at once. The tin-knockers, trying to hang ducts, were bumping into the electricians, trying to string wiring, who were banging into the glaziers, who were trying to set windows while screaming at the plumbers who put an occasional pipe through an occasional sheet of glass. Those panes, called "lights," were over seven feet high and thirteen feet long, and after seeing the mess made when one fell, I decided that on the street I would never again walk near an unfinished building.

The pusher stopped as he came to an outside wall in which the glass was already installed. A short dark fellow was standing by the window, holding a three-button electrical box in one hand and a two-way radio in the other. "Julie," said the pusher, "this is your bullstick man. He's on permit, but he's what you get, so don't bitch." The man shrugged his shoulders. The pusher turned to me. "What'd you say your name is?" I said, "Mike."

He looked at me as though he either hadn't heard or didn't care to listen, and went on without pause: "Okay. This is your engineer, Julie. He's a Guinea bastard, but he's your engineer. Now c'mere." He dropped to his hands and knees, opened a low casement window that formed the bottom foot and a half of the wall, and swung himself outside. I followed him and found that we were standing on a panel of sheet metal louvers some three feet wide, running like a horizontal and only slightly more heavily built venetian blind along the length of the building side, about ninety feet. The boom, two stories high (a virtual toy, I discovered later) was anchored to the base of these louvers a few feet along the wall. I could see down to the street through the spaces between the slats, and all I could think of was, What Am I Doing Here? I didn't get dizzy; I didn't get nauseous; I just kept thinking, What In Jesus' Holy Name Am I Doing Here? I grabbed genteely for the first piece of rigging I could reach. It was a manila line an inch thick, but to me it looked like thread. I tried very hard to keep my face empty. The pusher trotted off down the shades,

---

200,000 *tons* of steel? Probably not. There are 46,600 windows in it, but what kind of number is that? It's enough windows so that if a different resident of Elmira, New York, stood behind each one, there would still be a few hundred windows left unoccupied.

checking the rigging on the far side of the boom. When he turned and saw what I was holding onto he jumped back to where I was and yanked the line out of my hands.

"For Christ's sake, watch what you hold onto! You got the bitter end of a slipped hitch here, and if you put any weight on it, it'll pull out and you'll be holdin' ten feet of slack." Then he added, sneeringly, "The man said you could handle this."

"I *can* handle it," I insisted. "I just haven't had a chance to learn the rigging on this thing, yet." I was mad enough at being yelled at to forget for a moment that I was mainly scared.

"Well, don't try to learn by trial and error. When you want to know something, ask. In this business, you only get one mistake. Besides, you don't need to hang onto anything out here." He gave the entire sunshade a glance of withering dismissal. "You could roller skate on this thing." He gave the line I had been holding onto one quick jerk and it came free. My security had been wholly illusory.*

"That was only a tieback, see?" I said I saw. "Now look; when Julie signals you to swing left, stand here and push on this pipe. When you have to swing right, come over here and pull on this fall." A fall is a line riven through two blocks. Sailors call it a block and tackle. "That's all you do. Swing when Julie tells you to. Absolutely don't do anything else. If he goes to take a shit and you hear his radio

---

* Last summer we were doing a job in a factory in Jersey and needed a seam welded between two beams we had installed near the roof of the plant. The only welder available was a moonlighting fireman named Bob Henigan who took a quick look at the six-story open drop and decided it wasn't his cup of tea. He agreed, finally, to give it a shot, but wanted a length of line brought along with which to tie himself off (which means on) before starting the weld. (Tying off, by the way, is quite sensible, if you have time. You don't, very often.) He was determined but jittery, and it took him twenty minutes to crawl out to the work area. When he got there, I handed him his line, which he wrapped around himself about six times, around the beam he was sitting on about six times, then around himself a couple of times more before spending about ten minutes tying the biggest damned knot in the bitter end you ever saw. It began at his belly button and ended below his crotch. When he finished he gave the whole spaghetti dinner a reassured pat. I took one look and guessed that when he was finished welding we'd have to cut him loose. He set reasonably happily to work, unable, of course, to see anything from beneath his shield but the weld itself.

Five minutes later the whole thing had untied itself and hung in festoons all around him and every which way over the beam. I called the situation to his attention and helped him retie. Bobby is a sensible sort, however. To lunch the next day he brought a ham sandwich and the Boy Scout Manual of Knots.

squawking, don't answer it. Just stay put. I'll check on you later." He gave me a patronizing thump on the helmet, danced along the louvers, ducked in a single motion through the low casement, and was gone. I stood motionless, examining all the lines for safe holds. Julie's agitated knocking at the window went unheeded until I felt I knew where I could and could not go. Eventually I began to respond, but in spite of his repeated gestures of exasperation, I moved very slowly. I was functioning, but just barely.

The scene smacked of a dumb show. Julie would beat on the glass in response to instructions that came from his walkie-talkie. He accompanied his tapping with exaggerated gesture and shouting. He knew I couldn't hear the yelling, but he kept it up anyway. (Possibly it made him feel better: Knowing that it couldn't be heard, he probably indulged in some pretty villainous Neapolitan language.) I pushed and pulled in virtual silence. The glass being raised was being landed on a lower floor, and I saw none of it. My vision ended where the load cable ran down past the louvers. I was not about to lean over the edge to see what was going on. The meaningless view of the street that came up through the narrow slits between the louvers was quite sufficient.

That afternoon, when I was changing clothes, Jack came over to ask how things had gone. I said all right. He asked if the height had bothered me. I said no, but by the way how high was it? He said he didn't know exactly, but the floors were unusually high, so it was probably 320 feet, give or take a dozen.

I lay awake most of the night wondering what the hell I was doing and why people like me tell lies about whether or not they are scared. I assumed there were people like me.

It got easier, though. I stayed on the boom for about a week, and although I can't say that in that time I learned to like it, I did get to where I wasn't terrified.

My first insight into the rigidity of union procedures occurred during that week. The boom was being used to lift glass for the glaziers. They were landing crates on the seventeenth floor, but they weren't allowed to handle the whole operation. In construction the job pie is carefully cut up and bitterly fought over. Control of the machinery that moves the boom and its load is the province of the operating engineers. Julie's bell box—the thing with three buttons, in this case (it signals the operator)—is Julie's, or a brother engineer's, alone. The Chicago boom is erected by ironworkers, and all its functions other than electromechanical belong to them. The glass belongs to the glaziers, who are the only ones with the right to unload it.

I was unaware of all this, or that it mattered, until lunchtime that first day. At 11:15 Julie put his hand in front of his mouth with his fingers toward his nose and flapped them against his thumb. This, I realized, was the signal for lunch. By the time I completed a cautious scramble in from the sunshade, he was gone. I headed on down, but found when I got to the shanty that none of the ironworkers was there, except for the super, who was bent over a blueprint. "What're you doing here?" he demanded.

"I came down for lunch."

"Lunch is at 12:00."

"But Julie went to lunch."

"He goes at 11:30."

"Then why don't I?"

"Because ironworkers eat at 12:00."

"But it wastes an hour. If I'm willing to go at the time the gang I'm working with goes, why not?"

"Because our contract says we go at 12." And, indeed, that is where the matter remained. Every day Julie and the glaziers started down at 11:15, to be on the ground by 11:30, and I stayed up top with my finger up my ass until 11:45. They came back at 12:00 and stood around with their fingers up their asses until I got to the top at about 12:45, after starting up at 12:30. This is the way it is, and everybody in the industry understands that this is the way it is. Devotion to the literal terms of the contract is categorically just this blind. It has its origins, however, in the fight for better conditions, and is not likely to lessen. Before the unions developed strength the employers called all the shots, and a man did what he was told or was replaced. If the company told a gang to erect iron in the rain, it was erected in the rain. Erection is never a safe job, and in the rain it becomes a great deal more hazardous, but a man did it under whatever conditions prevailed, because if he didn't, someone else got his job. In the dark hungry days of the thirties, gangs of out-of-work ironworkers hung about on the streets around job sites, so that when a man fell, they would be instantly available to take his place. The pay of a man who fell was stopped at the time of his fall. Today things are better. When a man falls today, his widow and children are paid for the full day, even if he fell at 8:15 in the morning.

In the fall of 1929, when construction was started on the Empire State Building, an ironworker grossed $15.40 for a day's work. His benefits beyond that were negligible. Yet, if he went to buy life insurance, he discovered that he was placed in one of the highest risk categories, and this remains true today. It is also true that one out of every fifteen ironworkers is killed within ten years of entering the trade.* Illness and accident benefits, union-sponsored life insurance, protection against overly hazardous working conditions—these are the results of constant struggle, and it is not greatly surprising that fights between the various unions over who is to be awarded what kind of work sometimes descend to the picayune.**

So during the time that I pushed that bullstick and pulled that rope fall, the operation stopped at 11:15 and resumed at 12:45. There were on the street a truck driver, his helper, and five glaziers. There were, on seventeen, where the glass was being landed, four more men. There was an engineer on top, and there was me. There was an operator for the engine. That's fourteen. Although there are some differences in the rates of pay, the average cost to the company of these men— hourly pay, insurance coverage, maintenance, medical services, book- keeping, and so forth—was around $20 per man per hour. It's considerably higher today.

---

* When my ex-wife found out what I was doing for a living, she said, "Well, if you're going into *that* line of work, you'd better get some life insurance for the kids' sakes." I talked with a number of agents. The best deal I could make was with one of the big mutuals: $25,000 straight life for just under $600 annual premium. They offered to renegotiate when I got out of the business.

I cannot recall ever meeting an ironworker with a private life policy of any size.

** White-collar workers, and to a considerable extent the younger blue-collar workers, have no gut understanding of the incredible bitterness of that struggle. Organized labor is regarded by many today as the most powerful force in the nation, but times of near destitution are well within the memories of the older men. Samuel Gompers' position hasn't been much changed: He explained what his members wanted with the word "more."

At every lunch I did nothing for the half hour after the others were gone. Ten bucks. Thirteen men waited a half hour daily for my return. Another $130. It comes to $700 a week. There was nothing the least unusual about this loss of time; in fact, it was so slight that no one at any level paid the least attention to it, nor would they have given a damn if told about it. It's a very small example, however, and could make one wonder about waste in a large building, such as, say, the Chrysler Building, which put to work 1500 men from twenty-two separate trade unions and uncounted numbers from more than fifty related subtrades and professions. Or the Empire State Building, on which at the peak of construction over 6000 men were at work.

The super summed it up for me neatly when I asked what I was expected to do between the time the gang went to lunch and the time I went to lunch: "Keep your damned ass out of the way." So I did.

I kept my ass out of the way, on the bullstick for a week, and for several more weeks when I was assigned to check for missing sash screws or to grind down welding beads on the decorative railings in the patio. And when the job was over, so that there was no longer any place to keep it out of the way, I went to the union hall and sat on it, along with everybody else whose job had come to an end, or who had gotten fired, or quit.

There is nothing about a hiring hall that would be within the ken of (or, probably, acceptable to) a white-collar worker, unless you'd care to stretch things enough to parallel it to an office temporary outfit. In theory, though by no means always in practice, a man in a hiring hall has no control over where he is going to work. The employer has no control over whom he is going to hire. The worker goes wherever he is sent; the employer accepts whoever arrives. The union has absolute power in this matter.

The worker, therefore, casts his primary loyalty to his union, and the employer, for his part, sees nothing to be gained by dangling extra incentives in front of his employees. It makes for minimal output, and it doesn't do a hell of a lot for a man's pride.

When a man is out of work, he goes to the hall. He sits, and if things are good, he is sent to a job. If he doesn't like it, he quits and goes back to the hall in hopes of being sent to a better place.

Jobs out of many locals are to a large extent a matter of patronage and good reputation. Supers' in-laws get work, and good men get work, most of the time. The business agents who run the halls can punish men whom they feel need punishing by not sending them out, or get even with men who might have opposed them in the previous local elections by not sending them out. There is less of this in the larger locals than the smaller, but there is always plenty. All locals are under the supervision of the International, but who goes out on what jobs is much too small a matter for International scrutiny.

So I had my first experience at sitting in the hall. It was a short one, because times were good. I've had some long ones. But this time in the hour between 7:00 and 8:00 nearly everybody was sent out. By 8:30 there were just two of us left. I had about concluded that we must both have leprosy when the B.A. (Business Agent), who had a voice like a tugboat full of whiskey, stuck his head over the counter and yelled to the other guy, "What're you doin' here, Harry? You get fired up in Utica?"

"Naw," said the one called Harry, who had shiny new teeth in a yellow leather face, "it was just a bad job."

"You layin' out a lot drinkin'?"

"I never lost no time to it." Harry rubbed at the stubble on his face. I couldn't tell whether I was watching the truth or consummate acting in his sudden conversion of defiance to diffidence. "Besides," he went on, "I got t'e wife and kids in an apartment here, now, and I'm gettin' too old to boom around all t'e time."

The B.A. looked disgusted. "Awright, Harry," he snorted, "you know Callahan?" Harry nodded. "Well, he's takin' out t'at railroad bridge on Sagamore. Go over t'ere." He wrote on a slip of paper and handed it to Harry, whose thank-yous were cut off as the man yelled at me, "Whadda *you* want?"

My God, I thought, he should be giving classes in Naked Aggression, Postgraduate Level. It would have seemed entirely appropriate if his squash-like sodden nose had suddenly flipped up to reveal a 105-millimeter howitzer swiveling in the bald turret of his head. Everything about him was altogether tank-like.

"A job," I said, trying to sound as guttural as he did.

"I don't know you." He looked at me appraisingly, apparently weighing whether it might dirty his treads to roll right over me. "You been workin'?"

"Yeah. I just finished up at the Frederick Building. I didn't get fired, Friday was layoff day for the whole . . ." He waved me into silence.

"I know it was layoff day. How long was you t'ere?"

"Seventeen weeks."

"You out-of-town book?"

"No, I'm on permit. I've never been here in the hall before; I got the job through Ja . . ." He waved me off again. You'd have thought I was a fly.

"T'at's just finishin' work," he sneered. "I got nuttin' for you."

I was dismissed. "Finishin' work" was apparently comparable to emptying bed pans. But there was no reason for Jack to sponsor me any further, and it looked to me as though if the B.A. didn't send me out now, he never would. He was right, of course; I didn't know anything about ironworking. But once, on a coffee break, one of the guys had spent five minutes showing me how to work an oxyacetylene torch, and I decided I'd better say so.

"I can burn."

"You can burn," he muttered, sounding exactly like me but an octave lower. His gun turret revolved idly about the room. There seemed to be some confusion at Command Level. "*What* can you burn?" Oh, derision! It was a tone evenly divided between Nasty and Long-Suffering.

"Anything that melts," I said, committed now to counterattacking.

"Don't shit me."

"I ain't shittin' you." We stood facing each other for a moment, then he looked away at the wall clock and finally down at the counter.

"Awright," he growled finally, "go to t'is address. Go burn." He wrote something on a slip of paper and handed it to me. I took it and turned to go. "Your assessments paid up?" he yelled after me.

"Yeah," I called back, and left before anything else could happen.*

---

* Assessments are monies paid to the local. All ironworkers pay them. The amount varies, depending upon whether one is a book man or working on permit, and upon what local has gotten you the job. In that local, at that time, I paid a base figure of $2.50 weekly plus $0.15 an hour for actual time worked. It came to $8.50 for a forty-hour week.

When I got to the parking lot, Harry was sitting in his car, drinking from a bottle in a brown paper bag. He called to me as I started by, "Hey, Mac! He send you out?" I nodded, looking at the slip for the first time. "Yes," I said, "I think it's the same place he's sending you." "Yeah, I t'ought he might," he replied, "t'ere's plenty of work." Harry had trouble working his new teeth, or so I thought. I hadn't yet realized that for a great many ironworkers there is no "th" sound. In fact, I wondered for a time what kind of entryway must grace a popular local gin mill called by everyone the Tree Doors Cafe, only to find out that all it had, of course, was an arrangement of three doors.

Harry started his engine. "You got wheels?" he asked. I nodded. "Okay, you folla me." I got in my car and followed him. We went a mile or so before pulling up in front of a gin mill. I put my car behind his and followed him inside. The bar had red vinyl stools with several layers of adhesive tape repairs in varying shades of dirt. Harry put a ten on the bar, ordered a seven and beer back. I ordered a bottle of beer. We exchanged names and small talk until I said, "I got sent out to go burning."

"So did I. T'at's all t'e job'll be."

"I don't know jack shit about burning."

"T'en why'd he send you out?"

"Because I told him I did. I haven't spent ten minutes with a torch in my whole life." When Harry laughed, I was sure it had been all right to say these things, and went on: "Tell me what I need to know, Harry. I need the job."

"Not much to it," he shrugged. "It'll be heavy iron, riveted panels. All railroad bridges are riveted. Watch if you have to burn one; rivets pop. Top and bottom flanges'll be four, maybe five ply, and rusty. You can't burn rust, it just makes slag, so try to keep t'e cuts clean. And wide. Weave t'e torch in t'e cut so's to make a nice wide slot. It helps if you're hung over, 'cause the shakes'll take care of t'e weave for you. I'll tell 'em you're my partner so you can work close to me 'til you get t'e hang of it. It's dirty work; you'll go home at night lookin' like a nigger." Harry put down two more drinks while telling me this. I realized that he'd recognized my greenness and was grateful that he wasn't using his knowledge to put me down. A lot of guys will do that, screaming that the hall only sends them assholes to work with, sending beginners off for tools that don't exist, explaining things backwards. Commonplace as such behavior is, it's a pain in the ass.

"It'll probably have a galvanized deck," Harry went on, "like a grid. We took out one a lot like it over t'e same canal a couple years back. You got to watch galvanized—it makes you sick. T'e steward is supposed to bring you milk when you burn galvanized."

"Why is that?"

"T'e burnin' makes a poison gas. Makes you vomit. T'e milk stops t'e sickness. Let's have a drink." He began making signals to the bartender.

I looked at the clock behind the bar. "Hadn't we ought to go?"

Harry looked at me disgustedly. "What t'e fuck for? T'e contract says we gotta be t'ere by 10:30." So we had another drink before going on to the job. I soon realized it is standard practice not to show up at a new job until the last minute. The company has to pay you from 8:00 anyway, and getting there at 8:30 would be giving something for nothing. You might try showing up at 9:30, which might lead your new bosses to think you were responsible and ambitious; but if you showed up at 8:30, they'd write you off as a fool.

We got there at 10:15, and I made my first mistake almost immediately. While dragging a length of torch hose across the ground, I knocked over another man's container of tea. His name was Timmy Shaughnessy, and he began to scream hideously, "You knocked over my iced tea! You knocked over my iced tea!" He was as skinny a man as I've ever seen, about six feet tall with red-grey thinning hair, large hands, and feet like canal boats. He was wearing straw-colored stovepipe levis whose baggy seat heightened my sudden impression that he was made of bones without flesh. He looked like Ichabod Crane, but was dancing around like an electrified scarecrow.

"Well, for crying out loud," I said, "I'll buy you another one."

"But it was *my* iced tea! Goddam it, it was *my* iced tea!"

"What's so special about your iced tea?" I asked, and went over to pick up the styrofoam cup. I smelled it, then looked at him. He didn't really seem to be angry so much as unstrung. His hands were shaking. I handed him my car keys. "In the trunk," I said, "there's a whole bottle of iced tea. Help yourself."

Timmy went immediately to the car and opened the trunk. When

31

he saw the bottle of vodka he turned, looking around on the dirt until he found an old coffee container. This he wiped out with his bandanna. Then he filled it with vodka and carried the cup with him back to work. His ill-humor vanished immediately, and for the balance of the day both he and Harry went out of their way to help me figure out what I was doing. They were equally solicitous of my car.

Since Timmy had no car, I soon found myself picking him up in the mornings and dropping him off at his gin mill in the afternoons. He shook worse at the beginning of the day than anybody else I've known. Some of the job could be reached only by walking across some light bracing—really small stuff, three inches wide, six inches deep. It was too small to crawl on; it had to be walked. A fall wouldn't have mattered much, beyond being embarrassing, since the bridge was only a few feet above the water, which was only a slow-moving canal with gently sloping banks. But there was no way that Timmy could get out there early in the morning. He would clean his torch, or help unload any trucks of gas and air that might have arrived, or set up other men's torches for them, but he would not cross over on that small stuff. By ten o'clock, when we'd normally have had our break and by which time he'd have had two or three containers of iced tea, he could dance across.

There were six of us in that gang: Callahan, who was the pusher, Harry, Timmy, two guys I've never seen since, and me. An ironworker is allowed a short break in the morning, a half hour for lunch, and a break in the afternoon. Somebody has to be the coffee boy. (Sometimes, a man *wants* to be the coffee boy. I had a job in Bridgeport one time when I was overjoyed to be the coffee boy. It was in the dead of winter, with the thermometer running from zero to four or five degrees, with the wind usually blowing half a gale, and everybody was volunteering to go for the coffee.) On a big job there are usually a number of apprentices, and one or more of these will be named coffee boy. Actually, apprentices are called "punks," which is not a pejorative term. (Should a punk be offended anyway, he can take some comfort in the realization that at some point in the past, his boss was a punk. Such are the compensations of the guild system.)

On the bridge job, though, we had no punks. Just the six of us, an engineer, and his oiler. The engineer ran the crane; his oiler fueled and maintained it. They belonged to a different union, and they got their own coffee. Sending two men for coffee for a total of eight people struck me as rather like the lunch problem on the Chicago boom, but by then I had learned not to suggest things. As the man who knew the least, I became the coffee boy. In the years since, I've worked in some strange gangs, but that one holds the drinking championship. I still have one of my lists, written on the back of a dues receipt. It's about average for that gang's morning needs: a pint of Schenley, a pint of vodka, a pint of V.O., six cans of beer, two Danish, one English, and one coffee, light and sweet.

Technically there was supposed to be no drinking. Some companies, such as American Bridge, pretty successfully enforce this rule. Some companies make noises but are careful not to look too closely. Some, like the little upstate outfit for whom we were taking down the bridge, ask only that it doesn't show in front of inspectors and mucky-mucks. Pints were carried in hip pockets and beer drunk from cans pushed inside gloves, and there was never any trouble. I never saw anybody behave stupidly on the job except Harry, once, and when he did Callahan merely sent him home to sleep it off. It was summer, the work was heavy, and a man using a cutting torch all day long can sweat out a hell of a lot of booze.

Most of the ironworkers in the town lived in the same neighborhood. There were frame two-story houses, elm and oak trees, squirrels, and a gin mill whose only identification was a tiny neon sign in one window that read, Utica Club Beer. Timmy and I stopped there a couple of nights a week after work. That is, I stopped there a couple of nights; Timmy stopped every night. There was no shanty on the job, and we were all so dirty after work that if we wanted to drink, we were pretty well forced to drink there; I doubt if any other bar would have let us in.

Once, after we'd been there for several hours and our conversation had lapsed completely, after Timmy had drunk perhaps a quart of vodka since work, after I had reached that point at which one merely wonders without moving what one is doing there, he suddenly said into his glass, "Cold, cold, cold, empty, empty, empty, dreadful, dreadful, dreadful." His voice had lost the street accents completely. He looked up at me, and I looked back at him without answering.

"Do you know what that is?" he said. "I'll tell you what it is, but you must never, never, reveal it." He lowered his voice to a whisper and leaned his head so close to mine that when he spoke the spit went all over my face. "It's Chekhov!" He turned away.

I watched him for a moment, then took a napkin from the bar to wipe my face. I looked at the dirt that came off on it and thought, "That bigot Harry is right: It is a dirty job; I am black."

Timmy seized his glass as though it were a snake, and when he swallowed, you'd have thought he was biting off its head. But he put it down quietly, and when he picked it up again, he drained it quietly. Then he signaled the bartender for another, got off his stool, and went into the bathroom. In a moment I could hear him throwing up. The sound almost had the same effect on me.

He was gone for some time, but when he came back he had washed his face and hands, his eyes had cleared somewhat, and his walk was reasonably steady. He picked up his drink and drained it. "Don't know a thing about me, do you?" he said, looking at the bottom of his glass. I agreed that I didn't. "Well," he reflected, "it's just as well. It's just as well. People spend too much time telling other people about themselves." He turned his glass upside down on the bar drain before continuing. "I will tell you this one important thing about myself, however: It's my bedtime." With that he walked out the door. I finished my beer and drove home. On Fulton Street a cat jumped out from between two cars and I ran over it.

The next morning, the night before was not mentioned. On the ride to work Timmy was completely silent. He seemed to be shaking, somehow, more than usual. I parked the car and reached in the back for the thermos as the 7:30 news was beginning. Work started at 8:00, but most of us got there at least a half hour early. Getting to work early has been a habit of mine in any job, but I was surprised to see how common it is among construction workers. Later I met many men who regularly showed up more than an hour early. Some were gin rummy freaks who came early to play, but many came to read the morning paper and drink coffee. There were also some who, even in the dead of winter, sat eating doughnuts and drinking cold beer.

I poured tea into the cap of the thermos and poked at a Danish. Timmy got a styrofoam cup from the glove compartment and half filled it with vodka. On top he poured a finger of tea. His day had begun.

The bridge was 90 feet long: two 45-foot spans supported in the center by a concrete piling. We worked from one shore to the center for three weeks, then moved the crane to the opposite shore and repeated the operation. The main spans were just as Harry had said they would be: riveted multilayer I-beams. They were five feet from the top flange to the bottom. The flanges were five-ply in most places, each ply made of half-inch steel. They were cinched to one another with rivets. There were so many rivets—one every four inches in both directions—that walking along the top of the beams was like walking on a pebble beach. Joining each of the main spans to its neighbor were a series of slightly smaller beams, three to four feet deep, spaced about every ten feet. There were diagonal braces at the joints, and a good deal of light iron at stress points. It was this maze of small stuff, often called "needle beams," that Timmy avoided in the early morning. Over this entire assembly there was a grid of galvanized iron, nothing more than a heavier version of the ventilation grids to be found in the sidewalks above the cellars of city buildings.

In order to lift out the grid, we cut it into sections some ten by fifteen feet. They were lifted from the bridge and landed on shore by the crane, cut into much smaller pieces, then loaded onto trucks. Harry and I, by default the two most agile men in the gang (Timmy generally had the shakes and the other two were old men), were generally the ones sent down into the substructure of the bridge to cut loose the grid's bottom welds. The two old guys sat on the surface of the grid, cutting it into sections and complaining about working with galvanized. Our torches were hooked to "banks." These are interconnected bottles of, respectively, gas and air.* Timmy was in charge of

---

* Oxyacetylene torches develop considerable heat—on the order of 2300 degrees. In a moment of exceptional stupidity one day, while burning sitting down, I managed to pass the torch across my own calf. It melted my green synthetic socks into my leg,

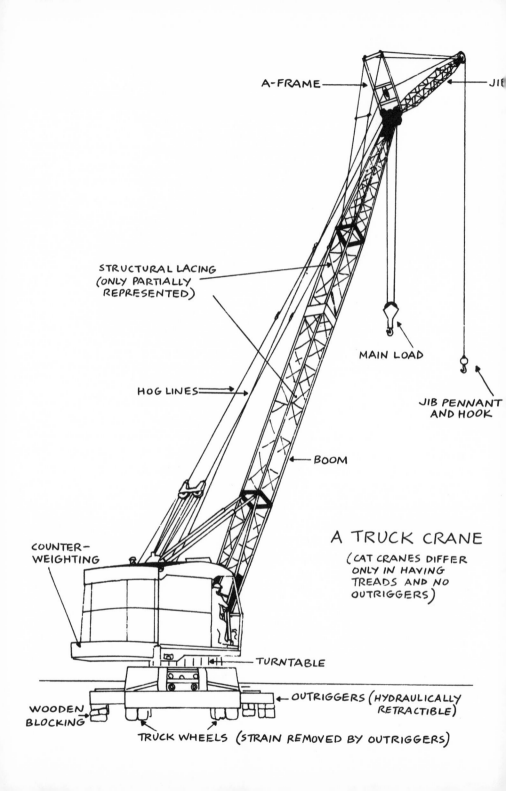

A-FRAME

JIB

STRUCTURAL LACING
(ONLY PARTIALLY
REPRESENTED)

MAIN LOAD

HOG LINES

JIB PENNANT
AND HOOK

BOOM

A TRUCK CRANE
(CAT CRANES DIFFER
ONLY IN HAVING
TREADS AND NO
OUTRIGGERS)

COUNTER-
WEIGHTING

TURNTABLE

WOODEN
BLOCKING

OUTRIGGERS (HYDRAULICALLY
RETRACTIBLE)

TRUCK WHEELS (STRAIN REMOVED BY OUTRIGGERS)

seeing that these were properly hooked up and in good supply. Callahan, the pusher, oversaw the work and did the requisite yelling. By union rules he is not allowed to do any labor. (The origin and aim of this will come up later.)

The crane we were working with was a "cat" crane. It sat on tracks and moved the way a tank moves. Its operator was a short, hairy Italian named Angie, who had big brass balls and a club foot. His machine was a hundred-ton P&H with ninety feet of stick. ("P&H" is a brand name. The "hundred-ton" part is a size rating, but not an actual description of lifting capacity. All cranes are rated in "tons," generally in increments of twenty-five. A "twenty-five tonner" is a very small crane; a "hundred tonner" is middling; a "two-hundred tonner" is pretty large.) The operation of a crane is in some ways similar to that of a Chicago boom: The stick can go up or down, and the load can go up or down. The lateral swing of the stick, unlike that of the Chicago boom, is powered.

This particular P&H was capable of handling a load of about twelve tons when boomed out far enough from its place on the bank of the canal to reach the pieces we were cutting loose.* It was Callahan's responsibility to decide where we should make those cuts. Cutting the bridge into unnecessarily small pieces would add to the length of time required to complete the job, but cutting loose something too large could put the crane in the canal, at the worst, or give us the messy problem of cutting up a girder underwater, at the least.

When a section of grid was ready for removal, the signalman would motion for Angie to swing his stick out over the load. Hand signals were used, since an operator cannot ordinarily hear anything over the noise of his engine. For lifting out grid sections, we used spreader

---

instantly destroyed all the skin in the area, and gave to the muscle tissue an emerald patina that looked for all the world like formica. It took several months to heal, during which time I swore a lot.

* Obviously, the more nearly horizontal a boom is, the smaller a safe load is. "Losing" a crane (that is, allowing it to tip over) is bad form. The cranes used in erecting Co-Op City (a high-rise housing development in the Bronx) were rigged with so much stick—something on the order of 450 feet—that after being assembled they were unable to pick themselves up. Other cranes were used to raise the long booms to a working position. Once up at a working angle (75°–80°), they were able to handle useful loads. It was an unusual situation, but not a unique one.

hooks. These are simply two twenty-foot lengths of wire rope, one end of each connected to a common ring, the other ends terminating in six-inch fish hooks. The ring end is place on the large hook attached to the bottom of the weight ball,* which forms the bitter end of the crane's load cable, and the hooks are taken to opposite outer portions of the grid, shoved into place, and the lift is made.

Timmy was ordinarily the signalman; sometimes Harry; sometimes Callahan—but never me. I didn't know enough yet, and would have sought a way out if asked. The signalman's responsibility is too great to be taken on by a beginner. When there is an accident, the signalman must be able to come up with explanations. The pusher can escape responsibility (if not a diminished reputation) by showing that his instructions were standard for the situation. The operator's only overt duty is to follow signals. The signalman should be an accomplished bullshitter. (He often is; I've known three or four who, by their own admission, have led utterly mistake-free lives.)

The operator demonstrates his skill in a variety of ways, but most visible are the smoothness with which he gets up and down on a load, the effectiveness with which he damps the lateral motion (once a load begins to swing it keeps on indefinitely if unchecked), and the accuracy with which he can make small changes (he is often asked to move a load up or down distances as short as an inch or two).

The signalman, for his part, must direct the exact placement of the boom prior to the lift and see that the hooks are put in the proper spots for a horizontal pick. If the load comes up on a slant, it may bind in adjacent parts of the structure. He must have some idea of the weight of the load being picked, since this affects the apparent center of gravity. If he puts the hook directly above the center of a heavy load, it will swing out, instead of coming straight up, when lifted, because the crane will unavoidably tilt forward as it takes the weight. Knowing how far it will tilt is part of the signalman's job. He compensates for the tilt by placing the boom a little back toward the crane (from the center of gravity). This is called leaving the boom "high."

---

* There is always a weight attached to the end of the cable of a lifting device. If there weren't, there wouldn't be any way to make the cable pay out: You can't push a flexible line. On large cranes and derricks, weight balls of two tons or more may be required.

Callahan made one major gaffe on that job, but since no one was hurt, it didn't really matter. He had decided we could save one lift if we could pick one of the next-to-largest girders in one shot. (On the first side of the bridge we'd cut its twin in two before lifting it, but it had come up very light.) He asked Angie if he thought the P&H could handle it, and Angie said he thought it would be pretty close. He agreed to try it if there were no men nearby when he picked it; Callahan agreed and said he would make the last cut himself.

The spreader hooks were not used for picking beams. They had a total capacity of some six tons only and were both the wrong tool and far too light to be used in picking a piece weighing ten or twelve tons. Instead, chokers were used. A choker is a length of wire rope with an eye riven at each end. Chokers in common use may be short and light (six feet of quarter-inch cable) through numbers of intermediate sizes on to long and heavy (twenty feet long and an inch and a half in diameter). There are innumerable ways to use these most common devices, but perhaps the most ordinary is to pass the choker around the piece to be lifted, taking one eye through the other, then pulling it up tight: "choking" it. To get a beam to come up flat (horizontally), it is obviously necessary to be sure that the choker is hooked in the exact center. In lifting the beams out of the bridge two chokers were used, set about six feet either side of center, leading up to a single hook. This gives a little margin of error for being off center, and in the case of the beams we were taking out was necessary anyway, since a single choker would not have taken the weight. As it was, the wire ropes we used were seven-eighths of an inch in diameter. Chokers that heavy are quite stiff, and wrestling one around a beam five feet deep is a two-man job.

When Harry and I had cut away a section of grid from below, and the other men had cut it away from above, and it had been lifted out and put ashore, we all went to work cutting the beams themselves from their anchors on the concrete piers. We left a few inches at the top uncut, so that the beam remained attached at each end by just about enough to hold it in place. Then two men walked to the center of the piece and waited for the crane to boom out over them, delivering the chokers. They were taken off the hook, put in place around the beam, and rehooked. The signalman then had the operator take a careful strain on the piece—a strain hopefully equal to the weight of the thing, so that when cut loose it would go neither up nor down. Once the strain was judged satisfactory, a man would take his torch and cut loose the far end. The signalman and operator would then make any necessary adjustments in the strain, and the near end would be cut loose. When the beam was completely free, it was lifted away, swung around, and landed on shore for cutting into smaller, truck-sized pieces.

When we tried to do this with the long piece, everything went all right until time to make the last cut. After the first cut Callahan had looked at Angie for his opinion, and Angie had simultaneously shaken his head and shrugged his shoulders, an indication of a marginal situation. (Operators, of course, know more about what their machines will do than anybody else does.) Callahan went over to Angie and asked if that meant he wouldn't try it. Angie said he didn't care one way or another; it wasn't up to him to make the cut. He shrugged again and sat back down in his cab. Callahan walked out on the beam to the center and looked up at the ball. Then he walked back to the end, grabbed a torch, and called for Timmy.

"I'm gonna cut it from t'e bank; I don't want t'e friggin' t'ing to put me in t'e drink. You hold my legs."

Timmy put down his iced tea and stretched out in the dirt. Callahan got down on his stomach and wriggled downhill toward the beam, with Timmy holding him by the legs. He placed himself somewhat over to one side of the piece, so that if it jumped up it wouldn't get him in the face.

As he finished the cut, the piece jerked up and inward, forcing Callahan to squirm back uphill as fast as he could. Then the piece began to swing slowly outward. With ninety feet of stick above it, its motion was slow, almost stately. But as it moved outward, the back of the crane began to leave the ground. Everything happened so slowly that it all seemed unreal: a foot, two feet, three feet, until the whole rig was balanced on its toes. I was convinced that everything was going into the canal. Angie still had an option, however, about which everybody but I knew: He could drop the load. With all cranes, except for telescoping boom types called cherry pickers, the operator can, in this kind of emergency, release his friction and drop his load instantly. I was ignorant of this, but Angie knew that (if he didn't wait until past the point of no return) he could save the rig by dropping the load in the drink.

In the end, this is what he did. With the crane tipped so far over that it seemed to me it *had* to keep on going, he dropped the load. The P&H slammed back down on the bank with a noise that sounded as though it were disintegrating. The stick jerked about so wildly that I was sure all the bolts that held its sections together were going to shear at once.

But when the dust and waves had settled, everything seemed to be still in one piece. Angie leaned out of his cab and said, sourly, "A little heavy, maybe." Callahan answered, "It don't matter. We'll drag t'e fuckin' t'ing out." Harry and Timmy stripped down to their underwear and clambered down the beam into the water, where they cut loose the chokers.* They dragged them up to the near end of the beam, which was sticking out of the canal, and reattached them. We then spent the rest of the afternoon dragging the beam slowly up the canal bank, a little at a time, the ass end of the crane sticking up in the air whenever there was a major strain taken. Angie seemed to know exactly how far he could push his rig, which impressed me because I couldn't see how he could be so sure of himself if he hadn't at some time lost one. I didn't ask him, however. He kept his cab door open, ready to jump, I guessed, wondering how well a man with a club foot could do that.

When the beam was halfway up the bank, I cut it apart. As we loaded the halves onto the truck, I wondered why a man who'd been working in the trade for twenty-odd years hadn't been able to figure the weight a little better.**

---

* Everything depends on where you are. If you asked a Local Forty (New York) man to get wet, he'd be more likely to throw *you* in. No ironworker likes water, but in the city, it's anathema. These guys didn't have to do it either, as far as that goes: It's not in the contract.

** Figuring weight becomes intuitive. There are lots of manuals with charts showing how much it's safe to lift with a given diameter and type of cable, but I don't know many men who could from memory fill in any part of one. If a fellow goes to apprentice school, he's required to commit such data to memory, but he seldom seems to retain it very long after his last test. In practice such particularization just doesn't happen. "Get a heavier choker, stupid," a man will say. Or, "What're ya usin' a beast like t'at for? Get

I had noticed a curious thing, watching Timmy from the time he held Callahan's legs during the cut through to when I chopped the beam in half: He hadn't touched his iced tea. As soon as the piece was cut, though, he took his styrofoam cup and made a quick trip to my car.

He was quiet all afternoon and didn't speak on the ride home until we got back to his neighborhood. Then he asked me to come in for a drink. I shrugged and parked the car; I'm not hard to get along with.

We drank for an hour in virtual silence, until finally I realized that although he wanted to talk, he couldn't start.

"How much vodka have you put back today, Timmy?" I asked.

"A coupla quarts, I guess," he said. "Not enough." He wasn't looking at me while he spoke, but waved his glass at the bartender. I pointed at the glass he was waving. "Look at the waves in your glass, man. It's six o'clock in the evening, and you're still shaking. It's no good, like that."

"I know," he said, "I know." His voice went up and down a strangled scale as though he were searching for a tune that kept escaping him. "It gets this way. The shaking. I guess I'll be leaving soon." I looked at him questioningly, but did not speak. "It gets this way," he went on. "Everybody knows about me. You notice Callahan leaves me alone in the mornings? He knows." He took a long breath. "I'm a drunk. I come from a long line of drunks. My father was. . . ." Here he stopped, and I thought he was going to quit altogether, but it was only a pause to drain his glass and gather speed. "My father was a stone mason. He did really beautiful work when he worked, but he was a drinker, and mostly he drank. He built our house and he sold it for bourbon, and the day we moved out he wouldn't help with the moving. He just sat in his chair and listened to his music until my uncle unplugged the phonograph and carried it out to the truck. He liked opera. Nobody else in the family knew anything about opera, but he listened to it all the time. You'd have thought he was a Guinea. Nights he would come home blind drunk and put records on

somet'in' smaller." He'll be right. He may not be able to guess the weight of the piece, nor to tell you the capacity of the cable he's picked, but the two will prove to be properly matched. Generally.

so loud it woke up everybody in the house. My mother used to try to stop him, until one night he beat the shit out of her. Then she left him alone. When I was little, he tried to get me to listen to the records, but I didn't like them, because I thought he was crazy because everybody else did, so I laughed at him the way they did, and after awhile he left me alone, too. There were six of us kids, and we all laughed at him. I was the youngest. My brother Sean used to do imitations of him staggering home drunk, and all the others laughed at him pretending to stagger, and I used to laugh, too. By the time I was in high school, we were in bad trouble, living in a flat on Front Street, and he hardly came home at all. He met some Guineas and got a permit to go with the concrete workers and went to New York on the Semmes Building. He sent some money home from time to time, but it never came to much."

Timmy took both our glasses and waved them at the bartender. He didn't look at me while the drinks were being made, but when they were in front of us and we had had a sip, he gave me an examining stare. "You don't mind me talking?" I shook my head. "That's good. It's a stage, you know. I mean, one I'm in, not one I'm on. When it gets to this point, I always talk. I don't always talk about my father, understand, but I do always talk." I took a sip of my drink, but said nothing.

"He was on that job more'n a year. He was on it when it was still in the hole, but he didn't make it to the topping out. We got a call from the super one day, and Sean and I had to go down to identify the body." Timmy stopped talking for so long that I finally said, "What happened?" He began fishing in his pocket for change, putting some three dollars worth of quarters on the bar and arranging them in a rectangle. His drink was gone, and he slid three of the quarters out for the next one.

"Well, it's ironic, really. You'll forgive the bad pun. They said he was sober at the time. They said he'd been on a big bender the week before and was taking it easy." He gave a half-believing snort. "You know what a Guinea Cadillac is?" I said no. "Well, don't ever say that in front of an Italian. It's a concrete buggy. It has a dump bucket up front that must hold about a yard of concrete, and behind it there's a small gas engine that's attached to two little drive wheels on the bottom and a steering wheel on top. There's a seat for the driver. It's just a kind of power tricycle for taking the concrete from the hopper to wherever they're pouring the floor. The drivers all race 'em around as fast as they can. They go around corners on two wheels, screech to a stop, dump their loads, and go tear-assing back to the hoist. I think that's why they call the Guineas Zips. Anyway, he was driving one. Part of the floor was already set, and a little piece of pipe was sticking an inch or two out of it. He hit it, going flat out, and the buggy flipped. It, and him, and the concrete all went down the elevator shaft." Timmy imitated the path of the buggy with two fingers of his left hand, swooping up first, then bouncing off imaginary obstacles on the way down to the bar, finally plunging them into his vodka and orange juice. The splash went all over the bar. He was laughing as he licked off his hand, but it was not a funny laugh.

"Fifty-one floors," he said, tonelessly.

"My God, what was left?"

"Nothing, really. Sean and I didn't get there until maybe six hours after it happened, and they had cleaned things up as much as they could and sort of put it all in one pile, but it was a small pile. I don't think most of him ever made it to the bottom. What there was was sort of packed in concrete. The identification was a joke. They said it was him, and we nodded, and that was that.

"It was better, in a way. It was better than watching him take years to do it with a bottle."

Timmy got up and went to the john. When he returned we talked about little things for awhile, things that had happened on the job that day, how much longer the job would last, what kind of work was likely to be available after this job was over.

"You don't seem to talk much," he suddenly said to me.

"I'm like you in some ways," I replied. "Sometimes I talk continuously."

"Like I said, it's a stage." He pursed his mouth.

"What did you mean when you said you guessed you'd be leaving soon? You got another job in mind?"

Timmy shook his head. "No, no other job. It's what I meant about stages. I'm about ready to go up country to dry out."

I said, "Oh." Timmy said, "Yep." We sat through the next drink without speaking, and in the silence I found myself thinking more about myself than about him. I was beginning to feel the liquor and was trying to remind myself that it was still a fifteen-mile drive home.

"I take the cure," he laughed, "about once a year. My wife leaves me about once a year. They coincide. She leaves me, then I go dry out, then she comes back and I don't drink. Then I take a social drink, then she hassles me, then I drink some more, she leaves, I drink 'til it won't stop the shaking any more, I go dry out, she comes back . . ." he trailed off.

"How many children you got?"

"A little girl, six. They go to my wife's mother's. She hates me. Mother-in-law, not the child."

"Well, at least you've got it down to a science."

"Oh, yes, it's a regular formula." The words were slower, now, both in coming and from one to the next. Still, he seemed more exhausted than drunk. He had stopped shaking. He noticed it the same time I did. "Lookit that, will you?" He held his hands out parallel to the bartop with his fingers spread. "It's stopped. I guess I've got a little more time after all."

"Why do you use the shaking as the stop sign? Why don't you quit when she threatens to leave you?"

He seemed to have difficulty settling upon an answer, and it was some time before he spoke. "Well, two reasons, I guess. She doesn't threaten to leave me. She's pretty quiet, until the time comes she's made up her mind to leave. Then she just leaves. We hardly ever fight about it. I guess I said it wrong before; she doesn't really hassle me much. The most she ever says when I'm drinking is something like, 'You're drinking again; you know what'll happen, I guess.' Then one day I'll come home late at night and she'll tell me she can't take anymore and she leaves.

"But, you see, it isn't because of her that I drink, at least I don't think it is, so I don't quit because of her, either. I'm drunk and I'm talking too much which I warned you was a thing which happens, but let's make sure we've got one thing . . ." he belched over the finger he had pointed at me, then made a fist of the same hand and tapped his stomach twice and belched again before continuing, "straight, right now. I'm talking to you, because like I said it's a stage in this fucking mess and also because you're not a real ironworker anyway, so it doesn't matter what you think of me. But by the Virgin Mary, it's you I'm talking to, and not anybody else, and nobody else is gonna hear any part of this conversation, or speech, or vomit, or whatever the hell it is, right?" He was aiming a finger at me, with such an intense expression on his face that I thought a long moment before deciding to try to lighten things up.

"I think," I said, "I'll tell the guys you tried to get funny with me in the men's room." It was quite a while before he showed any response to that at all. Then he laughed, "All right. As long as it's the men's room."

I had to take a leak so badly that getting off the bar stool required considerable care. Before rounding the corner, I turned back and shook a finger at him. "Don't try to follow me."

When I came back there were fresh drinks in front of both our places, and his pile of silver was nearly gone. I realized I was being hired to listen, so I said, "What's the other reason?"

"Other reason for what?" He was having real trouble getting his words out now. The effort he was making to pull himself together was quite visible. Actually, it was impressive that he was conscious at all; he should have been comatose. "Other reason for what?" he repeated.

"For drying out."

"Oh." He stopped there, so I went on. "Did you drink much before your father was killed?" Cheap psychology! But I *was* wondering about it, and I *did* say so. There was a delay before every answer now, but he was still able to respond. I had the feeling that his thinking hadn't slowed appreciably, that it was only the motor functions that were impaired.

"Some." He looked at the rotating Utica Club clock behind the bar. "It wasn't that, though, I don't think. There was a thing that happened not long after that, but I think it was, what is the word? Unrelated."

"What happened?"

"I got scared. Hoo, boy, I got scared, the first time I was ever really scared, on the iron, I mean, and I wasn't even very high up."

He was drunk enough so that his mind showed, and I could see him start to let the thought out and then pull it back. Then it started out of him again, and he stopped it again. It was as though everything in him was visible: vomit and swallow, spill and mop . . . He couldn't solve it, and the period of oscillation kept shortening. Soon he was practically vibrating with it. I caught myself, ultimately, getting more involved with the process than the man and realized that I wouldn't have allowed it to go on for so long if I hadn't been drinking, too.

"I think it's time to quit for tonight, Timmy." I tried to slip this remark in during one of the Stop cycles.

"No, no, no, you think I'm afraid to answer but that isn't it at all. That isn't it." His voice had risen in pitch and volume. The bartender, normally so deliberately distant, gave us a glance of question. "You don't know me," he continued in a tone that had acquired a very hard edge. "I told you when we were here before you didn't know me. Nobody knows me; not Sean, not Mary, certainly not *you!*" This last was practically a shout, and the bartender strode down to stand in front of us. When he spoke it was to me, with his fat, florid, fleshy nose right in my face. "You! I like a quiet place!" He had a mouthful of gravel. I immediately decided he must be related to the B.A. "You make Timmy upset, so he makes noise, I figger t'at's *your* noise. So you quiet down. You don't get quiet, I t'row you out, you unnerstan'? Shuddup!"

I stiffened and had opened my mouth to reply when Timmy put his hand on my forearm. I think he thought I was going to throw the drink at the bartender. Perhaps I was; I hadn't thought it out. But when Timmy grabbed my arm, all other thoughts left, his grip was several times stronger than I would have thought he could manage. For a moment everything left me but my surprise at his strength. While he was holding my arm, he spoke to the other man.

"He dint do nuttin, Paddy. I'm drinkin' is all. He don't even hardly talk. Go away." The man stared at Timmy and was left with his mad hanging out and no place to put it. He made a disgusted Why Me gesture with his hands and went back to the other end of the bar. Timmy turned to me and began making apologies for himself and the bartender, but I barely heard him. I was still hearing Timmy's voice from before, when he'd been talking to the man with the three-F nose: "He dint do nuttin, Paddy. . . . He don't even hardly talk." It was the first time I'd noticed that up until then he hadn't been speaking blue collar that evening. I didn't reply to his apologies, and he kept on talking. I guess he thought I was sore at the bartender, but that wasn't it at all. I was just curious about Timmy.

His voice trailed off halfway through a sentence. I had been listening only to the words and had no real idea what he was saying. I got off the stool, went to the john, came back, and stood finishing my drink and gathering change from the bar. Timmy didn't look up from his vodka.

"Time for me to leave," I said. "You'll be on the corner in the morning?" He nodded but didn't look up.

"You ought to get out of this business," he said, over his shoulder.

"Not 'til I know why," I answered, as he was massaging the back of his neck with both hands. "Besides, you said I wasn't a real ironworker anyway."

"Yeah."

I went to the door saying, "I'll see you in the morning." He waved me off and made his final statement without turning.

"You bein' stupid," he said.

Stop here for a moment while I try to explain myself: I expect to be asked, certainly by guys who knew Timmy—which is one of the changed names, by the way, though those men will recognize him—why I've gotten into such heavy stuff as the scene above. The answer is complicated, and I'm not sure it can be approached directly. It revolves, somehow, about Death, and how one decides what it means. Does Death focus Life? Does Life give meaning to Death? Does the fact that most of us have learned how to stick out our tongues at the sophomoric naïveté of these questions make them invalid? How sophisticated are *you* at three o'clock in the morning?

It is Timmy's death, of course, that is referred to in the Note at the beginning of these pages. He tripped on a warped plank and fell to the street. It was not the only death of my life, but it has remained the most affecting.

Still, to the question of Why Hang the Laundry in the Front Yard? the answer has to be Because It Is Important that It's Seen. I keep hoping it might yield Generalizations—to me, you understand, as well as to anyone else. Generalizations eventually yield Theorems, and Theorems are but a step away from the Truth. In theory. Perhaps.

The materials of Timmy's life aren't unique. In having a drunken father he had plenty of company; in his own alcoholism he had as much. There is no striking uniqueness in his father's having been killed at work, nor in his father's virtual abandonment of his family.

It is certainly natural that he should know fear—only the very stupid have never been afraid. What *is* unusual is that he chose a whole life-style which *had* to aggravate fear. It becomes, therefore, very important to know whether Timmy's fear was a precondition or a perquisite.

An answer to that might help explain why he fell. Or shed some light on What Is An Accident, which is a question that has intermittently cost me sleep since I was a boy.

In 1947 I belonged, briefly, to the Boy Scouts. We met in the basement of a church. It wasn't much of a troop and the meetings tended toward utter boredom, so what fun I had came when I was able for a few minutes every now and then to sneak up into the church proper and play the organ. I didn't know anything about it except that it made a hell of a lot of noise. It made so much noise that I kept getting caught because I couldn't hear the scoutmaster coming for me.

I remember the Scouts mainly because one of those meetings marked my first direct exposure to death. One of the boys in the group, a Jack Somebody, came to the church one night wearing, instead of his uniform slacks, shiny blue serge trousers. They were so shiny that we teased him about being unable to look at him for the brilliance of the reflected light. We asked him what kind of polish he used. We asked him to walk us home to light the way, and similar idiocies. He said, with no special rancor, that if we didn't leave him alone he was going to hang himself. We said go right ahead.

During instruction on leaf recognition no one realized he wasn't in the main room. When we went to the kitchen to get sodas, we found him hanging by a piece of knot-tying rope from a pipe that ran across the low ceiling. There was an overturned chair beneath him. His face was as blue as his pants.

I never thought it was suicide. It was more likely a joke that went awry. An Accident. However, I quit the Scouts.

Still, even now, after almost *any* Accident, I am unable to avoid the midnight picture of Jack's slowly swinging blue body.

In the final week of the bridge job I had my first mishap. It wasn't much of one, really, since it broke nothing and didn't even cut me up, but it scared hell out of me:

As the days on the job had gone by, and as I began to acquire a little skill with the torch, Callahan had begun yelling at me less and showing me more. He had told me that he'd originally thought the B.A. had sent him an amateur as a personal insult, and that he'd thought I was probably a spy to boot, but that he'd now decided that I was all right. I'd told him to drop dead, which had struck the right note, and at this point things were reasonably friendly. I'd reached the point where I felt I could ask questions when I didn't know something, instead of trying to fake it. Over drinks after work Callahan would often review the day, explaining why he'd done a thing one way instead of another.

On this occasion I was sent out on the last beam to make the next-to-last cut. Both ends of the piece were cut through to the top flange, and the chokers were in place and under strain. I was trying to do the job right, or at least look like I was, so I laid the torch down on the end and walked to the center of the piece, where I shook the chokers to see how tight they were. I hollered back to Callahan on the bank that I thought Angie had too much on the load. Callahan's response to this was to smack himself in the forehead with his palm and yell, "Jesus, Mary, and Joseph! Hey, Angie! Meet the new pusher!"

So I said, "Ah, screw it!" and sat down and made the cut. The flange was sixteen inches wide, and when I got all but about three inches burned away, the remainder began to tear. It was obvious what was going to happen, but I didn't react fast enough to do anything about it except to flip my goggles off, which was probably about all that anyone could have done—except look for a place to land: There was far too much strain on the load. When it tore through, the beam popped up like a catapult, and I went straight up above it and into a somersault. On the way down I intersected the piece with one arm and a leg and managed to hang on. At the moment hanging on seemed vitally important, although if I'd been unable to, all I'd have gotten would have been a bump and a bath. When I looked over at the bank, the gang was in stitches. Harry and Callahan were rolling in the dirt with their arms around their stomachs, and Timmy was draped over the crane cat, tears running down his face and his iced tea slopping out of its cup.

Angie was the only one not laughing. He had his face pressed up against the windshield of his cab, the whites showing all around the pupils of his eyes. He very slowly let the load back down until the end of the beam was level with the bank, then scrambled out of his cab and limped over toward me.

"Hey!" he shouted, "You alla right? You okay?"

"Yeah," I answered, "I'm all right. I got a sore ass is all."

"Callahan, 'at dumba bastard, he saysa strain is justa right. I tell him beam is not so heavy, but he saysa strain isa just right."

"It's okay, Angie, I'm tellin' you. No damage."

Angie then turned to Callahan. "Hey! you dumba bastard! You insista strain isa all right. I tell you itsa too much; you insista. 'At man coulda get hurt." Callahan had picked himself up out of the dirt and was brushing himself off. He made a gesture to Angie as though he were stuffing him in a closet, saying, "He didn't t'ough, did he?" Angie shrugged. Callahan shrugged. Then he began picking up gear and shouted to everybody, "Arright! It's late. Let's clean up and get outta here."

It took me awhile to get my torch disconnected and coiled, because I was shaking. It took me even longer to realize that I was not shaking from fright, but because I was sore at Callahan.

We spent three more days on that job, cutting up pieces and loading them into trucks, knocking down the crane, and shipping out tools. The incident didn't come up again until we were at the gin mill celebrating the end of the job.

The contractor had taken us all for the traditional drink, bought his obligatory rounds, and left. Time passed, and the four of us who were still there—Harry, Timmy, Callahan, and me—were getting drunk.

Harry was talking with another ironworker who had wandered by about what work was around. The other man said that he'd been in the hall that morning and that only five men had been sent out, but that there was talk that a big job in Charlesburg was supposed to be opening up soon. Harry said he wasn't crazy about traveling that far, but who was running the job?

"The evil Gill," replied the other.

"Screw t'at," said Harry, "I'll sit in t'e hall, t'en. I'll never work for t'at bastard."

Timmy was sitting at the end, where the bar turned a corner to run into the wall, with one hand in his pocket, trying to strike a paper match with the other. The hand seemed a foreign object to him, and his water-colored eyes strove to will its shaking to stop. Everyone understood that it was a private contest, and no one spoke to him. He had succeeded in folding the match roughly in the middle so that the head would reach to the striking surface, but his thumb, with which he was trying to scrape the one against the other, kept sliding off to the side. I was so engrossed in watching the thumb struggle to the match head only to lose it every time that when Callahan's voice finally reached me I realized he must have spoken several times.

"Hey, Mike! Where t'e hell are you? You ready?"

"Am I ready," I answered, trying to guess what it was I was supposed to be ready for. It took me a moment to focus on Callahan. "Ready for what?"

"For a drink, you dumb bastard." I nodded that I was. Callahan paid for the round out of a thick pile of money. As I stared at it, I realized that he intended to stay there until he'd drunk it up. When the drinks appeared, I raised my glass and uttered the required, "Luck." Harry did so also, and Callahan dipped his glass at each of us. It is as formal and necessary a ritual as is the expression, "First one for the day," which accompanies the initial barroom drink after work, regardless of how much has been put down on the job. Timmy, however, was so involved with his thumb that the new drink and the one before stood equally unattended next to his Pall Malls.

"I hate wreckin' work," said Callahan.

" 'Sa job," said Harry, some of his V.O. dribbling out of the left corner of his mouth.

"Yeah, but it's shitty work," answered Callahan.

"What he means," said Harry, winking conspiratorially at me, "is t'at it was all slag and rust and old iron, and no mungo."

"Up yours, Harry," Callahan went on, "it ain't what I meant at all." He neatened up his pile of money as though it were a pile of poker chips, squinting intensely. "What I meant was, well . . ." He was able to make a unit of his bills, but couldn't put his thoughts together. "It has somet'in' to do wit' buildin' holes in t'e ground." He got up from his stool. "You don't know not'in, anyway, you dumb Polack. I gotta piss." He hiccuped once on the way to the men's room.

"Got'm, didn't I," said Harry, gleefully. It wasn't a question.

"Did you?"

"Sure I did. I sure did." More V.O. trickled out of the left corner of Harry's mouth. I wondered why nothing ever came out of the right side of Harry's mouth, and said so.

"Took a flop in a powerhouse down in Bridgeport, once, about t'e same's six floors. Landed on bags of asbestos, which saved me, but I caught a brace on t'e way down wit' t'e left side of my head. Shattered my jaw; t'e left side don't feel much." Harry hadn't seemed to mind the question, but his answer left me with no desire to pursue it further, so I asked him instead about "mungo."

Mungo is salvage: metal scrap that has a per-pound price high enough to make it worth, to some, carrying home. It is resold, when a worthwhile quantity has been accumulated, to dealers in scrap. Depending upon the current state of the market, copper or brass will bring anywhere from thirty to seventy cents a pound.*

"You don't know about Melvin, do you, Mike?" asked Harry. He'd been buying his share of the drinks, but augmenting them with off-speed shots to the side, and he was beginning to slur and grin.

* The word itself is interesting. According to the dictionary, it comes from Yorkshire, probably after the personal name Mungo, and has come to mean the waste of milled wool used with cotton, and so forth, to form a cheap cloth. The "waste" part makes sense, but it is to be suspected that our usage of the word more likely relates to "monger," as in "ironmonger," "fishmonger," et cetera. The roots of that word are also Anglo-Saxon, meaning, as a noun, a merchant or dealer; as a verb, to traffic in a specific commodity.

At any rate, metal scoffed for resale is "mungo." I know an Italian in New York, a guy named Leo, who is so fanatic that he'll even steal the lead bricks which the plumbers use. I watched him take home ten pounds a night for three months. He keeps it in his attic, waiting for the price to rise, and I fully expect to pick up a paper some day and learn that he's been crushed by his own collapsing house.

"Melvin?"

"Melvin the Mungo Master." Harry wore an expression of professorial self-contentment. "If you stay in t'is, ah"—watching Harry search for language was physically debilitating,—"business any lengt' of time, you'll meet Melvin, t'ough he works outta Forty mostly t'e last few years. He was Callahan's pusher on a job in White Plains, once, and t'at's why I'm breakin' his balls."

"Don't you like Callahan? Why break his balls?"

"Why not?" Harry countered. I shrugged. He fixed me with a curious stare. "I t'ink you're gonna be all right," he went on, "but you ain't an ironworker yet, and . . ." he trailed off.

Callahan reappeared from the men's room, his face an agony of remembered concentration, grabbing Harry by a shoulder and spinning him around on his stool so that they were facing each other.

"What I meant," he said, "was t'at all we made was a hole, which is not as good as a somet'ing."

"You're right, t'ere," said Harry, sounding as though he were tolerating an aging Mongoloid. Callahan, however, seemed not to perceive the tone of voice. He grabbed me by the elbow and half lifted me off my stool.

"I wanna talk to you," he said. I jerked my arm loose.

"What about?"

"About you, numbnuts."

"If you're gonna tell me I'm not a real ironworker, you'll have to get in line. Timmy's told me that repeatedly, and Harry started in tonight, and, well, you're just way down the list."

"T'at wasn't it, exactly," Callahan said.

"Callahan, you remember three or four weeks ago when you were swung out over the canal, standing on the ball, hollering for a three-eighths choker—at *me*—and I didn't know what you meant?" He nodded. "Well, I felt about as stupid right then as I ever care to feel. Do you understand that?"

"You *were* stupid."

"Oh, screw you. I give up."

"*You* give up? You shmuck! I carried you. I kept you employed, you dumb bastard."

"You set up that little scene when I made the last cut on that girder, though, didn't you? You knew damn well the strain was too great. You let me walk and go through the whole bit, shaking the chokers, pretending to know a little something of what I was about, just to see me get whipped into the air like that, didn't you?" Callahan concentrated on arranging his left eye directly above its reflection in the center of his shot glass. "Angie did what you told him. You knew it wouldn't kill me, but you knew it would scare hell out of me." Callahan, still looking at his own eye, nodded. "Monday," I said, "we'll both be in the hall, and the way things are going, according to that guy Harry was talking to, neither of us will get sent out, and then we can go drinking, and you can tell me what the devil you thought you were doing, and I'll listen to you. Tonight I don't feel like screwing with it." I banged my glass to catch the bartender's attention. When he looked over, I waved at everybody's glass, and he began filling another round. About then, Timmy suddenly let out a sigh of great satisfaction.

"What t'e hell is he doin' over t'ere, anyway?" asked Harry, "Comin'?" Timmy's face was a broad slack smile as he waved the lit match for all to see. While he held it up for approval, it ignited the rest of the book, and he shook it hurriedly off his hand to the floor, where he jumped up and down on it.

"Cheez," said Harry.

Now that Timmy's labors with the matches were completed, he set about catching up on his drinking. He had three glasses before him, and now drained all without stopping. Harry watched him. "You goina hall Monday, Timmy?" he asked.

"I'll be there," Timmy replied. We looked at each other's faces for signs that the conversation would continue, but no one seemed to have anything to say. Finally, Harry went on, "What about you, Mike?"

"I'll be there," I said. Another pause and round of glances. The bartender brought a round and tapped his knuckles on the bar when Timmy pushed money toward him.

"That's on me, gentlemen," he said. We nodded, and Harry, whose old glass was empty, picked up the new one and dipped it in salute before knocking it back. Silence resumed, and it struck me that as a group we never talked about anything except the job, and that, with the bridge down, there just wasn't anything to talk about. Harry kept squirming on his stool, obviously hoping something would happen.

"Hey, Callahan," said Harry, jabbing his fingers into the man's ribs with some force, "you goina hall Monday?"

Callahan was jerked erect by the blow, but his head still tilted forward and his concentration remained on the shot glass.

"Lemme tell you," he said, trying again to get his eye above its image, " 'assa good ol' sky-blue Irish eye, t'at is. T'e only t'ing is, it looks sorta brown."

"Switch to aquavit," I said.

"Huh?"

"Try some aqua—oh, to hell with it." Callahan stared at me intently, but didn't question me again. I stared back. He broke off first, turning to look at Timmy, then Harry.

"You gennlemen know what?" he inquired rhetorically. "Misser Permit Man here," Callahan put his arm around my shoulders, patting me several times, "Misser Permit Man here din't know his ass from a hole inna ground a few weeks ago, but he's learned a lot, an' he can use a torch pretty good, too, if you don' mind waitin' aroun' on him." He stopped for breath. I used the time to move away a couple of feet, so that he patted space a few times before realizing it and putting his arm down.

"Howsomever," he continued, "lemme tell you what he *t'inks*." He looked at me with a smile too boozy to interpret. "You remember when Misser Permit Man did his li'l somersault a couple days ago?" He looked at Timmy and Harry, nodding his head elaborately, as though he were leading a chorus. "Well, he's got a 'spicious nature. He *t'inks* I set it up on purpose. Now, what kinda way to t'ink is t'at?" Again he looked at the other men, still wearing his slack and featureless smile. Neither Harry nor Timmy answered him nor changed their blank expressions, and as Callahan finished his speech, he was again arranging his eye above his drink. "Would I do t'at? Like t'at Guinea operator said, a man could get hurt." There was silence until Harry began to giggle. He picked up his empty glass and twirled it in a slow loop while making a kind of whistling sound effect.

"Plump!" he said. "Landed right back on it, he did. Could have gone right on burnin'."

Callahan scrunched down in his stool and began burning the bartop with an imaginary torch. As he talked his voice got louder, and he straightened up his body with gathering speed until at the end of the cut he threw himself backward off the stool, shouting, "Okay, meeen, t'e cut is maaade!" He stumbled as he landed and wound up sitting on the floor.

"You all right, Callahan?" I asked.

"Umph," he said. There was laughter from Harry, and more laughter at the fall from people at the back of the bar, but our group lapsed again into silence. Callahan brushed himself off and sat down. The bartender asked if he were all right. Callahan made motions that he was and to bring another round. I put my hands out palms down. Callahan looked at my gesture and shrugged. I tapped Timmy on the shoulder, told him I was leaving, and asked if he wanted a ride. He shook his head. I scooped up my money, leaving a buck for the bartender, told everyone I'd enjoyed working with them, and started for the door. As I went out, I could hear Callahan.

"Was only a joke," he said.

Job availability changes quickly in the construction industry, and, of course, most quickly in the smallest towns. In Megalopolis a man might work on a single skyscraper for a year or more. In Hicksville he might work for ten or fifteen companies in a year. One large building going up in a place like Binghamton, or two or three in Hartford or New Haven, can constitute a boom. Conversely, when a large job in a small town finishes, the hall is suddenly full of men. This happened now: A big job wound up the day we finished the bridge, and the hall was crowded.

There were two rooms to the hall: a smallish one, perhaps twenty feet by thirty, holding file cabinets and desks for the B.A. and his clerical staff, and an anteroom about twice that size in which the men assembled, waiting to be sent to work. The two were connected by a dutch door, and from time to time the B.A. would lumber up to the closed lower half, look at a piece of paper in his hand, then glare around the room at the men. "Hey, Charlie," he'd growl, "you got wheels?"

"Yeah, sure," Charlie would answer, or if he had money in the bank, or it was coming on to deer season, or if he was hung over and half of a mind to go drinking, he might reply instead, "Don't run too good, where'd you want me to go?" Or, if he had a particular buddy with whom he wanted to work, he might say, "No, Tom's got the car; we have to go out together."

As in any group, some men were more ambitious or more in need than others, and they tended to cluster near the door, hoping to be seen. Some made a social club of it all, sending each other out for coffee and doughnuts. Some tried to kiss ass by going to the dutch door and yelling, "Hey, Fred, I'm going for coffee. Can I get you anything?" Some stayed near the outer door, hanging around just long enough not to be lying when they went home to tell their wives that they'd shaped the hall. Some just cruised around, lining up the day's drinking companions.

I sat in the middle of the room, feeling utterly invisible. On Monday a half-dozen men were sent out, but I got not a glance. On Tuesday it was raining, and at 7:30 the B.A. came to the door and said, "What t'e fuck are you jerks doin' here? Go home." On Wednesday it was still raining, and for the first time since we'd finished the bridge, I saw Harry and Callahan. I asked Callahan if he'd seen Timmy. He said no, and nobody's goin' out in t'is weat'er, let's go to O'Rourke's.

Driving over, I began to recognize that the feelings I got sitting in the hall weren't really much different from those I'd had while standing in the corner after some grade-school misdeed. Many of the other men wore expressions that seemed to suggest the same reaction.

I followed Callahan's car toward O'Rourke's. Harry was riding with him. Through their rear window I could see them passing a brown paper bag back and forth. The sight made my stomach knot, and I rolled down the window half expecting to throw up. At O'Rourke's I order a beer, but it didn't want to stay down. I told Harry and Callahan that I didn't feel like drinking, which was certainly the truth, and left. As I was opening the car door, the beer and the greasy egg I'd had for breakfast came up. I parked the car in the municipal lot downtown and went to a double feature. When I came out the rain had stopped, but the skies were still dirty. I bought a couple of paperbacks in the drugstore, went to my room, and spent the rest of the day reading.

Thursday, four men were sent out. No one at all went out on Friday, but there was a lot of speculation about the Charlesburg job opening soon and about how many men might be needed for it. I spent the weekend reading and seeing the only two movies in the area I hadn't already been to.

On Monday the Charlesburg job broke and the hall was virtually emptied. Still, I didn't get called. Callahan didn't get called. Harry did, but he asked the B.A. who the super was, and when it was confirmed that the evil Gill was running the job, Harry, true to his word, said no thanks, he wouldn't work for that prick if it was the only job in the state. The B.A. said that it just about was. Harry said he didn't give a damn and stormed out. By a quarter to nine I'd read everything in the paper and all the notices and tool advertisements on the walls and was down to my last three cigarettes. The only others in the room besides Callahan and myself were two teenagers. One wore dress khakis and a button-down denim shirt that was more likely from Brooks Brothers than Sears; the other had three inches of hair down the nape of his neck and kept fiddling with his headband. All four of us were standing. Callahan was studying the naked ladies on a calendar advertising the Try Me Body Works.

When I caught his eye, I folded the three middle fingers of my left hand, sticking out the thumb and little finger, put the thumb to my mouth, and waggled the hand up and down. Callahan nodded assent, and without bothering to speak we got in our cars and went to O'Rourke's.

The first beer was drunk in silence. Callahan took a swallow of the second, then sighed. "Hippie bastards," he said.

"Only one of 'em had long hair," I answered. This in no way altered Callahan's judgment.

"Hippies," he repeated. "T'e skinny one don't look like he could lift a spud wrench."

"You know who they are?" I asked.

"T'e hairy one is Joey Firello's kid. I never seen t'e ot'er one before. He's somebody's kid, t'ough, you can bet your ass on t'at." Callahan looked at his beer disgustedly, took a swallow, looked pained, then said, "I don't see how you drink t'is shit; t'ere's not'in' in it." He called the bartender over and ordered a double V.O. He motioned for the man to pour me one, but I told him not to. I said I'd stick to beer.

As we sat there I kept seeing the scene in the hall: the B.A. coming to the door just after seven, surveying the room, returning to his desk to make notes, then coming every few minutes to the door with slips of paper in his hand, hurling his whiskey voice into the smoky, almost silent room. "Jones, Ruark, Johnson, Reilly!" The men went to the door, and there was conversation in guttural, uncatchable whispers. Then they would cross the room quickly, heading for the door to the outside. Someone would grab one by the elbow, saying, "Hey, Ruark, where'd he send you?"

"Charlesburg," Ruark would reply.

"All of youse goin' t'ere?"

"Yeah." Then Ruark would tear his arm loose and they would be gone. In a few minutes the voice would come again. "O'Neill, Paterson, Kelso!" More men would get up.

This had continued until only the four of us were left. Seven men had gone to nearby jobs, all the others to Charlesburg. I had begun to be fascinated by the B.A.'s selective vision. He could scan the room from wall to wall, registering only those men whom he intended to send out. It gave me the feeling that if I were standing there with a pistol pointed at him, I would still be invisible. This picture expanded. Callahan and I, standing in the middle of the room full of men, the guns in our hands pointed toward the dutch door as the B.A. stood there with his eyes focused ten feet beyond us, growling, "McHenry, Tabor, Elliot, Brown . . ."

But Callahan was a wrong element; he didn't belong on my side of it. With the picture revealed as false, it vanished, and I returned to look at Callahan in the present. He was making faces at that part of his reflection that showed between the whiskey bottles shelved in front of the bar mirror. I laughed at him. "You're no prettier'n you were yesterday, Callahan; give it up."

"I look better over at t'e T'ree Doors," he said, shaking his head in exaggerated sadness. "T'e mirror's tinted blue."

"How come you're not pretty enough for the B.A. to see you? He looks through you the same way he looks through me." Callahan took a swallow of his drink but didn't answer. "You on his shit list, chief?"

"Nah," he answered, shaking his head with some force, "it ain't t'at. Fred knows I won't work for Gill is all. Hell, I coulda gone out if I really wanted. Some of t'e guys t'at went out were permit men, you know."

"You lost me."

"Some of t'em guys are on permit. A permit man can't go out before a book man, dummy." When I looked at him without saying anything, he continued. "All I got to do is tell Fred I want a permit man's job, and he's got to give it to me."

"In the hall, you mean, before the man goes out."

"Anytime, stupid. T'at's what permits are for. If a man wit' a book had come by t'e bridge job and seen you he'd have known you were on permit—because you don't *walk* like a book man—and he could've come to me and demanded your job and I'd have given it to him."

"Thanks a lot," I said. "How the hell can you fire me without cause?"

"Oh, what t'e hell's t'e matter wit' you? T'e *permit* is t'e cause. What'd you t'ink t'e union *is*, for Chrissake? It's our protection." Callahan ordered another drink, asked for a large glass, and added a little water to his V.O. I remarked that I'd never seen him water his drinks before, and he said that he was thinking of taking his kids to the movies in the afternoon and didn't want to get stiff.

"T'ere are," he went on, "about t'ree hundred books in t'is local. It ain't changed in years. We don't even have an apprentice program anymore. Talk has it t'e government's gonna put t'e screws to us, but it ain't happened yet. We've let a few men transfer in here from ot'er locals, but I can't even remember t'e last time a new book was let. T'ere's four, maybe five hundred permit men workin' outta here, off and on. T'at's how we cover slow times. When it tightens up we don't put t'e permit men to work, and we can keep t'e book men goin'. Most of t'e time, anyway. But when t'ere's a real recession t'e buildin' trades get hit first of all, and t'en *nobody* works.

"T'e goddam government don't understand any of t'is, t'ough, and you just watch. All t'is civil rights shit and everyt'in'. T'ey'll come suckin' around here pretty soon, and louse it all up." Callahan poured a new shot into his glass, splashing a little water on top. "Commie clerks and longhairs and schoolteachers and Johnsonites—t'ey don't know shit. But t'at don't keep 'em from buttin' in. 'Here, now,' t'ey say. 'Take t'is here poor black bastard into your union and let him get some of t'at wonderful money you're makin'. He's starvin' to deat' and runnin' up t'e welfare rolls.' So you say, 'Why don't *you* take him into *your* business? Let him be a big banker, or a school principal, or somet'in'.'

" 'Oh, well,' t'ey say, 'we couldn't do *t'at*. He's uneducated, you see, so he wouldn't fit in wit' our kind. But you guys are all dumbhead dropouts anyhow, and he'll fit in wit' *you* just fine. Besides, you *know* you're way overpaid for just plain old manual labor, and you ought to share the pie.' "

Callahan's voice, when imitating the "other side," was a rather effective parody of Camp Swish. " 'It ain't right, you know,' " he said, wiggling his hips and wearing a very superior smirk, " 'to be so *pred*—jew-diced.'

"Shit!" he exploded in his own voice, "I'm not prejudiced; I'm tryin' to make a livin'!"

There didn't seem to be anything to say, so I used the silence to go to the men's room. When I came back into the main room I saw that he had just drained a shot to the side of his regular drink. I waited a few feet down the bar until he'd had a chance to move the extra glass to the wash tray.

"Kidneys are goin', I think," I said, straddling the stool. "Goddam beer goes right through me."

"I made sixteen t'ousand dollars last year," he said, "and eleven and a half t'e year before last. But t'e year before t'at I made less t'an six, and I bet if you averaged out my whole ironworkin' life, it wouldn't come to eight. I pay t'ree times what a regular person does for a little bit of life insurance, and I get no pension, and when my beat-up body starts to slow down it'll be harder to get work, and if I lose even just a hand, I'm t'rough on t'e spot. Sometimes I t'ink if t'e niggers and P.R.s want t'e stinkin' trade, t'ey can have it."

I said nothing. Callahan stood up while finishing his drink. "Sit in t'e hall mornin's," he said, "so's Freddie'll get to know your face. But don't feel bad if he don't send you out right away. Go to t'e gin mills around quittin' time, hang out wit' t'e guys. Listen to 'em talk about t'eir jobs, and don't be afraid to talk about your own. Let 'em know you can burn. Get to be one of 'em. In t'e long run, you'll get more work t'at way t'an you will outta t'e hall. Your pal Patrick is a good hand; it wouldn't hurt none to let him know you're outta work."

"I can't do that, Callahan. He got me the first job; I can't ask him again."

"I don't know why in hell not. T'e B.A. sure as hell isn't gonna come lookin' for you wit' a 'Please sir won't you do us t'e favor of takin' t'is job.'"

I nodded and asked if he wanted another drink.

"Nope. Gonna take t'e kids to t'e movies, soon's t'e older one's home from school."

When he got to the door, he pushed on it hard twice before he realized he had to pull it. He glared at the knob. "Stupid fuck," he said to it.

When I was sent out next it was as a bolter-up. I'd been going in every morning with coffee and a paper, conditioned to sitting there for a couple of hours until the B.A. told those of us who hadn't been sent out to go home, when one morning he came to the door and yelled, "Cherry!" I was so surprised I had to look around the room to see if I'd heard him wrong; perhaps he'd called somebody else. But no one else got up, so I put down the paper and went over. When he dropped his voice to a whisper there was so much phlegm in it I began to wonder if he had T.B.

"How long you outta work?"

"Two and a half weeks," I answered.

"You bolt up?"

"Sure."

"You're a fuckin' liar. You never been boltin' up in your life."

"Well, stick 'em, pull the erection bolts, gun the mothers up," I said. "I can do it." He studied me, apparently deciding if I were trying to be cute. Then he bent over and wrote an address on a slip of paper, which he then handed to me. I thanked him and turned to leave.

"*Any*body can do it," he growled.

The job was in a little industrial park some thirty miles down the main road. There were seven buildings in a two-acre clearing. They were all in the terminal stages of erection, each by a different builder. Their shapes were intended to reflect the nature of their occupants' businesses. One was circular, divided into twelve wedge-shaped bays, roofed by a shallow inverted saucer. It was to be the home office of a watch company. One, the business office of a chemical company, was shaped like a giant retort. I never found out the business of the firm that was to occupy the building I was on. It was shaped like half a tire. It still bothers me that I don't know. There was a round reflecting pond being dug where the hub cap should have been.

A bit wiser now in the ways of the business, I didn't drive directly into the job site, but having located it, went on down the road until I found a diner, where I drank coffee until ten-fifteen. Then I drove back to the park and nosed around until I found a trailer marked Seneca Construction Company. I opened the door to find Jack sitting on a stool before a drafting table, looking at blueprints.

"Hullo, Jack," I said, glad to see him, "I didn't know you were here."

"You didn't?"

"Nope."

"You got tools?" He was being rather unfriendly, I thought, wondering why.

"Just a crescent and a gas key is all. What do I need?"

"Patrick's up on the fourth floor; he'll straighten you out. Here. Sign these. He pushed the usual tax forms and employment papers in front of me, at the same time handing me a pencil.

"Patrick's here?" I asked.

"You didn't know that?" he countered.

"I haven't seen Patrick in a couple of months," I said. I began signing the papers, confused by his manner but glad to learn that Patrick was on the job.

"He's up welding bar joists. You can bum tools from him, because he isn't using his while he's welding. But don't get to jawin' until after 4:30." I nodded, put the pencil on top of the papers I had signed, and started for the door.

"Your partner's a kid named Dan. He's even greener than you are, so the both of you be careful. You've got some angles to put in, and I don't want an accident." I started to speak, but he waved me off. "Your pusher's name is Dan, too. After you've seen Patrick, report to him." He looked at his watch, sighed, then glared at me. "I hope you didn't pick up bad habits on your last job. We're behind, here, and everybody has to put out. Work, and I'll keep you here as long as I can. Goof off, and I'll throw you out tonight."

When I found Patrick, I asked him what the matter with Jack was. He said that Jack had a piece of the profits and there weren't going to be any. He told me to get his tool belt out of his car and to take everything out of it except the wescot,* bull pin, seven-eighths spud, and four-pound beater.

The belt itself, a Miller with a serial number so low it must have been made in the forties, was a piece of heavy oiled leather two and a half inches wide by nearly a quarter of an inch thick. It was reinforced for several inches along each side with additional pieces of leather riveted to the main length. At these points, scabbards were hung. One was designed to hold two spud wrenches; another held Patrick's bull pin. Behind the pin scabbard was a canvas bag about four inches by eight inches by eight inches, meant to hold bolts. I strapped the belt on, replacing the smaller spud wrench with his wescot, dropping the beater into the bolt bag, emptying miscellaneous junk into a cardboard box in his trunk. I guessed the weight of this portable tool kit at twenty to twenty-five pounds right like it was, and wondered how in hell the connectors, who carry all of this plus another spud wrench, a connecting bar, and a whole bag of bolts, manage to climb a flight of stairs, let alone spend all day shinnying up columns. It didn't seem to me that anyone could climb the columns on this job anyway; they were too small. The building was only four stories high and, with the exception of the center bay, had no iron in it more than eight inches wide. Iron this light—it's steel, of course, but it's called "iron" anyhow—is sneeringly referred to as "small stuff," and jobs containing a lot of it are held in very low esteem. This is not a *macho* thing, but a practical one. Light iron is a drag to work with. It's easily bent, so that

---

* I've spelled this phonetically, in terms of the place we were. In other places it's pronounced other ways: "westcott," "wescock," "westcock." It probably was once a brand name. In New York City it's generally called a "crescent." Sometimes it is even referred to as an "adjustable," which is what it is—a twelve-inch adjustable wrench.

minor collisions in offloading or erection can ruin pieces. It is hard to climb, since the flanges are too skinny for one's hands to get a good purchase. It's hard to walk across, not so much because of the narrow gauge, but because it shakes with a man's weight. Worst of all, a load landed roughly on any part of a light structure will shake the entire job, and a man working on open iron out of sight of the raising gang has no way of knowing when the next jolt will come.

This building was so flimsy-looking that I wondered if it satisfied the safety code. The hole it stood in was only one-story deep, and the columns ran in one piece from the footings to the roof. The principal horizontal members connecting the columns* are called "headers." Horizontal members running from one header to another are called "beams." On a large building, or a smaller one designed to bear a heavy load, the beams are usually four to six feet apart. After they (and some even smaller pieces) are in place, heavy corrugated iron sheets are spread out across the beams and tackwelded in place, wire mesh is spread on top of the sheets, and three to six inches of concrete poured on top. On this job, however, the support for the floors was composed of bar joists. Bar joists are usual in smaller structures. A bar joist is a welded truss resembling a side of one type of bridge. It is made of two parallel lengths of T-shaped steel separated by a triangular arrangement of light rod struts. These struts (half-inch rod, in this case) are welded to the longitudinal members at sixty-degree angles, thus forming a series of equilateral triangles, thereby making the unit quite rigid. The joists are tacked-welded at either end to the headers, and the corrugated iron sheets, called "decking," are laid on top.

A "bay" is the area bounded by any four columns and their connecting headers. The bays on this job, because of its peculiar configuration, were fan-shaped, meaning that the joists, ten or twelve in each bay, were closer together at the inner end than the outer. When I reported to Dan Pusher, he and Dan Permit were having considerable trouble with the arithmetic involved in placing the joists where they belonged. Dan Pusher kept referring to the drawings but

* This must be pronounced "kol-yooms." If you say it the other way, no one will know what you're talking about.

66

could find no listing of the spacings. Dan Permit had a piece of "keel" (crayon) with which he was doing division problems all over the nearest column.

"God damn it," Dan Permit said, "there's twelve joists go in this bay. It's twenty-four feet between the columns at this end. They have to be two feet apart on center."

"Well, it ain't right," said Dan Pusher. "Any fool can see t'at."

"I see it, I see it," mumbled Dan Permit, "but, Judas Priest, two times twelve is twenty-four." He kept scratching the back of his head in confusion.

"Try dividing by thirteen," I said.

"Who t'e hell are *you?*" asked Dan Pusher. I told him my name, and that the hall had sent me out to bolt up. During my explanation the two of them eyed me suspiciously.

"Why by thirteen?" asked Dan Permit.

"Because twelve joists make thirteen spaces," I replied. Understanding dawned in Dan Permit's face. He began again scratching the column with the keel. In a moment, however, it was once more cloudy weather.

"It don't go even," he said, "and what good is a friggin' decimal point with friggin' feet?"

"Change everything to inches first," I suggested.

"Listen, smart ass," put in Dan Pusher, "you know how to do t'is shit, *you* do it. What local you out of, anyway?"

"I'm on permit."

"Jesus, Mary and Joseph," he sputtered, "another one! I'll go friggin' nuts; t'ere ain't a book man in t'e state." He paced back and forth on a bundle of decking for a minute or two, then wheeled on me. "All right, Mister Mike Permit, you're in charge on layin' out t'e joists. Take Dan's keel and mark centers. When a bay is marked, lay out t'e joists. Work your way from t'is end to t'at one, and stay in front of t'e welders. I don't want nobody standin' around waitin' on you. Dan, you work wit' him. I'll send somebody else boltin' up." He hurried off, muttering, "My God," over and over to himself.

Dan Permit and I laid out bar joists for six days. Through the last two we had a hell of a time keeping ahead of Patrick and his swamper, who were laying out and tacking decking at top speed and threatening to overrun us. Over a beer one night I asked Patrick if he always worked at such speed.

"Not exactly," he said, reflectively, "but close to it. I do good work and I like to go fast, but in this case that ain't the whole thing." He shuffled his feet around on the bottom rung of his stool before continuing. "This's a bad job. I'd like to get it over with, that's all."

"What's the matter with it?" I asked. "Are you talking about Jack being bent out of shape?"

"Not especially. It ain't any one thing; it's just a rinky-dink job. Small as it is, it's still the biggest job this outfit ever took on, and some things are wrong. The gear is too light. You didn't see the crane we used to set the iron, but you will next week. They're bringin' it back to set the coolin' tower. It's too small, but it's all the company's got. Everything's too small. Wait'll you go boltin' up, you'll see. They're usin' electric guns, like this was a goddam garage, for Chrissake. At the far end of the building you have to use so much extension cord that there's a bad drop in the line voltage. Hell, they subbed out the concrete to a guy named Jackson, and he paid his men the week before last in cold checks—every one of 'em bounced. Now he has to pay his men in cash, and the bank doesn't even want to do business with us." He paused long enough to order us another round, and the break seemed to destroy any further desire to go into details. "I just want to finish up and get out," he said. "That's all."

We shot two games of snooker before I spoke. When I did, it was just to ask why he didn't quit.

"Can't. Promised Jack if he'd put you on I'd stay to the end."

"Put me on? You're behind that?" Patrick looked at me and laughed. I had to raise my voice to get through the noise he was making. "Nobody told me that, man. Freddy called me and sent me here; that's all I know."

"Don't make a big deal out of it. I asked Jack to call for you and he did, that's all."

"Why?"

"Because you don't seem to realize what was being done to you. How'd you like working with Callahan's gang?"

"I didn't mind. We got along all right."

"I know you did. I talked to Callahan. What you don't know is that if you stay with them any length of time you'll get a rep you don't want. That gang is famous. They nearly always go out together because nobody else will have them. They're known as the Drunk Gang. Every goddam one of 'em's a lush, from Callahan, who can at least carry it off, through Harry all the way down to Timmy, who's a knock-down, drag-out rummy."

"Well, he shakes pretty bad most mornings, but he gets his job done."

"Some job. He used to be a *connector.* Now he works on the ground, when he works at all. You don't ever want to be in a raising gang if he's in it. At least, *I* don't, and I don't know anybody else who would want to. Four or five years ago he was one of the best there was, but he poured it all down a bottle. Hell, do you know he's got a *college* education?"

"Yeah. I know."

"Then you tell me, you know so much about it, why in hell a man with a fuckin' *college* education would go ironworkin'. It don't make any fuckin' sense."

"I never said I knew anything about it; maybe it does make sense. Maybe he likes the work, for all I know."

"*Likes the work?* What's to like? All you do is hump yourself blue in the face. You freeze your balls right up into your belly in the winter and sweat 'em down to your knees in the summer—what's to like? *I* like the work. I *got* to like the work, because it's all I know. *You* like the work, because it ain't as bad as the wire mill, and the reason it ain't as bad as the wire mill is it pays five dollars an hour more than the wire mill. Why would *Timmy* like it?" Patrick shook his head in belligerent confusion.

"You like to connect?" I asked. He nodded. "You rather connect or bolt up?"

"Well, I'd rather connect, of course."

"Why do you say 'of course'?"

"Well, because connectin' is where it's at, that's all."

"You think I'd like to connect?"

"My God. Well, you're always complainin' that everybody keeps tellin' you you're not a real ironworker, so there you are. They'll quit when you learn to connect."

"You think Timmy likes to connect?"

"I think Timmy's scared shitless."

"I think I'm gonna be scared shitless, too."

"You got time. It'll be awhile before you go connecting. You ain't even been in a raisin' gang, yet. You'll get used to it."

"We weren't talking about getting used to it; we were talking about liking it."

"You're losing me, man."

"I'm just wondering if Timmy likes to connect."

Patrick shook his head with conviction. "Maybe once. Not now. Now he *can't* connect. Period."

We had one more drink apiece before Patrick went through his "Quittin' time!" routine.

In the years since that night I've tried to remember what I thought about on the way home, but I've never been sure I've got it right. I've told the story of what happened on that job often, when out drinking with other ironworkers and into the miasma of fatalism that sometimes takes hold, and I've usually presented Patrick's remarks about it being a "bad" job as though they constituted an omen. But I don't really remember if I took them that way. The bare truth is simply that two days after Patrick expressed his distaste for the job, Dan Permit was knocked over the side.

The crane had been brought back to set the cooling tower. "Tower" is rather too grand a word, but the term is used irrespective of the size of the unit. It was simply a cube-shaped frame of light iron about sixteen feet on a side. Its function was to house a water tank, pumps, and related equipment. It was put together on the ground, bolted up and welded, then hoisted atop the building.

A thirty-foot jib had been added to the eighty-foot stick of the crane so that it would be possible to reach in far enough beyond the lip of the roof to place the tower where it belonged, which was well to the rear of the roof. A "jib" is simply an extension. Cranes are counterbalanced, of course, by massive weights fitted to their rear ends, and the farther out the stick is boomed, the less effective is this weight. Placing the tower where it belonged involved being able to boom out to an extreme angle, and Jack, after an argument with the operator, had us drag over a couple of tons of stuff and hang it off the counterweight. With this additional counterbalancing, the operator agreed to make the lift. Patrick was stationed on the edge of the roof as the signalman, since the final placement of the tower was to be so far back that it would be out of the operator's sight.

The tower was hooked on, and the crane lifted it until it was nearly two-blocked.* Once it was up, the crane swung round until it faced directly toward its destination. Patrick then extended his arm with his fist clenched and his thumb pointing down. This means "boom out," and the operator began easing the boom forward. As the load neared the edge of the roof it of course came lower. Patrick made a twisting motion with his other hand, as though he were driving a screw into the ceiling. This is the signal to "get up" on the load. There were about four feet of space left between the blocks, and the operator began to come up through this distance with the load. He was booming out at the same time—all of this is ordinary procedure—when his cats began to leave the ground. He was no Angie, though (or perhaps the additional weights we'd hung confused his feel for his rig), and things began to happen very quickly. The balance point shot past, and the crane continued going over. He let go the load, but it was too late. The boom struck the edge of the roof, bent, and collapsed. In a sequence that no one was ever able to agree on, the rig went over on its nose, the boom folded over the roof, the cooling tower tore through the rear outside header and plunged to the ground in back of the building, and the cable that had hoisted it snapped. The breaking of the cable must not have happened until the tower had nearly reached the ground, because there were sixty-five feet of it beyond the jib sheave when the inspectors measured it later.

When all this hell broke loose, I ran like a madman for the back of

---

* "Two-blocking" occurs when a load is hoisted as far as it can go. There is a sheave, or block, for the cable to pass through at the end of a boom or jib, and if the cable is in more than one "part"—each part being a run between the blocks—there is also a sheave at the hook end. The higher a load is lifted the closer together come the sheaves. When they have come all the way together the load is "two-blocked." By extension, therefore, "two-blocking" is carrying anything to its limit. (To take up on a turnbuckle all the way is to "two-block" it.)

the building. Dan Permit was astride a back header on the third floor, shoving bar joists around to the keel marks I had made for him. The flying cable snaked in a giant diagonal arc, took a turn around a column, and whipped him over the side. He only fell thirty-five feet, but he landed on his head in a pile of rocks that had been removed from the hole. I took one look at him and threw up.

When I finished vomiting, I took off my sweatshirt and pitched it across his face. As I started around the building, I realized that no one else had come around back and that therefore no one else had seen Dan fall. I looked up to see Patrick climbing down the broken boom, which was curled around the roof header and led down to the crane cab at about a fifty-degree angle. Several men were helping the operator out of the rig. There was a lot of noise. As the man was lifted out, Jack kept shouting, "Is he okay?" The man answered for himself that he was. Patrick dropped from the lower end of the boom to the ground, leaned against one of the upturned cats, and lit a cigarette. He shook his head when Jack asked him if he were hurt. Jack looked at me. I said, "Dan Permit's dead." When he just stood there, I shouted at him, "Dead, you slow-witted prick!" He and Dan Pusher, who had come up behind him, took off running toward the back of the building. Patrick pushed himself off the cat and walked slowly after them.

"Not much point in running," he said, to no one in particular.

It is traditional to take up a collection for the family of a man who has been killed. In Dan Permit's case, the money came to $212. The local deposited the money to its account and made out a check to the widow for the same amount. Freddy came out to the job and handed the check to me, saying that since I was his partner I should be the one to give it to his wife, and for me to get some sort of card to put it in.

There was insurance coverage through the local, in the amount of $2500. Since he was not a book man, there was no coverage through the International. Had there been, his estate would have received another $10,000.

Jack, Dan Pusher, Patrick, and I attended the funeral. I tried, while attempting to give the widow the absurd lily-decorated envelope that contained the $212, to make a speech of condolence, but she seemed to hear nothing, nor did she extend her hand. I finally gave it to the elder of the two small girls beside her.

Drinking sessions for the next several days shaped themselves variously as Postmortems, Courts of Inquiry, or Symposia on The Meaning of Life. In the Postmortem phase, one man would begin by remarking that, "He only went thirty, thirty-five feet, the poor prick." All would nod. "My God, Jack himself went five floors on that job in Syracuse and come out of it wit' nothin' more'n a pair of broken legs." It was mandatory that the next man point out that Dan Permit had landed on his head. Then someone would mention another flop, and swapping tales of who had gone how far when and with what damage might last an hour or more. Inevitably, someone would hold that since he was only a permit man, and a brand new one to boot, he shouldn't have been put where he could get hurt in the first place. Another man would snort, "And where the hell is there that a man can't get hurt?" That would open the Court of Inquiry: Should he have been on open iron anyway? Was the lift of a fairly heavy tower with a toy crane inherently unsafe? Why wasn't the man told to get out of the area while the lift was being made? What caused the tower to drop almost to the ground before the load cable parted? Had the operator done all he could?

I was surprised at the lack of agreement and the murkiness of the answers. Even after an investigation of sorts had been conducted, there was less clarity than passion, and The Meaning of Life stage of a conversation was generally made up of a series of discrete and unattended manifestos. There was lip service to When Your Number's Up It's Up, which sometimes arose in abbreviated form as You Never Know, and there was a nodding of heads when one man said that Dan Permit should have kept his job with the railroad. Patrick repeated his desire to finish the job and get out.

The accident was the main subject of conversation for about four days, gradually being replaced by expressions of hostility at the approach of winter.

I finished pushing Dan's bar joists into place, and once looked over the side at the rocks. Some still bore bloodstains. There was a mound of loose sand two or three feet from where he had landed, but it might just as well have been two or three miles away.

PART 2

FOUNDATIONS

I am not so much afraid of death, as ashamed thereof. 'Tis the very disgrace and ignominy of our natures, that in a moment can so disfigure us, that our nearest friends, wife, and children, stand afraid and start at us.

—SIR THOMAS BROWNE

THE most obvious, relentless, whimsically malevolent enemy of the man who works outdoors is the weather. He is more aware of the state of the weather than of that of the nation's economic health. The weather is more immediate. Construction slows in a recession and stops in a depression, but these conditions develop through longish blocks of time, and a man has an opportunity to make adjustments and seek solutions. But if the rent is due on Friday and he is rained out on Wednesday and Thursday, his problem is in the here and now.

The savings account is the sensible outdoor worker's answer. Any reasonable man expects to lose time in the winter. His savings account is his cushion, and he hangs onto it for dear life. Where other groups may measure status in automobiles, dress, or housing, the construction worker tends to salute available funds. He does not trust abstractions. If you work in an office, it's unlikely that you know how much money the man who works next to you has in the bank. It would be gauche to ask him. But I can tell you exactly how much money most of my friends have tucked away. We brag about it; it's part of our daily conversation.

And a run of bad weather can wipe us out. More easily than slow times, in fact, because if we *know* there'll be no work, we'll look around for something else to do: tending bar, pushing a hack, loading trucks in a warehouse. If we can prove that there's no work, we can draw unemployment insurance. But bad weather happens one day at a time.

Many people outside the industry seem to think it's seasonal, that we shut down in the winter. This isn't so; we work, or try to, twelve months of the year. In bad weather we get sent home—but we go in every day.

What weather can do to a man's income shows in these figures: In 1970 I worked in New York City from March 1st on. That was a famous year among construction people, because the winter was virtually snowless and the spring was almost without rain. In those ten months I lost a day and a half to the weather. The following year I lost forty-three days, which comes to about $3400. Thus in spite of the fact that I worked *two months* more, I earned about the same.

Still, financial vagaries aren't the worst problem. The worst thing is sheer physical discomfort. Hell, call it pain. Some people can take it better than others, but none of us is happy about it. Too hot versus too cold is a Hobson's Choice, but I'd rather be too hot. "Youse Rebs got t'in blood," my friend Leo tells me every winter.

But he hates cold weather, too. Any construction worker who tells you he doesn't hate it is either a madman or a liar. In winter the whole notion of what distinguishes a good job from a bad job is turned upside down: Tit work is to be avoided, and if a man must work, he is well-advised to seek bull work. When the temperature gets down near zero, a man who would in summer absolutely refuse to carry planks or bust rods may happily accept such work.

I had one tit job in December that first year and went to work each day fully expecting to freeze to death. It was a small office building much like the one I'd been on with Dan Permit. Bar joists supported the decking. On top of the decking we spread five-foot-by-ten-foot sheets of wire mesh, tying them to each other with wire. At the perimeter of each floor and around every column we laid four-foot lengths of reinforcing rod every six inches, tying these into the mesh also. (Concrete stuffed with such rods, in this case ranging from three-eighths to three-quarters of an inch in diameter, is a great deal stronger than concrete without reinforcing. The wire mesh serves a similar purpose.) Since the building was not tall, the concrete was pumped up from the trucks by hose, the nozzle of which was wrestled around by two giant Italians in hip boots. Other Italians and blacks with shovels and lengths of two-by-four and trowels and spatulas did the spreading and smoothing. These people belonged to a different trade union, of course, but even so they couldn't work without an ironworker being on hand. This was because they weren't allowed—by the terms of their contract and ours—to handle any of the rods, wire, or mesh that would occasionally stick up through the wet concrete. If something had to be retied or pushed back down, an ironworker had to do it. Thus we had essentially the same kind of situation that had existed with the glaziers on my first job: The concrete gang couldn't pour unless the ironworker was present, while the ironworker had nothing to do if the concrete gang wasn't there.

That job is called "pour-watching" and is ordinarily given to the eldest man as a sop to his age, since there is virtually nothing to do. However, there were no old men on that job, and it fell to me. I was handed a rod-tier's belt and pointed toward the pour. The belt is merely a leather strap with a six-inch aluminum-shelled drum of tie-wire attached on one side, and a scabbard holding a pair of side-cutting pliers (for seizing the tie and snipping its ends) on the other.

The pouring gang did half a floor a day, making eight scheduled working days for the four floors of the building. Because of sleet, freezing rain, and one major snowfall, it took three weeks to find the eight days. On the first day I wore my thermal underwear, jeans, and a heavy jacket, and sent out for whiskey at the afternoon coffee break because I thought I was going to die. On the second day I added a sweatshirt and overalls and decided that my feet were going to have to be amputated. By the fourth day I had reached maximum clothing capacity: regular undershorts and tee-shirt, thermal bottoms and tops, heavy levis, a cotton turtle-neck, wool turtle-neck sweater, thermal-lined hooded sweatshirt, bib-top overalls and blanket-lined canvas jacket, wool inner socks, wool knit outer socks, thermal-lined water-proof boots, cotton inner gloves under leather outer gloves, and a woolen ski mask with ear flaps fitted under my hardhat. In order to get all this gear on and off, I became regularly the first man in the shanty in the morning and the last man out at night. Fortunately, nothing ever needed retying; I couldn't possibly have bent over to do it. In the entire three weeks I tied nothing at all, though several times I pushed things down out of sight with my boot.

Winter! I began each day by listening to the weather report, praying to hear that the temperature was either over twenty-five or under twenty below. If it was in the twenties, I felt I could survive; at twenty below not even Mad Johnson, the foreman, could expect us to work. I listened for the wind that sneaked into my room under the door and became expert at computing the wind-chill factor. Each morning after the weather report I made coffee, using a little immersion coil, and went back to bed, where it was possible to think of thousands of reasons for not going to work. I thought enviously of the welder who had left a few weeks before. I had worked with him for a couple of days, laying out buttons. Buttons are little steel stampings less than an inch square which one man places at intervals so that a welder can at those points tack the decking sheets in place on their supporting bar joists. During coffee break on the first really cold day he told me that he always went to Florida to work in the winter. He'd been doing it, he said, for twenty years, so that he knew everyone there and was seldom stuck for a job. He hated snow. He would be off, he announced, the moment there was the least little bit of it.

The next day was warmer; by midmorning it must have been up in the thirties. It was a beautiful blue day with one very tiny gray-white cloud down near the horizon. But that cloud worked its way slowly over us, and out of it came one little snowflake, which settled very gently on the welder's nose. On the instant he dropped his welding lead, shook my hand, and went off yelling for the Madman to get his money. I never saw him again.

Envying the welder, though, changed nothing, and when my coffee was done I would get up and begin girding my loins to face the day.

There was only one day on which I talked myself out of going in, and that was the day the beer froze. I had heard the weatherman say that at the airport it was four degrees above zero with the wind from the north at twelve miles an hour. I had then made up a dozen reasons for staying home, rejected them all, and gotten dressed. To open the door, however, I had first to move a couple of cans of beer which I had left in front of it the night before so that they would keep cool. When I realized that they were frozen solid I denounced the reporter for a fool and a liar and went happily back to bed.

Some men accept ordinary cold weather genially, saying little about it other than that they would rather be too cold than too hot. Others, like me, would rather be too hot, and bitch unendingly. A frequent subject of January gin mill debate is What's The Best Job In Winter? Callahan annually manages to draw unemployment insurance during December, January, and February. I'll-Drink-To-That never mentions the weather, hot or cold. Harry likes to carry rods. Timmy, despite a body full of antifreeze, complained without pause. And there is always *some* idiot around who demonstrates his masculinity by trotting along the iron in his T-shirt.

Patrick, however, speaks for the majority and sums up the matter properly when he announces over his four-thirty tequila, "Winter sucks."

There was enough work that winter to keep most of us busy, but it was all small stuff. Patrick and I spent two weeks as partners carrying rods at a small shopping center. I'll-Drink-To-That and I carried rods for a week at a suburban restaurant. I carried rods for three or four days at a gas station with a young boy whose name I've forgotten. It seems to me in memory that, with the exception of a week in the raising gang on a steakhouse, I spent the entire winter either sitting in the hall or carrying rods. I carried rods so often that I began to worry if I were being typecast.

And it is dull work, perhaps the dullest nonassemblyline work there is. Virtually all construction concrete is larded with rods. Floors are laced with them, laid over wire mesh. Walls are gridded with them, the verticals anchored to those protruding from the concrete of the section below and the horizontals fastened to these with tie wire. Bridge supports are often (when they aren't solid metal columns) basically rod armatures around which the carpenters build wooden frames into which the concrete is poured. The molded cast concrete panels which make up the roofs of the more fanciful modernistic buildings begin life in female molds built on the ground. Rodmen build "mats" into these molds, bending the individual rods to their proper shape with tools called "hickies." The formed longitudinal and transverse rods are tied together, concrete is poured and spread, and when it has set, the top of that panel is used as the bottom of the next mold. Everywhere there is concrete there are rods. Some men tie them; some men carry them.

Tying them is dull enough (and not precisely beneficial to any man with a back problem, since the work amounts to bending down to tie your shoes a thousand times a day), but carrying them is utterly moronic. When it is necessary to move rods from point A to point B, three decisions have to be made: Who is going to do the carrying, how many are going to be carried at one time, and where along their length should they be lifted. The first matter does not concern the carrier; the pusher says, "Mike! You and your idiot partner get t'ose number t'ree rods over to Sam's gang. Sometime today, if youse please!" (The phrase "sometime today" translates as "instantly.") The second matter is resolved by the accommodation of the carriers to each other: "Are you kiddin' me, or what? Put some a t'em sonofabitches down; I can't carry all t'at!" Or, conversely, "Jesus Christ, Mike! Whaddaya wanna do, walk back and fort' all day? Pick up more'n t'at, anyway!" The third decision requires some experience, although no more than an orangutan could acquire in an hour. Some rods are sixteen, twenty, even twenty-four feet long, and when lifted at each end sag in the middle. The solution lies in picking them up at the quarter-points—a fourth of the way in from the ends. This results in half the length of the rods being suspended between the carriers and thereby minimizes the sag. It also gives the man in back a chance, if he is so inclined, to give his partner a small screwing: By working his way aft along the bundle while they walk, he can throw some of the weight forward to the other man. As with the rest of the world, some men never do this; others try all the time.

But once a man has carried enough rods to prejudge the weight of his intended bundle, and once practice has given him enough of an eye to judge the quarters, there is nothing left but picking them up and putting them down. More than once I've been so lost in daydreaming that I've walked into mud holes and snowbanks.

Nevertheless, some men bust rods year in and year out. I know carriers who've never been ten feet off the ground in their lives.* And who don't intend to go. Carriers are recognizable by their clothes: The

* Again, everything depends on where you are. Rodmen carry regular ironworking books in most places (called "mixed" locals), but not in New York City. In the city, the wire lathers, a different union, handle the rods. They shape, cut, and tie, but don't carry. They have laborers to do the carrying.

rough surface of the rods tears holes. Also, the men who habitually carry on one side develop the old postman's condition, high-shoulder.

It's a dull job, but like carrying plank, not so bad in cold weather. A man can pretty much set his pace to match the temperature, moving less quickly as he warms up. He can keep warm more easily than can, say, the bolter-up, who may spend two or three hours on the same "point," working with his hands but unable to do anything to increase the circulation in the rest of his body.

The steakhouse job was another kind of thing altogether. I was sent out as a rod buster, but went in the raising gang when a man was out sick, and stayed there for a week. It was one of dozens of identical buildings in a chain of restaurants which dots New York, Connecticut, and Massachusetts: an eight-sided one-story structure with eight radial gables butting on a center block resting on falsework. Falsework is temporary iron. In this instance, the falsework was the centerpost; when the job was complete, the middle column was removed, leaving what amounted to a rigid tent without a pole.

The foreman had put up ten or twelve of those buildings, and had no patience with anyone who didn't know exactly where everything went. He made my life miserable, though the discomfort was somewhat buffered by the fact that I'll-Drink-To-That was also in the gang, which at least gave me somebody to talk to. Not to listen to, however, for in spite of our now having known each other for some time, he seldom did more than repeat his nickname.

The crane with which the iron was handled was a hundred-ton P&H, a twin of the one we'd had on the bridge job. Rigged with a short stick, it was still plenty for so small a building.

The raising gang consisted of the two connectors (who never spoke to me, I suppose because they resented working with a beginner), the signalman, the hooker-on, the tagline man, and the pusher. I'll-Drink-To-That was the hooker-on, and I was pressed into service as the tagline man.

The job was so small that its erection was a model of simplicity: A truck would arrive at the site; the connectors would jump on it, wrapping heavy chokers around the load. When finished, they made signs to the signalman, who made signs to the operator, who made the lift. The load was put on the ground, the chokers disconnected, and the shaking-out process would begin: Spreader hooks were put on the crane hook, one hook was shoved into each end of a piece, and the piece was lifted and swung over to be landed home. "Home" is directly below where a given piece will be when it is set. The pusher directs a shaking-out, and a main difference between good and bad in pushers lies in how well they plan these moves. When the shaking-out was done, the connectors loaded their bolt bags from kegs of bolts and scaled the columns. The hooker-on then choked a piece at its center, the tagline man attached a line to one end, and the piece was sent up. The connectors fastened each piece to the pieces already erected with just enough bolts to keep it there—one at each end in many cases, two if the connection was of a type in which the use of only one bolt would allow the piece to "roll" (wobble) if walked upon. The moment a piece is "made," one of the connectors trots along it to the choker, cuts it loose, throws down the choker, and trots over to where the next piece will be coming up.

A good raising gang is an impressive sight. This one was not so good, but at that time I had little with which to compare them. It remained for my second gang to show me the real level of intragang competitiveness: each connector trying to be faster than his partner, the two together trying to be faster than the hooker-on, who is trying to get his chokers hooked and centered before the tagline man can get his line ready. If anyone has a moment to sit down, he tends to do so rather ostentatiously, because he is less interested in resting than in letting everybody see that he is so quick that he has to dawdle to let the gang catch up.

This competition flames and flickers, of course, from company to company, gang to gang, day to day. I've worked in gangs in which nobody gave a damn whether the building went up at all, and in gangs in which speed was placed at such a premium that accidents were commonplace. Both extremes are bad news, and I've seen more than one good ironworker arrive on a job at ten in the morning and ask for his money by noon.

I had never been in a raising gang before, and my involvement with this one was so brief that I didn't have a chance to learn much. My job was simply to wrap one end of a five-eighths diameter manila rope around one end of the piece of iron that was to be set, then to use this line to steer the piece clear of any part of the structure that it might be likely to hit on its way up, and finally to swing the piece so that the proper end arrived within the reach of the proper connector. At the moment that he grabbed it, my job with that piece was finished, and I was to take back my line after he had cut it loose, coil it, and run to get ready for the next.

I'll-Drink-To-That was my savior. My ignorance and the speed of the operation rattled me, which triggered constant abuse by the connectors and the pusher, and if it hadn't been for the little man's silent assistance—he often rigged a second line for me while I was still gathering up the first—I might soon have been bullied into quitting in disgust. In one of his rare verbal moments he assured me that the yelling was meaningless and suggested that I wasn't doing as badly as they made out. By the end of the second day, when I had begun to feel that I was catching on, I was less inclined to hold still for the hazing. One of the connectors hollered down, "Hey, numbnuts! Quit givin' us this shit end-for-end, for Chrissake! You got it backwards again." I had checked the piece carefully before it went up and was certain it had gone up right.

"Up yours!" I yelled. "It's right."

"Bull*shit* it's right," he called back, as he and his partner pushed it laterally so that it swung end-for-end. One of them signaled for the crane to ease down on the load so that they could make the piece up.

"Go ahead, you illiterate asshole," I yelled, "make it up backwards. I'll tell the pusher it ain't your fault because you can't read." He had thrown down my tagline when he first grabbed the piece; I picked it up and walked away while coiling it.

At one end of each piece of iron a number indicating its place in the scheme of things had been painted. Although no one had seen fit to explain it to me, I had finally realized that these numbers were painted on the west end of east-west pieces and the south end of north-south pieces. I had walked away because I knew I was right. As I bent to attach my line to the next piece I could see out of the corner of my eye that the connectors were shrugging at each other, and recognized then that they had known all along which end was which and had merely been, as they would have put it, "bustin' balls." They spun the piece around once more and made it up properly, and thereafter yelled at me somewhat less.

Many beams, especially in simple box structures, could go in one way as well as another. Obviously, it won't do if the piece has holes punched somewhere along its length (other than dead center) to receive the end of a smaller piece. To avoid mistakes, the practice of standardizing the location of the numbers is universal. I cared less about that than about finding a chance to be sure I was right so that I could do a little yelling of my own. It was several jobs later before I had it brought home to me that the painters of the numbers might make an occasional mistake.

One day one of the connectors went to pieces. There are endless stories of men freezing on the iron, but I've seen it happen only once. I didn't know the man in any way beyond his name, which was MacDonald. I never heard him called by a first name nor a nickname; he was just MacDonald.

He was cooning out from his connection toward the choker to cut the piece loose ("cooning" is a rapid shuffle along a beam accomplished by putting the feet on either side of the bottom flange, then bending over so that the hands can grip either side of the top flange), when one of his feet slipped off. This caused a momentary lurch, but nothing more. He still had both hands and the other foot on the iron and was never really in danger of falling. It's practically impossible to fall off a beam while cooning. He kept on moving to the choker, grabbed it, and while standing erect on the bottom flange, slipped it from its hook. The operator swung the hook away, and as MacDonald stooped to free the choker from the beam, the same foot went out from under him again. He dropped to the beam, curled his arms and legs around it, and put the side of his face down on the top flange, which knocked his hat off. His partner began to laugh, and the pusher looked up and yelled to him to do his humping after four-thirty. The other connector checked his laughter long enough to chime in, "Yeah, MacDonald, do your screwin' on your own time; we got a goddam buildin' to put up!"

But MacDonald remained motionless. I was almost directly below him, a vertical distance of no more than twenty-five feet, and could see his hands gripping the bottom flanges. The knuckles were white. His nose and chin showed over the edge of the beam, and they, too, were white. The crane had swung over the next piece and I'll-Drink-To-That was slipping the eye of the choker over the hook, hollering to me at the same time, "C'mon, Mike; getcher line on t'is t'ing." The pusher and the other connector were still yelling at MacDonald to stop fooling around and get up, but he wasn't moving.

"Forget the damned piece," I called, "somethin's happened over here." I'll-Drink-To-That ran over and we stood together, staring idiotically up at MacDonald. The other connector went out the beam to the man, sat down, and began talking to him. He tried to pry one of MacDonald's hands away from the flange, but failed.

"I can't budge him," he called down, "he's welded on."

As the pusher had realized what was happening, he had skimmed up the opposite column, gone out the beam, and now sat at MacDonald's feet. Wrapping his legs around the piece, he used both arms to try to pry loose one of MacDonald's legs, but couldn't do it. The other man was talking softly to MacDonald, "Hey, man, it's okay . . . everyt'in's okay; it's okay, MacDonald; say *somet'in'*, will you?" He got no answer.

"Is he breathin'?" asked the pusher.

"I can't tell," said the other in considerable agitation, "I don't know."

It was the signalman who came to his senses first. He placed himself so that he could see the men on the beam and so that the crane operator could see him, then had the operator swing his hook directly over MacDonald. As he did this, I'll-Drink-To-That ran to get a three-eighths choker and hollered for the pusher to catch it. He yelled several times before he was able to get the man's attention, and even then the pusher just looked dopey until I'll-Drink-To-That pointed at MacDonald while making circling gestures with the choker around his own waist. When understanding dawned in the pusher's eyes, I'll-Drink-To-That threw him the choker. He worked it between the man's stomach and the beam, choking it at the spine, slipping the eye over the hook. When they tried to pull him off the beam, however,

MacDonald began to scream. The noise was proof he was alive, but it wasn't words and it wasn't very helpful. His grip didn't loosen; his knuckles were still white.

"Stop it, for God's sake!" I yelled. "You'll pull the poor son of a bitch in half!" There were exchanges of confused glances, but the pulling stopped.

"Hit him in t'e head, dammit!" yelled somebody. The other connector, after a moment's hesitation, gave MacDonald a vicious but openhanded slap in the face. Nothing changed.

"Love pats won't help," called the signalman, "you got to cold-conk him." He and the other connector exchanged stares. The connector shrugged, put a three-inch bolt in his fist, and gave MacDonald a shot that should have knocked all his teeth out. Blood spurted everywhere, and MacDonald's body went limp. The crane lifted him up, swung him a couple of feet to one side, and lowered him to the ground. As the other connector slid down a column to the ground, he kept repeating, "What could I do? What could I do? There wasn't any other place to hit him."

MacDonald's face looked like it had been in a train wreck. A half-pound bolt, I saw, added considerably to the effectiveness of a blow. The bleeding was mostly from the nose, and we had it pretty well stanched by the time the ambulance arrived. By then MacDonald was awake but silent. His eyes were unfocused, giving the impression that he was looking inwards. I'll-Drink-To-That stood him up and steered him into the ambulance as though he were blind.

As we stood watching the car drive off somebody said, "What t'e hell caused t'at?"

"Damned if I know."

"He stumbled twice just before he froze."

"So what? He was always stumbling. He never fell."

"Well, what'm *I* supposed to know? I wasn't even watchin'."

"Hook jerk t'e piece?"

"Hell, no; steady as a dance floor."

"You got a smoke, man?"

"Was he new to connectin'?" That was me, asking out of ignorance.

"Good Christ, no," came the answer, "him and me did t'e

Satterwhite Buildin', some time back. He's connected four, five years, anyway."

There were a few more questions without answers before the pusher said that it was a quarter to four and he had no one else to send up anyway and to hell with it, everybody go home. By ten after four all the tools had been put in the box and the box hung in the sky off the crane for the night (an antitheft move) and everybody had driven off, except me. I stayed sitting in my car, smoking a cigarette. When it was finished, I suddenly felt very dirty and drove home to shower.

"You hear about MacDonald?" I asked Patrick.

"Yeah," he said, "I heard."

"Well, what do you think?"

· "What do you mean, what do *I* think? You were there, not me."

"Whoo-ee, mister," I said, surprised, "what makes you so touchy?"

"Who said I was touchy?" he said, touchily.

"I mean, what do you think was the reason for it? Nothing happened, you know. He stumbled a little bit, not enough to blow a man's mind."

"What does anybody know about what it takes to blow a man's mind?"

"Well, I guess that's what I'm asking. You knew him, didn't you?" I wanted very badly to get Patrick to talk about what had happened to MacDonald, but even when he answered direct questions, his shoulders remained hunched halfway between apathy and distaste.

"Worked with him a few times, that's all."

"What's his first name?"

"Don't know." I sighed and let it drop. I asked Patrick if he wanted to shoot some pool, but he said not right then. A man I didn't know stepped up and invited himself instead, so I left Patrick sitting there and spent the next half-hour at the table. When I went back to the bar, Callahan was sitting beside Patrick.

"D'ja hear about Timmy?" he asked. I said no. "He's up to Happy Dale again."

"That's a sanitarium?"

"His home away from home."

"Good," I said.

"Good?" said Callahan, "What in hell's good about it? It means I got no signalman and t'e hall'll probably send me out some dummy like you, t'at's all."

"What're you doin' workin' this time of year, anyway?" asked Patrick.

"Couldn't pass it up," replied Callahan, "It's only about a five- or six-day job, and t'e unemployment people don't ever need to know about it." He turned to me, "Listen, dummy, you want a few days' work?"

"I'm workin'," I answered. "I'm taglinin' on a steakhouse."

"Oh, yeah?" said Callahan, showing signs of interest. "Is t'at t'e job where MacDonald did a number?"

"Yeah," I answered.

"Aw, shit," said Patrick.

"Well, what t'e hell happened to him?" Callahan asked. "T'e story I got was all mixed up."

"Screw everybody," said Patrick.

"He had a—a seizure, I guess you'd call it," I said.

"Whaddaya mean, a seizure?" Callahan asked. Patrick put his tequila glass loudly on the bar.

"He *froze*, birdbrain," he declared. I suppose it was the word "froze" that triggered it, but whatever the reason I had a sudden and painfully vivid memory of what had been inside my head for a moment as I had stood motionlessly looking down through the louvers that very first day on the Frederick Building.

But I had been up three hundred feet and change that day, and had never previously worked at height at all, irrespective of the width of the platform. How could that feeling relate to what had happened to MacDonald? Why would a man who had been ironworking for several years, and, judging by rumor, been working capably, go berserk twenty feet off the ground? And why had *I* had the shakes at the end of that day? It hadn't happened to me. Would it happen to me when I went connecting? Somehow it seemed to have something to do with absolute height, but why would that be so? In no realistic way did that make any sense: A man doesn't have to fall very far before his death is a foregone conclusion. Why should greater height produce deeper anxiety? Or does it? Doesn't he get forty or fifty feet off the ground and say to hell with it? From here on up it's downhill all the way?

I could have brought these things up if I'd been talking to Timmy, despite the likelihood that he'd have prefaced any response by asking what it could possibly matter to me since I wasn't a real ironworker anyway, but I could not bring them up with Patrick. It was a different kind of relationship. Patrick conducted his affairs on a let-it-rip basis and generally refused to be drawn into any discussion of insides, his or anybody else's. If there were dark things in Patrick's house, they were down with the amontillado.

"What caused it?" Callahan asked.

"Nobody seems to know," I answered. "He just dropped down on the piece and got it in a regular death grip."

"Wanna play a little snooker?" asked Patrick.

"T'at's t'e same t'ing happened to Timmy," Callahan said.

"He froze?" I asked.

"I got ten bucks here says I can beat any man in the house at the pool table," said Patrick.

"Stuck to a column so tight I t'ought we'd never get him off," Callahan said, shaking his head in remembered wonder.

"When did that happen?" I asked.

"Every time I get to thinkin' you might have some sense, Callahan," said Patrick, pointing a fresh drink at him, "you reconvince me you're a complete asshole."

"Must have been about t'e time t'e baby was born," Callahan replied, ignoring Patrick. "Somewhere around t'ere, anyway."

"Are you shmucks really going to get into this?" Patrick demanded.

"Unless you want to explain to me what happened to MacDonald," I said, "I think it's unavoidable." Patrick threw up his arms.

"Stop with all the words," he said. "You asked me before and I told you then what I tell you now—I don't know."

"It bugs me not to understand things," I said. "I never saw a thing like that before, and I don't understand it. I don't know what caused it."

"A whole lot of things happen in this business that you never saw before."

"Right. I mean, after all, I'm not a *real* ironworker, am I?"

"Not yet."

"If MacDonald's not there in the morning, I'm going to ask for his job."

"Don't be super-stupid. In the first place, they won't give it to you. In the second, you don't know enough to be able to do it, anyway."

"Why do you want it?" asked Callahan, giving me a peculiar stare. Why, indeed? It was an idiot thing that had popped out of my mouth before I knew it was there.

"I'm not sure I do want it," I answered, "but I think I ought to ask for it."

"They'll send a man out from the hall," said Patrick wearily. "Your turn comes later."

"You don't expect MacDonald back."

"No," Patrick said, slowly, "he won't be back."

"Then you do know what's going on here."

"Not the way you mean. I haven't talked to him; I haven't talked to anybody. But he won't be back."

Callahan had been observing this exchange with such a bemused expression on his face that I began to think he thought it was all funny. When Patrick and I fell silent, he began toying with his shot glass. After a few moments he said, "Timmy went back."

"Well," said Patrick, heavily, "there you have it." He downed his drink, jumped off the stool, gave me a tap on the shoulder that was a shade too hard to be merely friendly, said, "Change the subject, numbnuts," and walked off. He took his hat and belt from the coatrack and left without saying goodnight to anyone nor going through his "Quittin' time" speech.

Callahan asked for a detailed account of the "t'ing wit' MacDonald," and I gave it to him. When I finished, he said, "T'at's pretty close to t'e way it was wit' Timmy, as well as I can remember it. Except t'at when he was on t'e ground he started cryin' like a baby. He couldn't stop. When we got him to t'e hospital, t'ey had to give him a shot to make him stop." He paused to take a drink. "Just like you said about MacDonald, t'ough, it didn't seem to be any one t'ing. T'e ball hit a column and shook t'e iron, but not hard enough to knock anyt'in' down. Patrick yelled at t'e operator, but it wasn't his fault."

"Patrick was on the same job?" I asked.

"Patrick was t'e ot'er connector," he answered.

"Oh," I said. In the silence which followed I ordered drinks and went to the men's room.

MacDonald did not return. The foreman did not call the hall, but somehow knowing what Patrick had known and I had not, he had called a friend of his the same night. The new man was on the job before eight o'clock, which precluded my asking to go connecting. Months later, after I had done some connecting, I was retroactively grateful to that fellow, for by then I realized how laughable my request would have been. I could not have done an acceptable job of it, even though it was as straightforward and simple-minded as connecting ever gets. That statement has nothing to do with anxiety; it has to do with experience. Being a good observer, or even being able to read the drawings or to understand the engineering factors which underlie the techniques, are all equally useless; it all comes down to experience.

My favorite example of experience versus book knowledge-engineering-math-trained brains revolves around Black Tom Martin, a man whom I roundly hated. By the time I went to work for him I'd dealt with a number of unpleasant bosses, but none before or since could drive me up a wall as easily as he. I worked for him on a three-derrick job on Seventh Avenue, where he had the center derrick. He was seventy years old and seemed to me to have gotten himself confused with Captain Bligh. At first I assumed it was the cantankerousness of old age, but other old men who knew him said he'd been that way forever. He was reputed to have pushed a derrick on the Empire State Building, which could be true—it went up in the winter of twenty-nine. But whatever he'd been like then, at seventy he was a foul-tempered son of a bitch. He'd come from St. Johns originally and had never lost his very thick accent. (The Newfoundland accent has a Scotch quality to it and can be full of burrs and mushy.) His false teeth were so yellow that he seemed to have an old lemon peel in his mouth, and he chewed incessantly upon the fat and frayed stump of a black cigar. We were all convinced that it was the only cigar he'd ever bought, because week in and week out it looked exactly the same.

When I was put in Black Tom's gang, I was still pretty new at connecting, and the super had told me that he was doing me a favor because the old man knew more about derricks than anyone else alive, that he had—the super couldn't pass up the cliché—"forgotten more about derricks than you will ever learn." At first I was afraid this might be literally true. He often did things so strangely that neither my partner nor I knew what was coming off, which made us speculate that perhaps he had finally forgotten it all. We were wrong; it soon became obvious that our iron was going up considerably faster than the other gangs'. It soon got to the point where we spent a half-day or more a week doing other things so that the other gangs could catch up. But at learning I was utterly frustrated, because with the false teeth, the accent, and the cigar all working against me, I could never understand what he wanted. My partner could understand a little; he was a Newfie, too, and the accent didn't bother him. I had to depend on him to keep me posted on what the old man was saying, which didn't solve everything, since I had trouble understanding *him*. Once, when the boom cable had jumped its sheave and my partner and I were on the spider (the very top of the derrick) trying to fix it, the old man paced back and forth on the plank floor 135 feet beneath us, screaming so loud and so constantly in his anger at our apparent slowness (though from where he was he couldn't possibly have seen the exact nature of the problem) that I lost my temper and threw my hat at him. The instant it left my hand I thought, "Holy shit, what have I done? If it hits him I'll never work in New York again." It missed him by several yards, however, and I gave thanks to the high wind. He continued his screaming and never gave any indication that he knew I'd thrown it at him.

After work I stopped in at the super's bar—he and we didn't usually drink in the same place—seeking him out to tell him that I'd decided there wasn't any point in my being in a gang where I got so mad I started throwing things at the boss and that I thought he'd better put me somewhere else or get my money. He bought me a beer and patted me on the shoulder. "Now, Babe," he said, mock-soothingly. (He called everybody either "Babe" or "Once-in-Awhile," depending upon whether or not the man being addressed had been at work the day before.) "Now, Babe, take it easy. I never said he was easy to get along with. I just said that you'd learn from him." I denied this, pointing out that I couldn't learn anything from a man whose speech was totally unintelligible. He shook his head and grinned and continued to try to calm me down. We passed an hour or so at this exercise, I bitching and he placating, until finally the anger began to drain away. When the super saw that I was beginning to unwind, he began telling me little stories about the old man. I remember thinking to myself that the super was a con artist, which probably was at least part of the reason he was a good super. Most of the stories he told about the old man are long since lost to me, but "The Day The Engineers Blew It" is still in mind and still, I imagine, in general circulation:

The first five floors of what was to be a forty-two-story job were set with a crane, which was now to be used to trip (put in place) the derrick that would take over the erection of the remaining thirty-seven floors. This is standard procedure. (A derrick is one of those two-masted affairs you see atop buildings-in-progress. Newspaper articles inevitably and mistakenly refer to them as cranes. How they work will be explained, eventually, but isn't really important here.) The old man was pushing the crane and was therefore responsible for the tripping of the derrick, and he snorted in disgust when the trucks carrying its sections began to arrive. It was a new type and was accompanied by a large group of engineers. Although there was nothing radically new about the thing, it was their baby, and they had brought themselves, their drawings, their photographers, and a choice collection of dignitaries and political candidates. None of this foo-foo-rah did the old man's temper any good. He let it be known that he had a building to put up and that having all these "Jesus, Mary, and Joseph *people*" underfoot wasn't going to make things go any faster. However, that day not even his foul mouth could save him from being outflanked. In the middle of a tirade he was pushed unceremoniously aside by a number of fashionably suited young men in spotless hard hats who were helping the photographers pose the president of the company with one of Governor Rockefeller's brothers. Black Tom moved to new ground and again began to thunder, only to be shoved out of the way by the engineers, who were setting up a large field table and covering it with their countless drawings. Finally he gave up in disgust and went to sit morosely on the fender of a truck, muttering indecipherably through his lemon teeth and his black cigar.

He remained there throughout the several hours it took the engineers to ready themselves. The photographers left, and the dignitaries immediately after. They're probably still kicking themselves; they missed the best part of the show.

When the engineers were finally ready, they went to Black Tom and asked him to get his men together and began giving him instructions on what they wanted done. They explained their entire plan to him, showed him where they wanted the crane to hook the derrick when it was ready to go up, and told him their prescribed order of events. He listened to their speeches wordlessly, and when they had finished, he told them that it wouldn't work. They stared in disbelief. When he continued to insist that it wouldn't work, they became angry and went to the super of the job and complained that the old man was ignorant and unable to adjust to new techniques and obviously too stupid to see the logic in their plan. The super went to Black Tom and told him that he sympathized with him but that neither of them had a choice and the thing was just going to have to be put up the way the engineers wanted to do it. The old man repeated that it wouldn't work. One of the experts who overheard this blew up and accused Black Tom of about every lack known to humanity, including impotence, and concluded by demanding to know in what specific fashion it wouldn't work. For perhaps the only time in his life (we all believed he ate with it in place), the old man took out his cigar. He turned on the expert, addressing him with normal vehemence but unprecedented clarity, "It—will—fall—down!" The expert jumped back as though struck in the nose with garlic.

More argument ensued, until finally the old man said he'd do it the way they wanted if they'd all promise to "run thattaway," he said, pointing to the opposite end of the block from the projected collapse. Having secured from the engineers their condescending promises, he put his men to work.

As they began, he went to the super. "Might's well call t'hall," he said.

"What for?" asked the super.

"Gonna need two more welders in t'morn', put t'is piece a'shit back t'get'r."

"Oh," said the super.

It went up, of course, exactly the way the engineers had said it would. And when they tried to slack off the load, it fell down exactly as the old man had said it would. He had moved himself and those of his men who weren't needed well out of the way. He had told the others which way to run.

The old man's expression, amid all the shouting and tumult, never changed. He wandered around long enough to make sure that all his men were okay, told the super that if there were no experts around the next day, he'd stick the derrick as soon as the extra welders had made the repairs, stepped carefully through the rubble, and took the subway home.

I admire the story, and I admire the old man, but all the admiration I could muster never helped me get along with him. The very knowledge that enabled him to defeat the engineers made it impossible for him to exercise any patience with us dummies.

I've known men who worry every payday because they are afraid they're being cheated. They can't reassure themselves because they can't add up the columns of deductions, or if they make the attempt, come up with the wrong answer and an earful of ballpoint pen ink. Yet they can suggest a dozen or more ways to make a recalcitrant piece of iron go where it's supposed to, ways that would simply not occur to a new man, even if he held a PhD. from M.I.T. It can be painful to have the same man who consulted you for an explanation of his paycheck stub come over to show you how to fit piece X into slot Y, but it happens:

Back in 1955, after a bout of pneumonia, I developed asthma. Although it eventually disappeared, it was for a few years a fairly spectacular case, and I spent much time in St. Joseph's Hospital in Louisville. Sometimes I was there for only a few hours, sometimes for several days. On one of the longer visits I became friendly with the man in the next bed, a fellow I called Nick the Butcher. That was not because of his behavior, but because he made his living at the Jefferson Street Market, cutting meat. He had had an accident with his car, and the doctors had removed his spleen, his gall gladder, most of his stomach, and a kidney. He had what looked like a water-damaged parchment scroll where his abdomen should have been, and I strongly suspected the surgeons of having lied to him. It seemed likely to me that they'd taken out his entire insides, leaving only a pacemaker and a spigot for connecting him to the dialysis machine.

Nick tried to teach me the game of Go. It's a board game, like chess in some ways, and its rules are simplicity itself. All the pieces are exactly the same, and they don't even move. They are either on or off the board. The object of the game is to surround space. The rules can be explained in less than a minute, and once they've been explained the student is in possession of as much material about which to think as is the teacher. It is not a game of chance. And yet I could not beat him. Ever. He didn't have a single bit of data unavailable to me, but he won every game. By wide margins. He gave me huge handicaps and still won. I looked across at him, torn and aging, dull-witted and apathetic, a widower whose only horizons were cutting meat and playing a silly game, and I saw, however uncharitably, that he was not a very bright man, and I tried to discover how it was that he always won.

I asked if he would like to borrow something to read, and he said, "No." I wondered if it were just that my books were the wrong kind of thing and asked what he liked to read. He said, "Nuzzink." I asked what he thought about the governorship of Happy Chandler, and he said, "Iz not my bizziniss." But he won every game. I asked him how long he'd been playing, and he said, "Fiftin yirs."

Patrick fell while spreading decking near Charlesburg and broke some ribs. I called Callahan to tell him about it, but he already knew. Nothing seemed to happen to anyone from that neighborhood that everybody didn't know about instantly. We decided to go together to pay him a visit.

As we stepped out of the elevator onto Patrick's floor, we could hear him shouting. The girl at the desk in the foyer had put her face in her hands and was muttering, "My God, there he goes again." She didn't look up as we walked past her toward the sound of Patrick's voice. We found him in a ward with perhaps a dozen other men. He was yelling for a nurse, loudly but without apparent rancor, and beating at the same time on the metal frame of his bed.

"Hey, man," he said when he saw us, "get one of them damn nurses or an orderly or somebody in here, will you? I got to take a leak, and they won't bring me a bottle."

"Why don't you just go to t'e john?" asked Callahan. "I t'ought it was your ribs you busted, not your legs."

"The doctor's afraid I'll hurt myself," Patrick answered, cheerfully. Then, adopting a theatrical leer, he added, "and the nurses are afraid I'll hurt them." He held his hands to his chest while he tried to laugh. "Oh, lemme tell you guys, the little girl that was on yesterday afternoon is some kind of good-lookin'. Only she won't talk to me. She's sore because I made her knock the piss bottle over on herself." Still trying to hold his ribs from wriggling he laughed again. We asked him to explain about the nurse and how he managed to take a flop. "Well, it was one of those boring days," he said, "and we'd been drinkin' beer all afternoon to help pass the time. I was on my way over to a column to take a leak, walkin' on the bar joists, and one of 'em rolled. They were supposed to be tacked down, but I guess some asshole skipped one. I just went right down between 'em." Callahan and I made cracks about the absurdity of getting hurt that way and suggested that perhaps he'd been drunk. "Naw, I wasn't drunk," Patrick said, "I just went in the hole is all. It was only one floor, and I didn't think it was too bad, but they sent for an ambulance and it didn't seem right to make it go away empty, so here I am. Anyway, in all the excitement I never did get to piss, so by the time I was in this bed here, after the X-rays and all, the situation was difficult if not impossible. I asked the nurse for a bottle, and she brought me this thing that was no bigger'n a milk carton. I told her it wasn't enough, but she kept tellin' me that it was." He began laughing again. The discomfort it caused him was obviously not enough to shut it off. "So I filled it right to the very brim, and the only way I could keep from lettin' it overflow was to use one hand for a hose clamp, and I held it out for her to come get it, and when she did, a little bit sloshed over on the front of her uniform, and she jumped when that happened, and the whole thing got dropped and I tried to get out of the way and let go the hose clamp and another couple quarts squirted all over the bed." By the time he said this last, he was laughing so much he could hardly talk, and the next part came out in gasps. "Oh, I tell you, it was a sight worth money. I mean, you could have sold tickets. It went all down the front of her uniform and into her shoes. She got mad at me laughing at her and picked up the empty bottle and threw it at me and ran out of here going *squish squish* and leaving footprints on the floor. It was beautiful."

Callahan contracted the dirty giggles. Patrick's face was a mixture of amusement and discomfort as he tried to stem his own laughter. When he finally managed to stop, he again asked me to find somebody who would bring him a bottle. He was very unpopular, he pointed out, and unable to get good service.

There was a bottle on the table beside the next bed. The man in the bed seemed to be asleep, so I took it. When Patrick saw what I was doing, however, he began to shriek, "Good God A'mighty, Mike, don't touch that thing!" I dropped it back in its place instantly. "Go wash your hands, quick. You'll probably get an infernal disease, anyway . . . It's probably too late already." Callahan looked confused.

"What've I got?" I asked.

"What's an infernal disease?" asked Callahan.

"Whatever *he's* got," said Patrick, apparently addressing us both.

"What's *he* got?" I demanded.

"I don't know," admitted Patrick, "but it's clearly terrible. I think it's fatal. He complains all the time. He complains about his head, and his stomach, and his feet. It could be anything except lockjaw."

"I hope it's priapism," I said, drawing blank stares from both.

"What the hell's that?" Patrick demanded, looking fiercely at Callahan as though he might know. "What the hell's that?" Callahan shrugged his shoulders.

"A very rare genitourinary affliction," I said, as I started out of the ward. Going down the hall, I could still hear Patrick loudly demanding, "What is it with him and his damned big words, anyway? What's a genito-whatever, anyhow? Answer me, Callahan." Then, louder yet, "Goddam it all to hell!"

I stopped a nurse and asked her politely where I could get a bottle into which my friend might urinate. She asked who that might be. When I told her, she said, "Oh, him," and crooked her finger for me to follow. We stopped in front of a supply pantry. She took down a bottle and handed it to me, saying that if I wanted to take over the nursing of that particular patient, she and the other nurses on the floor would be happy to take up a collection to pay my salary. I thanked her for the bottle and was in the middle of telling her that I'd consider her offer when she started backing away, fluttering her fingers at me as if there were some sticky substance on them that she was having difficulty shaking off.

When I got back near the entrance to the ward, I began to stagger. I lurched through the doorway to Patrick's bed and thrust the bottle at him. "Here, you take it; I can't make it anyway, Pat. You'd best go on without me. Tell Gertrude I was full of thoughts of her." I collapsed, half across the foot of his bed, half on the floor.

"My God!" Patrick fairly shouted, "He's got it! He's got that pri-whatever-it-was. Medic! Get a goddam medic in here, Callahan!" Out of the corner of my eye I could see him repeatedly squeezing the button of his paging device. I began to slide slowly to the floor.

"What t'e hell is t'is all about?" asked Callahan.

"That other bottle," I gasped, "it must have been contaminated." I clutched at my stomach and rolled over.

"Medic!" Patrick screamed continuously, hitting the button over and over again. When the nurse entered, I was sprawled on the floor, eyes shut and motionless.

"What happened to him?" she asked in a suspicious tone of voice.

"Damn if I know," said Callahan.

"He's got pri-something-or-other," said Patrick. "I think he's dead."

"Pri-what?" asked the nurse.

"That's close," Patrick answered.

"He said it was some kind of a genufliction," offered Callahan. The nurse, who was now crouched on the floor beside me, trying to take my pulse, gave Callahan a puzzled look.

"I never heard of a genu-whatever-you-said," she remarked.

"No, you're gettin' colder," put in Patrick.

"Pill," I muttered into the green floor tiles while trying manfully to reach into my pocket, "need . . . pill." I pulled my arm away from the nurse, put a hand in my pocket, and unwrapped a Rolaid before withdrawing the hand. I popped it quickly into my mouth.

"What was that?" asked the nurse.

"Aluminum hydroxide," I said, sitting up, "it helps, sometimes."

"I tell you," said Patrick, "he's got that pri-something, and he's gonna die. That son of a bitch in the next bed had it, and now look at him—he's *dead*. Now Mike's got it, because he touched that guy's piss pot, and *he's* gonna die, and he fell across this bed and touched my legs, and *I'm* gonna die!"

"That's an antacid," said the nurse.

"I'm gonna die!" shouted Patrick. "I want to *live*! I'm just a boy, for God's sake!"

"It's a specific for aplastic dyslexia," I explained.

"I can feel it coming over me," yelled Patrick. "Medic!"

"You want me to do somet'in'?" Callahan asked, moving towards Patrick's bed.

"Don't touch me!" Patrick hissed. "It'll get you, too." Callahan retreated. "Somebody's got to be alive to sue this stinkin' hospital."

"Sweet Jesus!" called a voice from the rear of the ward. "Shut the bloody hell up, will you?"

"I think I'll resign," said the nurse, still sitting on the floor. "I was never that sure I wanted to be a nurse, anyway." She got up, brushed herself off, and walked purposefully out of the room. I got up myself, and asked Patrick if that was the one he'd thought was so cute.

"What're you, kiddin' me or what?" he replied, shaking his head.

"Hey you," Callahan bellowed toward the rear, "you can go back to sleep, now." The voice did not answer. I wouldn't have, either. Callahan's voice can be almost as intimidating as the B.A.'s. When we told Patrick we had to go, he held his hands to his chest.

"Good," he said. "Don't come back. I think you're interfering with my recovery."

"Drop by the bar when you're out of here," I said. "I'll-Drink-To-That says there's a shopping center going up outside Cortland. Maybe we can go plumbing-up. You'll have to do something light for awhile, I guess."

"I'm fine," he answered. "The only thing wrong with me is a bad case of the malingerings."

"Sure," I said. Callahan had begun fidgeting.

"Timmy still up in Dry Gulch?" Patrick asked.

"Yeah, as far as I know." We started toward the hall.

"If you see that nurse," he called after us, "tell her the man next to me is definitely dead." We didn't answer. The elevator came, and as we got on it and the doors slipped closed behind us, we could hear him still carrying on: "Will somebody get this son of a bitch out of here? He's startin' to *smell*, for Jesus' sake!"

Patrick was in the hospital only a few days, but it was the better part of six weeks before he could move around well enough to consider going back to work. I had three different jobs during that time, bolting-up on one, taglining on another, plumbing-up on the third. Bolting-up struck me as a bore, as it has on other jobs since. It's a good job for the old men and the alcoholics, though, since one doesn't have to move around much and isn't usually in a very hazardous position. You can bolt up long after age has taken your legs or whiskey your balance.

There are a large number of different kinds of bolts used on buildings, varying in length, diameter, and hardness. Lengths and diameters are obvious functions of the sizes of the members being joined, and hardnesses are derived from studies of the stresses that will be involved. A bolter-up knows nothing of these stresses, and cares less. He does what he's told, generally, and will happily put any bolt he has at hand into any hole that needs filling, if practical experience has taught him that the use of bolt A instead of bolt B isn't going to cause the building to fall down, or if he knows that the inspector is across the street in the gin mill. He has long since realized that steel buildings are far overbuilt. The pusher may tell him that the column splices are to be made up with 490 bolts, but if all he has handy are 324s and he thinks nobody will notice, he'll put them in without hesitation. (Those numbers are a measure of a bolt's hardness; the higher the number, the harder the steel.)

The use of the bolt, in an industry which through its reluctance to adopt new techniques is rapidly becoming an anachronism, represents a sweeping change. Not very many years ago most of the connections which today are bolted or welded were made with rivets.* Today, with exceptions made for some bridges, the rivet is gone. Two men, using a "gun" powdered by compressed air (except in Jerkwater, where if the job is small enough they might use an electric gun instead of taking the trouble to drag a compressor around), can make many more "points" (the intersections of columns and headers) than can a four-man riveting gang. There is also an advantage in safety, since it is no longer necessary to toss red-hot rivets from a furnace on the working-floor up to the men on the point. (Naturally, not every rivet arrived right in the catcher's bucket, and the stories told about where they went when they didn't go in the bucket are endless. Several involve men wearing sweatshirts with the hoods thrown back over their shoulders, who are said to have fallen while trying to dance free of the burning metal.)

Bolts get dropped, frequently. But at least they aren't red hot. I dropped once one that went thirty-six floors before making the neatest little hole you ever saw in the roof of a Buick. Even the guns get dropped every now and then, and since they weigh from about twelve pounds for a little one to twice that for a big one, damage has been done. But since they're powered by compressed air, they have hoses attached to them, and unless the couple breaks, they are usually thereby prevented from going very far. Guns are merely impact wrenches. They look like large versions of the tool with which your garageman takes a wheel off your car, or like a granddaddy home drill with a socket (to receive the bolt head) where the bit should be.

There are "hard" bolts and "soft" bolts. It's a technical distinction:

---

* A couple of years ago some engineers came to a job I was on to demonstrate a new device which in a sense combined the functions of a bolt and a rivet. They were as pleased with themselves as pigs in clover. Its use involved sticking the fastener through the aligned holes, then seizing it on the far side with a tool which flanged and crimped it—rather like an oversized pop-rivet or a dressmaker's grommet-setter. The engineers thought it was a wonderful little machine and talked much about the time it would save. They were not concerned with the half-inch-by-seven-eighths-inch cutoff which the thing left for garbage. We were, though. The idea of literally tens of thousands of little chunks of waste metal lying about, falling between the planks or over the side, was not appealing. As far as I know, nothing ever came of this system, which suggests that, however unlikely it may seem, the inventors came to their senses.

If either were to land on your head, you'd find it difficult to say which it had been. Soft bolts are generally used on intermediate pieces—beams that connect between headers, rather than at a column. They're stuck by hand and sucked up tight by hand. A soft-bolter is one of the few ironworkers who works alone. He fetches his bolts for himself, puts them in what looks like a heavy-gauge shopping basket, and carries this around with him as he works. His is one of the trade's dullest and least rewarding tasks. Generally, no one even knows whether he's getting anything done. A man who likes soft bolts is likely also to enjoy solitaire.

The sticking of hard bolts, which are tightened with guns, is done by men working in pairs. They begin work by hanging their float. A float is a wooden platform, usually made of inch-thick oak, generally about three feet by six feet, and always fitted with two lengths of rope. Each rope passes down through a corner of the float, leads diagonally across its bottom, and comes up through that corner. The men use these lines to secure the float to the building frame at a convenient working height. They then drag over their basket of tools, their gun, and their bolts. The bolt-up boss is supposed to have insured that his punks have filled one or more baskets with the proper bolts and brought them to a spot on the working floor directly beneath the point which is to be bolted. A lot of bolt-up bosses do this by writing on the columns lists of the bolts needed on the point just above.

This works fine, if the punks can read, except in the case of a fellow who was universally referred to in his brief career as "Bobby Backward." The fellow seemed to be able to read, but in every single case brought the men bolts of the wrong length. No one was able to learn how it could be that he *inevitably* brought the wrong lengths until his pusher in desperation opted for shadowing Bobby Backward's every move. All punks are required to carry a measuring device. Generally, they choose a standard six-foot folding rule, although they seldom have to measure anything longer than eight or nine inches. The pusher eventually noticed that Bobby Backward's rule was a single length of stick, rather longer than any section of a broken ordinary rule would be. He asked to see it and thereby solved the mystery: The fellow was using a piece of a special type of surveyor's rule, not knowing that the marks represented tenths of a foot, rather than inches. All the yelling about carelessness that the pusher could ever do, and all the caution that Bobby Backward could ever take, would never have resulted in the bolts being right. The mystery was that the kid didn't know what an inch looked like.

Pieces of iron are fastened to one another in a variety of ways. Often, several different types of connections are represented on a single point. All of them, however, require pushing and pulling, beating, reaming, smashing, pinning, and cursing. Newfies make the best bolter-ups, because they are the best cursers, although I know a pair of rednecks from Arkansas who are pretty good. Indians aren't in it at all, since they have to swear in a foreign language; the Indian tongues contain no curse words.

It is useful to have experience, but a neophyte can squeeze by. A pair of bolter-ups with experience and a familiarity with each other's methods are faster than beginners, and once in a while a situation will arise in which the job simply cannot be done without expertise, but not very often.

The monotony of hard bolts got to me almost as much as the solitude of soft bolts: driving drift pins (six-inch hard steel rods tapered to a point at either end) into some of the holes so that the others would line up (a large column-welded flange, called a "wing," might have a dozen to six dozen holes in it to receive presumably matching holes in the header), stuffing the holes with bolts, gunning them up tight—over and over and over. The worst aspect of bolting-up, however, is the noise. Running a gun against steel plates is like spending the day at a band concert with your head stuck in the bass drum. All attempts to talk to your partner are either utterly useless or lead directly to laryngitis. There is seldom any use in trying to talk to your partner even when the gun is not in use, for if he's been bolting-up for any length of time, he's odds-on to be stone deaf anyway. Bolting-up is relatively safe, which is about all it has to recommend it.

The time I spent taglining was better, but how it works has been mentioned before, and besides, the job didn't last long.

I was again one of the few men remaining in the hall one morning toward eight-thirty, when the B.A. came to the dutch door and fixed me with that baleful glare of his. "Hey, Cherry," he growled, "c'mere." I went. "What was youse doin' on t'at steakhouse?"

"Taglinin'," I growled back.

"Everyt'in' go okay?"

"Yeah," I answered, "everyt'in' was okay." He gave me another stare, but lately I had noticed that these examinations were becoming shorter and less hostile.

"Awright," he said, and wrote an address on a slip. "Go. It's a week's work." I left.

A week later to the day the job was uneventfully done, and I was back in the hall. Thinking now back to those days upstate and in Connecticut, my loathing for those short jobs returns undiminshed. I don't mind making changes, but when jobs get down to three or four days here followed by a week there, I don't have time to get acclimated. You meet too many people whose names you can't remember, and you eat in so many different places that you never get used to the food. You can't even keep track of the comic strips, for all the different papers.

With the coming of better weather a lot of things had opened up, and there were a lot of empty chairs in the big room. I didn't see anyone I knew, although the long-haired kid who had aroused such anger in Callahan was again studying the tool ads on the bulletin board. Two men were sent out, then I was called. I looked around the room to see why I had been called so early, but could get no clue. On the way to the door I decided I'd better just be pleased, and forget the analysis.

When I got to the door, the B.A. slouched down, resting his elbows on the narrow shelf that formed the top of the lower half, before speaking. When he spoke in confidential tones, the middle and high frequencies in what was left of his voice disappeared altogether, and I recalled that Timmy had once insisted that the man's whispers sounded like a load of shit gurling through a sewer.

"Youse finished up over t'ere," he said. It sounded more like a statement than a question, but I verified it.

"Yeah. We're t'rough."

"Ever go plumbin' up?" he asked. He knew, of course, that I hadn't.

A few months previously I would have tried to bluff my way through a scene like this for fear I wouldn't get a job, but I felt by this time that he'd throw me something of some sort, so I played it straight.

"No."

"Youse wanna learn?"

"Yeah."

He permitted himself the twisted beginnings of a grin as he handed me the slip. I thanked him and left, thinking, on the way to the car, that when my teeth were as torn up as his, I wouldn't smile much either.

The job was, for the area, fairly large, and was the first on which I'd seen a derrick. It was to be the plant of an industrial tool manufacturer, and since the machines in it were to be quite large, there was some comparatively heavy iron.

When I reported to the shanty—a trade's on-site headquarters are always a "shanty," whether the thing is a tarpaper shack, a plywood house, or a mobile home with wall-to-wall carpeting—I found that Jack was the super. He stood up and opened his mouth, but I spoke first. I put my hands on either side of my chest, palms up in an attitude of innocence. "This's a goddam coincidence, Jack, and that's all it is. I had no idea you were runnin' this job." I was surprised to see him, although I shouldn't have been, really. The same eight or ten men seemed to run most of the area jobs, so the odds on running into Jack from time to time were actually pretty short. I wasn't glad to see him, however. He'd been so short-tempered on the last job that working for him had been unnerving, and it seemed to me he might still be sore that I had yelled at him when Dan Permit fell.

He looked at his watch. "Nine-fifteen," he announced. "I see you've decided to take a middle course."

"I'll go back out for coffee if it'll make you any happier," I said, carefully.

"Relax," he said, sticking out his hand. I shook it. He pointed to a wooden milk carton container and invited me to sit down. "Forget the last job," he said. "You've been around long enough by now to know you can't afford to hold grudges." I nodded. "How's Patrick coming along?" he asked.

"Pretty good," I answered. "He won't do any climbing for a bit, and his snooker's pretty sorry, but he can get around some."

"I never did hear how it happened."

"Pilot error. He stepped on a bar joist that wasn't tacked, and it rolled with him. All he got was some ribs."

"You see him regularly?"

"Every few days."

"Tell him I'll make a slot for him as soon as he can make it look like he can work. No carrying. I've got two permit men in the plumbing-up gang, and one of 'em's so dumb he can't walk and chew gum at the same time. I'm moving him over to put you in there, and I'll move the other one out as soon as Patrick feels like going to work." It pleased me that Jack would do this, and I told him so. We talked on for a few minutes in what amounted to a testimonial for Patrick. When that lapsed, Jack said, "You're pretty friendly with Timmy Shaughnessy, aren't you?" I studied his face carefully, but could read nothing.

"That's right," I said.

"How's he gettin' along?" he asked.

I shrugged. "He's upstate dryin' out."

This brought our talk to an end. I wasn't going to ask why he'd brought Timmy up, and he didn't offer to tell me. I gatherered up my gear and went off to see what plumbing-up was all about.

From a structural point of view, it's too bad buildings aren't made of triangles. (Actually, to a certain extent, some are, notably the Hancock Building in Chicago, with its giant single X braces.) Noncontaining structures, such as bridges, radio and television transmission towers, and aerial signs are generally composed of groups of triangles. The triangle's great asset is that it does not wiggle. However, it contains less space per unit of enclosing material than does the rectangle. An equilateral triangle ten feet on a side encloses an area of about forty-three square feet, but a rectangle seven feet by eight feet—which would employ the same thirty feet of enclosing material—creates fifty-six square feet of space. This unfortunate relationship is not improved through translation into three dimensions: To make a rectangular pyramid that was of the same volume as a given cube (using the same base) we would have to *triple* the height.

Besides, the top of a pyramid by definition contains no space, and in a large building that is precisely where space is needed: for machinery, elevator engines, and such. So we don't build our cities of pyramids. However, towers and bridges, which are not essentially containers, usually employ them.

Rectangles do flex, and that is why there are ironworkers whose job it is to "plumb-up." If nobody plumbed-up, all the tall buildings in our cities would lean crazily into each other, their elevators would scrape and bang against the shaft walls, and the glaziers would have to redress all the windowglass into parallelograms. If you want a graphic example of this rigidity, get three sticks and arrange them to form a triangle. Drive just one nail into each corner and the structure becomes entirely rigid. Then try the same single-nail connections of a four-sided figure, and it will easily assume a variety of shapes. In fact, you can't make it stay in any one shape without bracing it, the most straightforward method of which is to nail a fifth stick across a diagonal—making the thing into two triangles. Buildings do the same thing without braces, happily flopping about like drunken sailors. The plumber-ups, in effect, provide the fifth stick.

They are responsible, first of all, for making sure the columns are vertical. This is done with a plumb bob (a length of string with a weight on the end), a gauge (a short metal strip with a notch a couple of inches along its length), a rule, and a collection of hooks, clamps, cables, and turnbuckles.

One man climbs to the top of whatever portion of the building then exists and lowers the weighted line down to another man on the working floor (generally two stories below). When the line is hanging, the man on top pushes it a known distance away from the side of the column by interposing his gauge. The notch receives the line. The man below measures the distance between the line and the column. If the gap is the same as that held by the top man, the column is plumb on that axis. (The process must obviously be repeated on an adjacent side if one cares to discover whether or not the column is "out" along the other axis.) If the measurements are different, the gang will rig a cable from near the top of the offending column to a spot rather away from the base of the column on the working floor, using their hooks, clamps, and a turnbuckle. The turnbuckles are three or four feet long, and the dumbest man in the gang gets to do the turning. Or the one who least likes to climb. He uses his wrench, or a stick, or a piece of "re-bar" (a short length of reinforcing rod, stolen from the lathers) to turn the buckle round and round, thus shortening the cable and pulling the column over. He gets to continue doing this until the pusher, for it is generally he who takes the measurements, decides that the column is "close enough." What "close enough" is depends upon the tolerances shown on the drawings and/or how the pusher is feeling at the time. An error—better to call it an "outage"—of as much as an inch in two floors is sometimes acceptable on the drawings, but the attitude of the pusher—or the field engineer, if he happens to be around—is more often the critical factor. In fact, the engineer and the pusher are apt to take differing but equally vehement views of what constitutes "close enough." The engineer, who makes his own measurements using surveying instruments, is likely to express his feelings through such remarks as, "My God, it's another tower of Pisa!" Or, "You boys are going to have to find *some* way to suck this end of the building back where it belongs; we haven't got air rights over the avenue, you know." The pusher, for his part, is more likely to shout, "C'mon, Mike, shake a leg! T'is is a buildin', for Chrissake, not a goddam watch!"

In the end, somehow, what leaned an inch west on the thirty-second floor is sucked back east on the thirty-fourth, and a column that refused to quit leaning south on forty-six can generally be brought over on forty-eight, and by the time the whole job is up the top is directly over the bottom. It always strikes me as rather impressive and mildly amusing to realize, in walking down the canyons of the city, that the giant buildings owe a good part of their verticality to a $1.98 fishing reel and an $.89 rule.

When the gang has finished plumbing-up a floor, or a pair of floors, actually, that part of the building is more or less inflexible. The dozens of cables they have strung have converted the rectangles or columns and headers into a series of triangles. These cables will stay in place until the concrete floors have been poured and had time to cure. By the time the cables on one pair of floors are ready to come off, the skeleton of the job may be ten or twelve floors above, so that there is an overlap function: plumb-up the twenty-second floor, strip the tenth; plumb-up twenty-four, strip twelve. This can make for a hell of a lot of climbing up and down stairs and ladders unless one works for a company that has a separate stripping gang, and not all of them do.

I enjoyed plumbing-up because my days weren't as much alike as usual. Sometimes a column simply wouldn't yield to ordinary measures for moving it over, and we would have to improvise a solution. We often employed reamers (to increase the diameters of holes) to gain some play; sometimes we had to use torches to alter the locations of bolt holes altogether; sometimes we had to cut loose a beam and redesign its ends in a major way—say, rebuild the whole mount—to make it fit.

I hadn't done any connecting then, and being the "up" man gave me a chance to practice climbing columns and walking beams without being in the spotlight of the raising gang. It also helped that the pusher, a young Irishman named Coley, was both a good teacher and categorically unable to get upset about anything.

A few weeks after I started plumbing-up, I had the pleasure of being able to play at offering Patrick a job. I was sitting in O'Rourke's late one evening, bored and trying to work up enough ambition to go out for something to eat, when he came in. Since his injury his entrances had become very quiet. He no longer carried a belt and hat to throw over the rack, and he no longer shouted "Injun whiskey!" He still drank it, but he didn't shout for it. I opened the conversation by suggesting that he looked a little peaked. He shook his head no.

"Aren't you sick of livin' on disability payments yet?"

"Now that you mention it," he answered, "yes."

"It just so happens that I have a tit job up for grabs, in case you're interested."

"I am indeed," he admitted, testing his ribs gingerly with the tips of his fingers, "if'n it ain't too haivey . . ." He had suddenly chosen to essay a southern drawl. "Ah cain't lift shee-it, Rafe. Took mah craydit card over to th' haouse of ill ree-pute last week, ah did, an' ah ain't been th' same since." I ignored the game.

"Want to go plumbin'-up?" Patrick tipped his head sharply this way and that, like a bird trying to get a good look at a worm, before answering.

"With who?" he asked. "I mean, with *whom?* I mean, goddam you, it's bad enough you win most of the snooker, but now you've gone and fixed it so's I can't even talk anymore."

"Me, Coley Branigan, and a kid."

"Why not?"

"I'll probably live to regret this," I said, raising my glass to him. He clicked his own against it, we drained them, then called for the bartender.

"When'm I spozed to start?"

"Tomorrow, of course; unless you need a couple of weeks to settle your affairs?"

"Write down the address." I started to tell him where he was to go, but he protested. "Don't tell me where it is, because I won't remember. You don't know what I've been doing today, my boy, do you?" I admitted that I didn't, though I was beginning to have my suspicions. "I have spent the day doing research on the local watering spots, in case I choose to stay in this area when I retire, which may be next month or possibly even next week, and there is absolutely no chance that I will remember tomorrow where'm spozed to go. I thank you very much for the job, but please write down the address."

I wrote it for him on a napkin. He folded it and put it in his cigarette package. "Constant habits are very useful, my son . . . the very first thing I do upon awakening, alive or dead, is reach for a cigarette. You understand, of course."

I said I did, and he left. Without a word to anyone.

Generally speaking, the only people who regularly have to climb columns are the connectors. By the time anybody else needs to go up top, there are ladders, usually. The bolter-ups, the plumber-ups, the plank gang, and welders are all allowed, and by and large insist upon, ladders. Punks will often climb when they don't have to (the ones who aren't scared silly) for practice or the hell of it, and twice a day—lunch and quitting time—whole bunches of younger men will go shooting down the columns or clamber down the framing of the concrete hoists or whatever else is handy, to avoid the traffic jams that develop at the ordinary exits.

The working floor of a building is normally attainable only by ladder. The stair erectors—who belong to a different union, naturally —can't very well install their stairs until the iron upon which they will rest is in place, and are therefore necessarily below the ironworkers. The elevator installers, who can't jump up until the ironworkers have picked their motors and placed them on platforms that have been bolted-up and inspected, are naturally even farther down. It's not uncommon, as a result, for an ironworker who wants to go to the street for lunch to have to descend perhaps four floors of ladders followed by eight or ten floors of stairs before he reaches an elevator that can take him the rest of the way. The rule says that no one is required to climb more than ten stories, but it is generally unenforceable.

The first week or so that Patrick worked with us he had a bad time with the ladders. On that job there always seemed to be five or six floors of them, and he took them very slowly. Coley helped Patrick out by letting him handle the rule much of the time, while he took the heavier work himself, and gradually Patrick rounded into shape. The job was a good one for all of us. Patrick was able to earn some money without ruining the repair work on his ribs; Coley learned to trust us enough to feel able to spend large chunks of his day off bullshitting with his buddies on other parts of the job without worrying that Patrick and I had sneaked off to a gin mill; and I was able to watch a raising gang work with a derrick. Whenever they were doing something I didn't understand, I asked Coley. He was up to then the only ironworker I'd met who was in any way willing or able to give explanations, and although Coley always began his lessons with a lot of cracks about my ignorance, I learned.

The three of us often stopped for a short beer in a bar a block away from the job, and often I'd continue asking questions in there. Every now and then one or the other of them would throw up his hands and scream that the day was over and couldn't we please talk about something else.

One afternoon Coley suddenly jumped up and ran outside to his car. He came back carrying several small books. "Here," he said, with

an air of having solved my inquisitiveness at last, "Take 'em. Read
'em—you can read, can't you? Good. Read 'em, and don't bug me
anymore."

The books were his old texts from apprentice school. They held
some answers, but I soon forgot them. There were tables showing the
theoretical breaking strengths of various lines and wire ropes, but only
experience can tell you whether a given line is adequate for a given
job. It is never smart, whatever field you're in, to use book figures
without thinking. This was illustrated one day in what might be called
smashing fashion by a huge, lumbering punk we called Ah-oogah. (His
nickname came from his habit of imitating, at random intervals, a
Model-T Ford. We never understood why he did this, and he never
explained himself, but three or four times a day he would open his
gigantic mouth and let loose a blast that would curdle your lunch. He
did it on the street one noon, and everybody in the crosswalk jumped
in terror for the curb.) We were finished (caught up) with our
plumbing-up for the day, and were passing the afternoon putting in
hand iron. "Hand iron" is (a) anything too small to justify tying up
the whole raising gang and its derrick; (b) anything inadvertently
forgotten when the raising gang was on that floor, regardless of size; or
(c) anything the architects chose to add to the floor(s) after the raising
gang had gone on.

We were putting in small U-shaped pieces, one on each floor, which
were to act as framing for a mail slot, when on twelve we found a
beam that belonged on two. It was a light piece about seven feet long.
Coley told us to lower the thing to its proper floor, then went off to
talk to somebody. Ah-oogah located a piece of three-quarter-inch
manila line, but it was too short. He suggested that we couple it to our
plumbing-up tagline, but we vetoed that.

"Well, I don't see nuttin' else," he said, petulantly, "what's t'e
matter wit' your line?"

"It's an old hunk of half-inch," I answered.

"Hell, t'at'll do okay," he persisted, "t'e t'ing don't weigh more'n
t'ree, t'ree hunnerd-fifty pounds."

"It's an old hunk of half-inch," I repeated.

"Steal one from the raisin' gang," said Patrick.

"Aw right," Ah-oogah agreed, "if you say so. You might's well go on

down t' two. I'll send it down t' you as soon's I get anot'er line."
Patrick took one end of the line and tied it to the beam, preferring
not to leave the choice of knots to a man whose work he didn't know.
He put a bowline (loop) in the other end and instructed Ah-oogah to
use another bowline through it when he added the second line.

"And don't try to hand-hold it," Patrick added, "take a turn on that
header." To "take a turn" means simply to wrap the line once around
the header, which would provide enough friction to take most of the
strain off the man doing the lowering.

Ah-oogah, acting a little sore at being treated like a rank beginner,
assured us that everything would be done properly, and Patrick and I
went down to the second floor to land the piece. We smoked a
cigarette and talked awhile before Patrick began to wonder aloud
what was holding things up. He leaned into the elevator shaft, looked
up, and reported that he could see nothing. We were looking at our
watches when a thunderous "Ah-oo-gah!" split the air.

"Never mind that shit!" Patrick shouted back. "Send the damn
thing down here!"

"I bet he has lung cancer before he's twenty-five," I said.

"Probably got it now," Patrick replied. We peered up into the shaft
and were just able to make out the piece eight or nine floors above us,
swinging from side to side as it descended. It was hard to see the
maneuver clearly in the shadows, but it appeared that Ah-oogah was
letting it down a foot or so at a time.

"For Jesus' sake, dummy," yelled Patrick, "don't jerk it like that!
Let it down smoothly!" Then he turned to me. "That guy is not only
dumber than you *are*," he said, "he's even dumber than you *used* to
be."

"How would you like to spend a few more weeks in the hospital?" I
offered. Patrick was shaping a response to that when there was a single
loud clang. We were already in flight as Patrick hollered, "Get away!"
to the men in the hole below us. The beam had broken loose and now
with great banging noises sounded like it was hitting everything in
town in its descent. It could very easily catch one end on something
and kick out on any floor, and realizing this we put considerable
distance between us and the shaft. It didn't kick out, however, but
went clattering past our floor like a subway train off its tracks and

landed in the hole with one hell of a noise. A lot of laborers had been at work in the basement, and we looked at each other speculatively as we walked toward the shaft. Patrick suggested that we not let ourselves be seen. As we peered cautiously into the hole, much shouting in Italian began. There were people moving agitatedly in all directions. Most of them began to move out of our field of vision when a white-shirted man, obviously their super, appeared. When the crowd thinned, we could see that one man was lying on his back near the base of a column. There was considerable blood on his face. It took a moment, though, to locate the beam. When I spotted it, I tugged on Patrick's arm and pointed. It lay a good thirty feet away from the injured man, and we stared uncomprehendingly at each other. The super asked what had happened, and a man in a sleeveless green undershirt answered in a very angry voice, with many gestures.

"This Godadammeda beam," he snarled, fixing the bent and battered piece with a glare that should have melted it, "coma down this Godadammeda hole, banga! banga! banga! Guido look up ina Godadammeda hole and see the Godadammeda thing, ana he runs. He runs right into thisa Godadammeda column!"

The man had more to say, but Patrick and I couldn't hear him. Patrick was rolling around on the floor holding his ribs, and I had my glove in my mouth to try to keep the laughter quiet. When we gained control of ourselves, I whispered, "Well, I guess it's probably just a bloody nose."

Patrick put his finger to his lips and signaled me to follow him as he tiptoed away from the shaft. When we were safely out of earshot he examined his watch, shook it, held it to his ear. "What time you got?" he asked.

"Two-thirty," I said.

"Long as we're down this far we might as well go get our own coffee," he declared, heading for the far stairs. We had no business doing this, of course, but it seemed, under the circumstances, the smartest thing to do. We walked across the street to the coffee shop and chose stools in the rear. At ten minutes to three I said, "You think it's been long enough?" He said he guessed so. Going back we again chose the far stairs. We found Coley and Ah-oogah putting in the mail slot frames on seventeen.

Coley just looked at us. Patrick went over to Ah-oogah.

"You get the piece back?"

"Where t'e hell was youse?" he countered.

"We made a discretionary withdrawal," I said. Ah-oogah gave me a long, confused look.

"T'em zips was sore," he said, finally.

"You're not surprised, are you?" Patrick asked. "You goddam near killed one of 'em."

"Awww."

"You know what happens when you squash a zip?" Patrick demanded.

"What do you mean, what happens?" Ah-oogah wondered. He appeared to be thinking about it for a few seconds, then gave it up. "Naw. I don't know what happens."

"You get rain," Patrick announced. Ah-oogah looked more unhappy than ever.

"Worse than that," interjected Coley, "his relatives go out to your car and pour olive oil in your gas tank."

"Nawww, . . ." said Ah-oogah. While this was going on I went over to a coil of line lying on the planking. It was my half-inch plumbing-up line, very neatly parted.

"We told you not to use this line," I said, waving the broken end at him. He became defensive.

"I couldn't find nuttin' else. Besides, half-inch line is supposed to be good for six, seven hunnerd pounds."

"You learned that at school, I suppose," said Coley.

"Yeah," Ah-oogah answered, "at school. An' it's right, too."

"I told you it was an old line," I said. "It's been lying out in the sun and rain for weeks. Didn't they teach you at school that weather weakens things?" Ah-oogah shrugged. When Patrick asked him how heavy he thought the piece was, Ah-oogah brightened.

"I tol' youse before, no more'n t'ree, t'ree-fifty."

"How heavy you figure it is when it's jerked?" Patrick continued. Ah-oogah's smile vanished in befuddlement.

"What do youse mean, 'jerked'?"

"You didn't let it down smoothly," said Patrick, "you let it down a foot or two at a time. When you stop something suddenly, it gets heavier. Much heavier."

"All right," said Coley, "forget it. Go to work."

"Where's the piece?" I asked.

"Ah-oogah dragged it off to the side," Coley answered. "It's too beat-up to use; we'll have to get another one made up."

"Which way does this stupid thing go?" asked Patrick, holding a piece of mail slot.

"I hope t'ey don't pour somet'in' in my tank," Ah-oogah mused.

"I hope they don't get my car by mistake," I said. Ah-oogah gave me a funny look.

During the next months there was no sign of Timmy. Word got around that he was home, but no one saw him. He didn't shape the hall, and he didn't show up in the gin mills. "Nothing unusual in that," said Patrick. "If a man's tryin' to stay off the bottle, he's not likely to hang around right next to one." I said I supposed he was right, but that it seemed odd he hadn't been to the hall.

"Not really," Patrick replied. "You don't know how much he hates the work."

"But it's all he talks about."

"He hates it. For the last five years he hasn't been able to do it at all without drinkin'."

"Since the time he froze, you mean. Callahan said you were his partner when that happened; when are you going to explain it to me?"

Patrick stiffened. "Never," he said. "It's none of your business."

He showed up, finally, at the topping-out party.

There are more stories revolving about topping-out parties than about the other social aspects of ironworking. Not that there are a whole bunch of social events, of course. There's the Annual Picnic, at which the married men who've brought their families behave while the single men get drunk; there are the occasional testimonial dinners honoring someone who is retiring, at which generally only the retiree gets drunk; there are the Friday-after-work get-togethers, consisting mainly of complaints about the job and speeches about how something ought to have been done. Topping-out parties at least embrace the twin illusions of accomplishment and relaxation. They are held nearly at the end of a job, when the super and the engineers and the architects and the fabricators and generally everybody at the management level can at last speak definitely of exactly when they will finally be done, which gives them the right to brag. The pushers can tell themselves that they've successfully gotten a job of work out of the indescribably lazy bastards that make up their gangs, and the men, who are by now sick to death of going to work in the same place every day, can gossip about what and where the next job might be.

When the first column on the last jump is stood up—in other words, when one piece reaches to the highest elevation of the building—an American flag is fastened to it. Company dignitaries strike poses at the foot of the column, while flunkies take pictures. Chief Assistants to the Assistant Chief abound. On topping-out day the coffee-boys work harder than anybody else, because as soon as the potentates retire to the highest-class cocktail lounge in the vicinity, the pushers send the kids out for cases of beer. And whiskey. If the column happens to go up in the morning, some effort to get some work done is made, but if a man puts in more beer than bolts he isn't likely to hear much criticism. The boss is inclined to tell himself that there isn't any point in firing the alcoholic son of a bitch this near the end of the job.

At three, or three-thirty, or even as late as four o'clock, depending on the company's avarice, everybody knocks off for a few hours of eating and drinking at company expense.* Sometimes it's just beer and skittles in the basement; sometimes the banquet room of a nearby restaurant is rented, perhaps even with a bartender to serve drinks and a waiter to pass out hors d'oeuvres. Some companies habitually throw better parties than others, and a part of the conversation at any party concerns how it stacks up against others.

Our party was held in the basement, with folding tables and kegs of

---

* Some of the men go to eat and drink as much and as fast as they can. In a field in which the employee's only fringe benefits are provided by his union—in effect, by the man himself—he has often more hostility than loyalty toward the company. He has no sick leave, no job security, no paid holidays (apart from four hours off just before Christmas and New Year's). Bosses at various levels have some benefits, but the man in the gang does not. He looks forward, therefore, to the topping-out party. It is his miniscule revenge.

improperly pressurized beer, trays of what were rumored to be sandwiches, and a self-service bar with some shot glasses and five or six bottles of house-brand whiskey; there was no ginger ale, no soda, and no ice. Condemnation of the company was universal.

Patrick, Coley, Ah-oogah, a couple of bolter-ups, and I sat with paper cups of beer at one of the folding tables. One of the bolter-ups said he was glad he hadn't brought his wife. The other one said, "Fuckin' aay right." Coley said it was the cheapest spread he'd ever seen; both bolter-ups said, "Fuckin' aay right." Patrick said he'd stay for one more beer and that was it. Coley agreed.

Ah-oogah, however, just sat with his untouched beer in front of him, his big raw face in a beatific smile. "Youse guys," he said, reflectively, "just don't know how t' do t'ings."

"He's stoned," said Patrick.

"I knew it," said Coley, leaning over to examine Ah-oogah's eyes, "he's one of them now, dope fiends." I stood up to go for beer, and Coley and Patrick quickly finished theirs and handed me their cups.

"One more," said Patrick, "and then we'll get out of here."

At the cooler I ran into the super, standing for the moment alone, wearing a large, fixed smile. " 'Scuse me, Jack," I said, "I'm playing barmaid." He moved to one side while I filled the three cups.

"This," he said through the fixed smile and sounding like the lady at the cocktail party complaining that her girdle is killing her, "is the worst party in the whole world."

"Your face is gonna get stuck like that," I replied, "and they won't let you go to any more funerals."

"I'd rather be at a funeral," he said.

"You see that punk over by the wall?" I asked. He nodded. "Well, he's been eating the sandwiches. You'll probably get to go to his."

"Who are you sitting with?" Jack asked.

"Coley and Patrick." He wagged his head up and down several times.

"The three of you," he said, lowering his voice to a whisper, "come by the Cock and Bull in an hour. Don't bring anybody else, though; the good guys are getting together."

"You're a 'good guy'?" I laughed.

"I turn back into a prick on Monday," he said, moving off.

I turned back toward the table and saw that Timmy was sitting there. I slowed my approach to gain time to see if he were drunk. He wasn't. The meeting was exaggeratedly normal, full of How-Are-Yous and You're-Lookin'-Greats, and things like How's It Feel To Top Out? It was all crap; Timmy looked terrible and everybody realized it. There were whole bunches of awkward silences. Coley finally remembered a joke, and Patrick affected great interest in it, bending across the table to make sure he caught every word. When Coley got well into the story, Timmy leaned over to whisper to me. "Why," I began to wonder to myself, "does everybody whisper to me? The B.A. whispers, and Jack, and now Timmy. What does this mean?"

"You a real ironworker yet?" Timmy was asking.

"Well, I'm gettin' there," I answered. Or something equally inane. It was difficult to understand why it was such an awkward confrontation, but it was, and Timmy was as aware of this as anyone.

"Hey, well," he said, rising, "it's good to see you guys, hear? I'll . . . see you around." He left amid a spasm of confused rejoinders.

"When is he goin' to straighten out?" Coley asked, watching Timmy's back disappear through the door.

"Never," answered Patrick, with more bitterness than I could see justification for.

"That's gettin' to be your favorite expression, lately, it seems to me, Patrick," I said.

"Who cares what seems to you?" he said, the bitterness still in his voice with a separate anger lying like cream on top.

He moved his chair a few inches farther away from the table. I slid my own chair back. It was not intended as a serious move, but I found to my surprise and confusion that I was sore. I was sore at Patrick for being sore. While I was trying to figure this out, Coley realized that we were about to get into it and responded by leaning back in his chair with a bad case of the giggles.

"My God!" he said, clapping his hands. "Cold sober! What are you guys like when you're drunk?" He began to laugh.

The laughter changed the whole scene. I stood up, putting my thumbs in the front of my belt à la Gary Cooper, and said, "Git up, yawl!" Patrick jumped up, facing me, his thumbs also in his belt. Both our pants were pushed so far down that Coley suddenly leaned forward in his chair.

"Hot damn," he said, "it's a pissin' contest!"

"Whut choo wahnt?" drawled Patrick.

"Thar's a train outta here at six pee em," I said, "be under it." Coley screeched and nearly tipped his chair over backward. Patrick's expression never changed. He remained motionless until Coley had quieted down. Then he drew his six-shooter with lightning speed, pushing the muzzle against my forehead.

"Yew know whut?" he asked.

"Naw," I answered, imperturbable, "whut?"

"Yew mess with me enny more," he said, his trigger finger twitching, "yew'r gonna have three eyes."

Coley fell off his chair altogether and lay writhing on the floor. Patrick and I sat back down. "Whatsa matter him?" Patrick asked. I shook my head in bewilderment. "I don't know. Gallstones, maybe?"

We piddled around through another beer. I said we'd been invited to the Cock and Bull to have a drink with Jack.

"What the hell for?" asked Coley. "Ain't it enough to work for him all day, I got to go drinkin' with him at night?"

But we went. It was packed, and dark, and very noisy. Everyone in the place seemed to be connected in some way with the job (though there were few ironworkers), and most of them were bosses. We hadn't got more than twenty feet beyond the door when Patrick and Coley decided that it wasn't their kind of group and that we should leave. Our retreat, however, was slowed by all the Hi Pats, Hello Freds, Whaddya Say Mikes, and Hows It Goin' Coleys that we had to get through. I was yanked out of the exit lane by an arm sticking through the crowd as a voice said, "Come over here, Mike, I want to talk to you." In the poor light it took me a moment to see that it was Jack. I followed him toward the outer wall, where the crowd was a bit thinner, wondering what was up.

"You have a job lined up when this one's done?" he asked, when we were relatively alone. I said that I didn't. "Do you want to come with me?" he went on.

"Where? Doin' what?"

"Binghamton. To put an addition on a hospital. It'll keep you busy the better part of a year."

"That sounds good," I admitted.

"In the raising gang," he added.

"I'll take it."

"Good. Now, you get hold of Patrick. If you can talk him into coming with you, and carrying you while you learn, you two can be my connectors, at least to start. If you do all right, you can stay connecting when the derricks go up."

It was too much. I was totally surprised and a little suspicious, and I said so. I asked him if he were offering me a job just to get Patrick.

"Don't be stupid," Jack said. "I can have Patrick without you. I'm not really doing you any favors. I've watched you plumbing-up and you get around the iron all right; you're in every day and you seem to be responsible and I think I can make money on you. If I didn't, I wouldn't offer you the job. But you don't really know anything, yet, and you'll need a lead connector, and Patrick's about the only guy around who hasn't got a regular partner. So you talk to him, and let me know by the end of the day Monday, because I'm not staying to the end of this job—we'll start in Binghamton in a week. If you two aren't coming, I want time to pick somebody else. I don't want to have to call the hall and take any Joe McGees they send out.* Talk to me Monday afternoon." With that he vanished.

I looked around for Patrick and Coley without success. Walking back to my car I kept waiting to feel elated, but it never happened. Was it because I didn't believe it? Did I expect Patrick to refuse? No. Patrick would jump at it. He hadn't connected in nearly a year and was forever complaining that he couldn't really give a damn about anything else. Was I scared? I didn't think so. I remembered that I

---

* A "Joe McGee" is a dumb, goof-off, careless ironworker. He is celebrated in the couplet:

> You can tell the Joes
> By their fingers and toes

which clearly explains what happens to men who don't pay adequate attention to what they're doing.

Nobody seems to know who the original Joe McGee was, but he's achieved immortality in the trade. His name has labeled every klutz for the last thirty or forty years.

had once thought the man on the Frederick Building who had said "You could roller-skate on this thing" must have been a sadist, but now I realized that he'd been right. It wasn't dangerous; it was only a matter of getting used to it.

Was I afraid I'd make a fool of myself? I gave this a little credence. I've never played the fool with equanimity, especially if I've been my own instrument. But the risk of looking foolish had never stopped me from trying things, so in the end I gave this explanation only a few points.

By the time I got to the car, I realized I wasn't going to find an answer, so I shut the thing out of my mind. I would find Patrick tomorrow and ask him to come with me and that would be that.

But as I drove home, I decided that I'd been lying to myself. I probably was scared, I probably was worried about making a fool of myself, and I probably was worried that Patrick would refuse.

During the time between then and the day I went to the job in Binghamton, that's the way it went: back and forth between It's Going To Be All Right and Oh No It's Not.

The building in Binghamton was an ordinary one, and we put it up in the ordinary way. The excavators dug a hole; the rodmen lined it with a mesh of re-bars; the dock builders poured the retaining walls and foundations for our columns. When they were out of the way, we built a ramp (the hole was three floors deep) and brought in the crane. With the crane we set billet plates atop the column piers. "Piers" (foundations) are subterranean stanchions of concrete reaching down, where possible, to bed rock; or, where not, to a point in the hard pan which the engineers compute will bear the load.* "Billet plates" are steel blocks placed atop the piers to receive the bottom ends of columns. They're often seven or eight inches thick and five or six feet square, weighing six to eight tons. When the billet plates were in place, we stood the first columns, which were three stories tall. When the columns were up, we set the first three floors of horizontal iron.

* Well, not always. There are some interesting exceptions. One is the Knights of Columbus Building in New Haven. It is twenty-three stories tall and rests on a single reinforced-concrete "pad" some five feet thick. There are no piers. The entire structure, in effect, floats.

When that was done, we brought in plank (fir slabs two inches by twelve inches by twenty-two feet, in this case) and spread it over what was at that point the roof.

Then, with the plank floor as a work surface, we used the crane to stand the first of our two derricks.

A derrick is simply a hoisting device, analogous in its setting to a Chicago boom and a crane in theirs. What is unique about a derrick is that it can be used to raise itself. It is made of two principal members: a fixed mast and a movable boom. On this particular derrick, a small one, the mast stood ninety feet high, the boom eighty. The boom is hinged to the base of the mast, and is swung toward or away from the mast (called up or down) by shortening or lengthening a cable—usually in several parts—which runs from the engine drum through the mast head to the boom head. The load is raised or lowered by shortening or lengthening a cable which runs from the load through a sheave at the end of the boom down the length of the boom to the base of the derrick and on to the engine. As with the Chicago boom, the engine does not provide lateral power. The cables which support the mast stretch from a round plate atop the mast (the "spider"), down to the building frame. These seven (sometimes eight) "guys" are made of heavy wire rope (generally an inch and a quarter in diameter). The whole affair looks like a giant May Pole. The spider's attachment to the mast is by a short axle; the base of the mast is similarly attached to its support by an axle. The mast-boom assembly can thus be rotated. There is an arrangement of drums and cables rigged near the base of the derrick to accomplish this. It all focuses at a wheel about two and a half feet in diameter, vertically oriented, called the "bull wheel." The bull wheel stands at right angles to its operator and generally has welded to it a six-inch length of pipe to serve as a handle. A small curved metal seat, like the seat of a tractor, sits atop a pedestal near the wheel. Thus the bull wheel operator gets to work sitting down if the strain on the wheel is little enough so that he can turn it without putting his weight on it. Before I tried it, I thought that being the "bullstick" man (he is still called that, in spite of the nearly universal adoption of the wheel) must be one of the trade's easier jobs, but it isn't.

The "bell" man, analogous to the signalman on a crane, wears

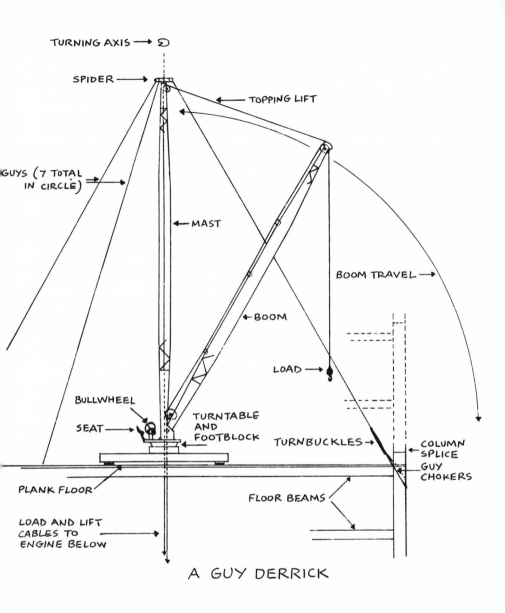

TURNING AXIS ⟶ ⊙

SPIDER ⟶

TOPPING LIFT

GUYS (7 TOTAL IN CIRCLE) ⟶

← MAST

BOOM TRAVEL ⟶

← BOOM

LOAD ⟶

BULLWHEEL

SEAT ⟶

TURNTABLE AND FOOTBLOCK

TURNBUCKLES ⟶

COLUMN SPLICE

GUY CHOKERS

PLANK FLOOR

FLOOR BEAMS

LOAD AND LIFT CABLES TO ENGINE BELOW ⟶

A GUY DERRICK

around his neck a small metal box hanging from a canvas strap. He pushes buttons on this box to give instructions to the operating engineer. Responding to the clanging of his bell and the blinking of the lights on his instrument panel, the operator works his double-drum gasoline-powered engine to take up or release the two cables, thereby raising or lowering the boom or the load. He can't see anything but the instrument panel, since his engine is far below the work area, and the relationship between a bell man and his engineer is therefore a crucial one. Either can drive the other nuts. If an accident happens as a result of a load or the boom continuing when it should have stopped, the likelihood of a near-lethal argument between the two is great. The bell man will insist that the operator didn't stop quickly enough; the operator will insist that he must have gotten a "slow" (read "delayed") bell. No one else is usually in any position to know what might really have happened, and sides are usually taken on the basis of reputation. Sometimes judicious use of fists or a connecting bar can help shorten the dispute.

Our bell man was Maxie—the same Maxie I'd heard talked about by the men who'd worked for the evil Gill. He turned out to be a nice guy, going to considerable lengths to be helpful, and, like I'll-Drink-To-That in my first raising gang, was instrumental in making me look better than I was. Maxie helped everybody. He would even—and this is unique, because a bell man jealously guards his status as the only nonboss who isn't required to do physical labor—jump on the platform to give the bullstick man a hand whenever the going was exceptionally rough.

When the derrick was in place, we were able to reach over the side with it to pick our iron directly from the delivering trucks. When the iron was on the plank floor, we "shook out" (separated the pieces and placed them around the floor in the general areas of their eventual installation) and stood up the columns. The columns were two stories tall, bolted and ultimately welded to projecting plates on either side of the tops of the columns below. When the columns were in place, we set the "intermediate" floor, then the "top" floor. When the top floor was complete, we planked it over. The derrick was then "jumped," that is, raised two floors, by separating the boom from the mast, then "guying off" (temporarily supporting) the boom and using it to raise the mast to the next level. Once the mast is in place, it is used to pull up the boom. From that point, the process was repeated every two stories. It's a procedure which could from a structural point of view be carried on more or less indefinitely; steel is wonderfully elastic, its compression strength is remarkable, and it is light.

People began gaping at the Cass Gilbert-designed Woolworth Tower's 765 feet back in 1912.* By 1930 they could stare at the more than 1046 feet of the Chrysler Tower, or walk downtown for a view of the marvel of the age—the Empire State Building, 1244 feet, 11½ inches from the street to the top of its light. Since then, of course, the world's highest television broadcast antenna has been added.

But the height of that building was the result of other design concerns, not a limit of technology. There was a fixed amount of money available; the cost of each cubic foot of space was known, and when the one was divided into the other, a maximum possible size of thirty-six million cubic feet was the result. The building was then designed to provide this volume.

The Empire State reigned as the world's tallest for over forty years, but now there are the World Trade Center, a double tower eight stories higher, and the Sears Building in Chicago. Like the Trade Center, the Sears Building is 110 stories high, but it has slightly higher floors, so that the result is a building something on the order of a hundred feet taller. Of course, it is only a single tower. However strange it may seem, the Empire State Building may yet regain her status: There is a plan (not a joke) to jack up the roof and insert another sixteen or twenty stories.

Perhaps the clearest idea of how large these buildings are can be had through comparisons. The Pan Am Building, which was built atop the tunneled foundations of New York City's Grand Central Station in the sixties, was at the time the largest high-rise office building in the world, encompassing 2.5 million square feet of usable

---

* For my money, this is not as impressive as the Great Pyramid of Gizeh, which originally stood 476 feet, or the Cathedral of Cologne, at 512 feet. Gizeh impresses because it was done without much in the way of hoisting machinery, and Cologne because it's hollow—which the pyramid, structurally speaking, is not. Cologne succeeded through the use of the "flying buttress," a free-standing brace which takes the lateral strain from a wall. Mortared stone has no torsion strength; without the buttresses a modest summer breeze would blow the place down.

floor space. Washington's Pentagon was once the largest office building in the world, high or low, with 5.5 million usable square feet. The Trade Center's nine million square feet exceeds the sum of both. The amount of material required to build such structures may become clearer if it is pointed out that the steel, stone, glass, pipe, wire, and whatever in the Empire State Building would fill a railroad train fifty-seven miles long.

Frank Lloyd Wright some years ago designed a building a mile high. It's never been built and probably never will be—but not because the techniques don't exist: The limiting factors in a building's height are financial and psychological, not structural.

A leading financial consideration is usable volume. Additional floors require additional access roads, that is, elevators, and there is no rental return on space occupied by elevator shafts. (The Empire State has seven linear miles of them.) Past a certain point, one is gaining negligible usable space because more and more of the lower floor space is filled by shaftways.

Psychologically, the public whimsy is beyond computation. "It sways in the wind" was a common criticism offered of the Empire State, implying that one of these days it is going to blow down. Flexing, of course, is common to all tall buildings. The Empire State has a maximum deflection of about eleven inches, and to detect it in a building that tall requires very sophisticated instruments. The people who foresaw the building's collapse seem finally to have shut up. Time, and the structural strength obviously demonstrated in the 1945 accident in which a military aircraft flew into the building (and stuck there) without causing more than localized and superficial damage, seem to have been responsible for that. However, largely as a result of this mythologizing and doomsaying, the upper floors stood under-leased for years. It was said that "lightning will strike it and electrify it." In point of fact, lightning does strike the building, as it strikes many tall buildings, harmlessly, a couple of dozen times a year. It's a pity that these same people never realized how impressive the strength of the structure really is. They seem never to have learned that the 205-foot needle which originally projected from the top of the building was in fact a mooring mast for dirigibles, and that to that end the top of the tower was designed to withstand safely a *horizontal* effort of fifty tons.*

Compared to these giants, our hospital was an outhouse. Part of the building was to be but five stories, the tower would be only twenty, and at that, one side would be tied into the mother building.

The erection process, however, was exactly the same. If you should see photographs of the Empire State taken during its construction, you would note derricks virtually identical to the ones we used some forty years later. We weren't using rivets, we had a bullwheel instead of a bullstick, and the power for the derrick was updated, but everything else, except for our refusal to go connecting in bibfront overalls with white shirt and tie, was pretty much the same.

The experience I'd gained in other trade operations—taglining, bullsticking, bolting-up—and the practice at moving about on the iron I'd gotten while plumbing-up were useful. I think now that I'd have fallen, through clumsiness or fright, without it. But none of it gave me the least clue to how much I'd need Patrick.

He spent the first days showing me one thing after another, and often continued his teaching, belligerently, over an end-of-the-day drink. "God *damn* it, man!" he'd shout, the moment he'd had the first swallow of his first tequila. "Don't give the bell man a signal 'til you've cleared it with me! If I hadn't of jumped off that lug this afternoon, you'd have had him land that fuckin' piece on my foot. I *need* my feet." I'd apologize, for whatever it was worth, and he'd go on. "When you get to where you know what you're doin', and when *I* know that you know what you're doin', *then* you can tell the man to come down. Not now." He looked sore as hell, but I soon learned that his true emotion was concern, not anger. "You just don't see yet," he said one afternoon, looking into his third tequila, after the shouting period was finished, "how easy it is to kill a man. It's no trouble at all." I just looked at him. "Let's say we're settin' an outside bay.

* When the mooring mast was built, the Hindenburg had not yet burned, and many people saw the lighter-than-air ship as the coming mode of transoceanic travel. Further gains in speed were to be realized by this downtown terminal, "permitting the Atlanticist," said a 1930 article in *Fortune*, "to slide down an elevator shaft into Fifth Avenue in five minutes, instead of steaming up from Lakehurst, New Jersey, in one hundred and twenty."

You're on the outside header, which is maybe two feet deep, and you're standin' on the outside of the bottom flange. It's wide enough for your toes and the balls of your feet, and it's where you've gotta stand to be able to handle the crossbeam when it comes up. You can't fall while you're waitin' for the piece, because until it gets there you can lean over the header and you've got the top flange to hold onto. I'm standin' on the top flange of my header, twenty feet to the inside. Up comes the piece. I grab my end and walk along the header, pushin' and turnin' until I get your end to where you can grab it. If it's a big beam, or one end's a little heavy, you'll grab it with both hands. The moment you do that, I'm responsible for you. All I've got to do is give it a little push and you're over the side. Then what're you gonna hold onto? The only thing you've got is the damned beam, and if I let go, or if you're heavier than I am so that my weight won't stop it from seesawing, you're gone. It's as simple as that." Patrick stopped to sip his drink and look at me; I remained silent. "And that's only *one* way. Harold Moustache went twelve floors onto the exhaust pipe of a diesel truck when his partner let a header bang into the empty column he was perched on. Shot him off like a catapult. An Indian kid I knew went off an apartment building when his partner cut loose before he'd got a bolt stuck. The partner landed on the plank floor, but the kid slid off the end and over the side. The partner swore he'd heard the kid tell him it was okay to unhook." He shook his head at the glass of tequila as though somehow it were at fault. "No, you don't see how it works, yet. You're busy learnin' the moves, and you're learnin' fairly quick, but it doesn't matter how fast you can climb a column, or how well you figure out a way to make a tough piece in a narrow space, if you don't learn that you never do *anythin'* without first makin' sure that your partner's all right."

Some nights, lying in bed after a day's work followed by one of Patrick's safety lectures, I'd have half-asleep fantasies of a faceless partner chuckling as he pushed a beam into my chest, knocking me over the side. Or of the weight ball banging into the column atop which I perched waiting for the header, making a terrible ringing noise that drowned out my falling screams.

Not often. Most of the time I loved it. But there were nights like that.

Some afternoons the lecture would be on technique. Patrick would usually find something to holler about, first, but would then settle into a relatively calm monologue on why things were done the way they were done, instead of the half-assed way I seemed determined to do them. "Now," he would say, taking a ball-point pen and drawing a square on a paper napkin, "here's a bay." I'd nod. "And here's three intermediate pieces that fill it out." He'd draw three lines, equally spaced, from one side of the square to the opposite. "You understand that because of the flanges on the headers, we can't just drop these three little beams in, bang, bang, bang," he said, retracing the three lines. "They have to go in at an angle, and get pried into place when they're at the right height. Yes." He used this "yes" every few sentences when he was lecturing. It meant that I was to indicate that I understood. I therefore nodded. "The piece comes up through the hole and keeps on comin' 'til it's higher than it has to be." I nodded again, to frustrate an additional "yes." "One man grabs an end and pushes the piece so that his partner can get the other end. Now, when the bell man sees that the tagline man has let go his line and the connectors therefore have the piece, he starts slowly comin' down. One man shoves his end to its proper place and spuds a hole." In the kind of connection Patrick was talking about there are a pair of L-shaped lugs welded to either side of the end of the piece being set. They have holes in them which are supposed to line up with matching holes in the web of the header. "Spudding" a hole means simply sticking the tapered end of a spud wrench through one of the holes in the header and impaling the matching hole in a beam lug upon the part of the wrench that sticks through. When this is done, the piece is wrestled around so that the other holes line up. Bolts are rammed through two of them, nuts run part way up, and the wrench withdrawn. "The other connector keeps the beam away at an angle to the header so that it'll fit beneath the top header flange as the bell man brings it down to proper height. Then he slides it, using his bar if he has to, along the web of the header until his holes line up. He spuds a hole, jams a couple of bolts in other holes, and hollers for the bell man to come down some more so that the choker goes slack and the piece can be cut loose. By the time it's ready to be cut loose, the first guy should be out in the middle waitin' to take the choker off."

133

Another nod from me. "Now," he said in the voice of a man coming to his punch line, "which connector makes up first?"

"What difference does it make?" I asked. He slapped his cheek in exaggerated frustration.

"A whole lot, dummy. The man the bell man *can't see* makes up first." He looked at me wearing an expression that suggested that anybody who didn't recognize the obviousness of this must be a prime-cut jerk. "The bell man is almost never in a position to have a good line on both connectors, but he can always see *one*. If that's the man who makes up last, the bell man can do what he has to do—because he can see what's happening—without waiting for a signal. It wouldn't work, the other way around."

This kind of thing went on so constantly that I began to wonder if it would ever stop. I said this out loud one night during a particularly critical session, and Patrick laughed. "Any day now," he said, "but, even then, all you'll know is what I know, and that's not all there is."

I was in O'Rourke's alone one night when Timmy came in and asked me to get him a job. "Freddy," he said, "doesn't want to know I exist." I told him I'd heard he wasn't even shaping the hall, but he said that he'd been there every morning for the past several weeks. Lots of other men were going out, but the B.A. wasn't even looking in Timmy's direction.

"Where's Callahan?" I asked.

"Camping with his kids in Pennsylvania somewhere."

"Harry?"

"Harry," he laughed, "is in jail. He got arrested for mopery."

"Mopery? What in hell is mopery?"

"Mopery is hanging around a whorehouse."

"I don't believe it."

"It's true, though, whether you do or not."

"Mopery? Hanging around a whorehouse? They don't put you in jail for hanging around a whorehouse."

"I didn't say they put him in jail for hanging around a whorehouse; I said they *arrested* him for hanging around a whorehouse. They put him in jail for hitting the cop that arrested him."

"Good old Harry," I said, or something equally inane. I asked

Timmy why he'd come to me for a job, considering that I had no book and therefore no clout, and he did a lot of mumbling before winding up with, "Well, if you get me on, I promise not to tell you anymore that you aren't a real ironworker."

"You're not drinking, these days, I gather."

"Nope," he replied. "Bone dry and a bachelor, too." I gave him an inquiring glance and he shrugged. "My wife's gone home to her mother."

When I went to talk to Jack about putting Timmy on, he was dubious, but not as hostile as I had expected. I think his curiosity got the better of him.

"You know he's an alky, don't you?" he demanded.

"He's sober," I said.

"But he's usually drunk," Jack insisted.

"When he gets drunk, fire him."

"Why are you so interested in gettin' him on?" he asked, walking around me as though I were an object up for sale.

"Maybe," I answered, "I'd like to see if he's any good." That was hardly out of my mouth before he was shaking his head in disagreement.

"You're not leveling."

"So what?" It was my turn to pace around and examine him. "You've got all the options," I went on. "You could come out smelling like a priest, if you wanted to. How can you get hurt? For Jesus' sake, Jack, I'm not asking you to put him connecting—or even in the raising gang at all. But who's he gonna hurt if he's carryin' plank, or maybe in the detail gang? It's your good deed for the year: salvaging a drunk. If he doesn't stay dry, cut him loose."

Jack played with a rolled-up blueprint while he considered this. He used one hand to push the tube to the end of the other hand's grip, then flopped that hand over and pushed the tube from the other end. He did this absently and repeatedly. "All this breakin' of my balls," he said, finally, "to get Timmy on." I made a face. "How do I know you won't break 'em all over again to get me to keep him on after a foulup?"

"No way," I answered. "When and if he blows it are no concerns of mine. All I'm asking is that you do me the one favor of putting him on; I won't ask you for anything else."

The conversation went on a bit longer, but the rest of it was essentially epilogue. Jack would hire Timmy, who would go in the detail gang, which was not the same as the raising gang but was better by a wide shot than not working.

The floor configuration of our annex was an L, with the extant part of the hospital nestled in the bend. Part of the new building was to be shorter than the old (five stories vs. twelve), and part was to be higher (twelve stories vs. twenty).

The columns of the annex were placed so that they almost touched the brick walls of the old building. When the new structure was complete, the original walls would be knocked down and the floors of the two buildings interlocked. This closeness was both annoying (it wasn't possible to get one's leg over any of the headers that paralleled the old building, which often made finding a place to hang on difficult) and amusing (strange sights were sometimes to be seen through the windows). This awkwardness wasn't confined just to my work and Patrick's, naturally. The bullstick operator was forced to attempt unaccustomed levels of precision. Every time he let the boom swing the least bit too far we wound up with the end of a piece knocking down a few bricks or sticking in a window. This led to a chronic adversary relationship between our super, Jack, and the hospital superintendent, a surly Magyar with one ear, named Shoetz. Shoetz was, upon the occasion of his first complaint, instantly renamed "Shitz," which didn't seem to help much. He apparently had no duties other than to harass us, and every time a beam or the ball banged into his precious walls his face would appear in the nearest window, contorted with distress. Patrick's stock greeting was, "Ah, good mornin', Mr. Shitz, and how are we today?" Shoetz would then begin his complaint, but Patrick and I were never able to hear what it was. "Speak up, Mr. Shitz," one of us would shout, "I can't hear you!" Shoetz generally sputtered on into the din for a few minutes before giving up to go ring our shanty to complain to Jack. This didn't often help his mood, since Jack's usual response was a counterattack: "In all honesty, Mr. Shitz, if you're goin' to keep stickin' your head into where the men are workin', you'll have to wear a hard hat; we wouldn't want you to get hurt, you know."

Mr. Shoetz's daily complaints continued, however, until Coley and Timmy settled the matter by presenting him with a white hat. Jack lent them the label maker, Timmy punched out "MR. SHITZ" on the tape, Coley stuck it neatly on the front of the hat, and the next time the man stuck his head out the window we all stopped work while the two of them dashed up a ladder to make their presentation. The superintendent admired the shiny symbol of position (bosses' hats are usually white) until he saw the label, whereupon his ear turned beet red, spittle formed at the corners of his mouth, and he fled from view. Future complaints were in written form, delivered by hospital orderly.

Nurses, much to the delight of us all, frequently leaned out of windows to watch. Over the months Coley went out with several of them. In the shanty the old guys tried to get him to verify The Myth Of The Nurse, but Coley perversely refused to enlighten them.

Doctors, too, often stopped to watch, and though they sometimes asked probing questions about construction techniques, they were all convinced that we were crazy. "Do you wear special shoes?" they asked, and Patrick would lift a leg to show the bottom of his boot, which was perfectly ordinary except that the front of the heel was beveled. "I just couldn't do that," said a young intern with a build like a sumo wrestler.

"Thank God," said Patrick. "If you fell we'd all have to run for our lives. You'd probably take half the iron down with you."

"What I meant," the massive one continued, "is that I know it wouldn't matter how much I tried to, I'd never be able to walk on those little beams."

"That's exactly the way I feel," I said, "about the likelihood I could ever take a scalpel and make the merest sort of incision into living tissues." We then shrugged at each other.

When another of the group ventured that we didn't look like Indians, Patrick turned to me and made a face. "*Hai*-ee kah-hahn-ah," he said.

"Hai-ee mai-*eer* kah-hahn-ah," I answered.

"What's that?" asked the doctor.

"*Who's* that, you mean," we replied. "It's a *who*." The doctor's face betrayed no understanding. "It's how you say good morning to a rabbi," Patrick explained. The man managed a weak smile in leaving, but he was clearly still out in left field.

We began the job on the low side, setting all five floors with the crane. (There would have been no point in standing up a derrick for such a short rise. The derricks were to be used around the corner, where the annex would rise twenty floors.) By the time we had set everything up to the roof headers I had begun to get some feel of the iron, and while I couldn't trot around as well as Patrick, I was at least not ashamed of myself. I had learned in those weeks that more practice produced less anxiety, and to implement progress had set certain standards for myself: I would never coon a beam that another man could walk; I would stand on the top flange when cutting a choker loose from the hook; I would never let Patrick have the easy end of a piece. Patrick and I generally had our coffee (delivered by tagline) sent up to us, instead of coming down to the plank floor to sit with the rest of the gang. Even this—dangling my legs over the side of the job, coffee in one hand and doughnut in the other—I regarded as practice. It all seems pompous and silly to me now, but then, when it was all new, it was important. It was important for a number of reasons, but principally as a demonstration to myself that I was neither going to fall nor to jump.*

This all soon changed, naturally. Once the first flush of a new skill

* True: I couldn't tell if I were more worried about the one or the other. I've known other ironworkers who would admit to such fears, but not many. Within the trade, this sort of response is apparently an exception. In the general populace, however, the proportions seem to be reversed. Dr. Leonard Elkun, a psychiatrist in the University of Chicago's School of Medicine, claims that a mild form of acrophobia is "ubiquitous— maybe 95 of 100 people have it." According to him, most people can't comfortably lean out of a second-story balcony. "What happens is that for a split second you realize how easy it would be to lose control and end it all by jumping. The impulse is quickly countered—you reassure yourself that your feet are firmly planted and you're not going to do it—but it lasts long enough to cause a slightly turned stomach or a tingle in the spine." Men who work daily in high, exposed places, he says, "are decidedly unaverage in that respect and probably others." (I wish I knew what he meant by "others.")

It's a pity Dr. Elkun hasn't chosen to pursue what might be called "conversion reactions," in which the hazard *is* the candle, the "slightly turned stomach" becoming at once the proof of victory and the victory itself—the desired condition.

was past, I began to realize that I was going home every night totally exhausted. I missed Patrick's "Quittin' Time" speeches because I was already in bed. If a good-looking nurse smiled at me, I smiled back and let it go at that. I began to realize that energy was a quantity, not a quality, and that I was one day going to come up empty. Patrick, after all, was seven or eight years younger than I, and as connectors go, he was old.

The day we set the last of the roof headers on the low side I was having such thoughts while we were sitting on a piece drinking our morning coffee. "Hey kid," I said to Patrick, who looked about as though checking to see if I might be talking to someone else, "when we go round to the other side, you have my permission to take the hard end every now and then."

"What's the matter, Pops?" said he. "You gettin' tired?" I allowed that I was. "There's older connectors than you," he went on.

"Maybe so," I admitted, "but they don't have to work with you." Patrick grinned. I sighed. He grinned again.

"Hey, fellas!" sang out a voice behind us. We turned to see a man in a plaid bathrobe leaning his head out of a nearby window.

"My Christ," said Patrick, "Shitz is hiring the patients to do his bitching."

"What can we do for you, sir?" I asked. Somebody was in the street refueling the compressor, so speech was easier than usual. The man's head was a mess of bandages and his left eye was blocked off with a huge patch anchored with flesh-colored plastic tape. He was quite wrinkled, and his voice rasped.

"How high you planning to go?" There was a querulousness in his voice that suggested he wasn't as pleased with our project as were the doctors and nurses.

"Forgive me, sir," I said, "but why do you ask?"

"You go any higher you'll block the sunlight," he explained.

"Block the sun?" said Patrick.

"That's right, young fella," said the old man, fingering the patch on his eye. "This's my room, you see, and if you go any higher you'll block the light." He stopped, but before either of us said anything he added, "Man my age needs sunlight. Haven't been well, lately, as any fool can see."

"Yes sir," I nodded, obviously one of the two intended fools, "as you say, that's quite evident, sir. May I ask what happened to your eye?"

"Bugs!" he snorted. "Bugs got it." He fingered his patch as though it were a scab he wanted to pick off. "Germs, anyway," he added.

"You'd rather we don't go any higher," Patrick said, not, apparently, caring to pursue the "bug" business. The man nodded vigorously.

"Won't be any light if you do," he pointed out, reasonably.

"Well, sir," I said, "we'll certainly make every effort to accommodate you. I'll talk to my superiors right away."

"Hmmph," said the old man.

"Hey, Claude!" yelled Patrick to the bullstick man, who was French-Canadian and spoke no English whatever, "Don't send up any more iron." At the sound of Patrick's voice, Claude and the whole gang looked up in mystification. "Hold everything right where it is," Patrick continued, "until we see the architect." Several profane expressions of confusion floated up to us, but we waved them off. Patrick and I tossed down our empty coffee containers, strapped on our belts, and stood up.

"Wait right here, sir," I said to the old fellow, "We'll be back shortly."

"Got nowhere to go," he replied. We slid down to the plank floor, answered the gang's questions about what was going on, and put in twenty minutes' work cleaning up the floor. Then I shinnied back up the column that gave on to the old man's window, where I found him still playing with his patch.

"Well, sir," I said, "you must be a person of some importance. I doubt if they'd have done this for just anybody, but I've been sent to inform you that this part of the building is going to be halted at this elevation. You need have no further anxiety."

"How's that?" he asked.

"We're stopping right here," I said, pointing to the header I was standing on, "not going to block the sunlight. Don't worry about a thing."

"Hmmph," he snorted, disappearing into the shadows of his room. I slid back down to the plank floor to meet Patrick's questioning smile.

"He's very grateful," I said.

One of the frustrations of construction work in general, and of "booming around" (traveling from place to place) in particular, is that you are forced continually to give up old friends and make new ones. Some people you seem to bump into every so often, but many you meet once and never see again. The foreknowledge we all have of this produces a certain shallowness in relationships.

The hospital was my first "big" job, employing a couple of hundred men (fifty or sixty of whom were ironworkers), and I've no idea what's become of most of the ones I knew. I realize, sitting here, that it was set up that way from the beginning: We worked together, had a few drinks after work together, but rarely socialized in areas unrelated to the job. It's largely self-protective. People who've seen this manuscript as I work on it ask me why so many of the conversations seem to take place in a bar, and the answer is merely that that is about the only kind of place in which we talk. I don't want that to be too sweeping a generalization, since it isn't an absolute. Patrick and I have known each other for several years, now, on and off jobs. Coley and I go sailing together regularly. But I haven't seen Callahan in five years; Harry was killed in 1971 when a building he was wrecking collapsed, but I hadn't seen him in some time and learned of his death by chance; I'll-Drink-To-That is still going about his taciturn business, which I know through having run into a fellow who's recently worked with him. Every man must wonder, sometimes, whatever became of so-and-so, but a construction worker can do it indefinitely.

On the positive side, it at least makes it easier to break the ice with a newcomer. "What local you outta, Sam?"

"Four-twenty-four."

"Oh, yeah? Say, is Williams still the B.A.?" The other man nods, and the speaker continues, "Well, next time you're up home, you say hello for me, hear? I worked in New Haven, once, on the, what was it . . . the Armstrong Building. Yeah, I remember Williams. Not a bad guy. Whatever happened to . . ." And so it goes.

Sometimes, asking after old acquaintances is merely curiosity (however hard this may be to believe, there was a connector on the Trade Center who had been a male model in Paris. He had an

141

apprentice book, and no one in the business knew he'd been a model, for obvious reasons. I've often wondered what became of him), and sometimes it's a little heavier (a bolter-up named Guffey once deflected a falling grinder that would surely have knocked me off the iron, and although we were good buddies for the six months either side of that event, I've not seen him since that job was finished).

Two people from the hospital job that I'm sometimes curious about are that old man who thought his need for sunshine changed the shape of the building and the connector who threw up (he's referred to this way when we're swapping stories with newly met men). "Hey, Mike," or "Hey, Patrick," someone will say, "tell these guys about the connector who threw up."

He was an Indian kid, maybe twenty years old, and was my partner for a few days while Patrick was recuperating from a sore leg he'd gotten when he caught most of the weight of a header that rolled over on the plank floor. His name was Eddie something, and I knew after working with him for half an hour that he was at his age a better connector than I'd ever be. The only thing I had over Eddie was that my stomach was in better shape than his.

We were setting the tenth floor iron, again working in a bay adjacent to the old building, when suddenly and for no apparent reason he began puking violently. The tagline man and the hooker-on were working beneath him and ran screeching out from under. I was at the other end of the header and saw what was going on only after I heard their curses. Eddie was standing on his end of the piece, retching miserably. When I ran to his end to ask what the matter was, he could only point to a window. It was an operating room. In it there were a variety of machines and bemasked medical personnel, and in the bright cone of light in the center of the room there was a man on the table with his entire middle open to view and more damned blood than you'd have expected at a small war. My most vivid memory of the scene centers about the blood. That's probably the way Eddie remembers it, too; I doubt if he's forgotten how sick it made him. He turned fishbelly white. When it dawned on me that he was going to faint and fall, I grabbed his arm and helped him sit down on the header. Satisfied that he was safe, I turned again to the window. The tagline man and the hooker-on shouted up to ask what the hell was going on.

"Come and look at this!" I called back, waving my arm in a sweeping invitational circle. "It's an *operation!*" Big Ben Bush, normally a phlegmatic sort of fellow, came shooting up the nearest column.

"I ain't never seen an operation," he said, several times, as I steered him to a vantage point. Coyle, the tagline man and as useless an individual as I've ever known, affected indifference.

"So friggin' what?" said he.

"Come on up, Coyle," I said. "It's worth a look." Coyle went slowly up a ladder two bays away and walked, wearing an expression that conveyed his distrust of being called, over to our header. As soon as he looked in the window, he turned around and sat down on the piece.

"Omigod," he said, holding his mouth with one hand and his stomach with the other, "Omigod." Big Ben Bush turned toward Coyle long enough to suggest that he go over by Eddie if he were going to vomit, so that there would be only one mess.

"C'mon, you little bastard," said Big Ben, "get outta here; you'll make t'e iron slippery." Coyle said "Omigod" a few more times, but managed to control himself.

"Whot ees?" called up Claude from his bullwheel platform, accompanying himself with a confused semaphore of arms, "Whot ees?"

"Alors," I called back, making cutting gestures across my stomach with an imaginary knife and pointing to the window, "Ici! Ici!"

"Can the phony French," shouted Patrick, limping into view with Coley and Timmy and a guy with an eye patch. (The detail gang was often fleshed out with whoever was getting over an injury.) "What the hell's going on up there?"

"It's either the operating room or the Disposall," I answered.

"No shit?" said Coley. "Make room for us." The four of them located a ladder and started up.

"Aayy," Claude fairly screamed, still gesturing, "whot ees!"

"Ohp-air-ah-shee-ohn!" I shouted back. "Ohp-air-ah-shee-ohn, you illiterate alien. Ici!" Claude put the brake on his derrick and came to join us.

Within a few minutes there assembled on the header and adjacent iron the entire raising gang, including their pusher, the detail gang, the plank gang, and assorted bolter-ups. After the first rush of questions, an intrigued silence fell over this entire group. You'd have thought we were all at a stag movie. Every now and then Coyle, who had recovered sufficiently to watch, said "Omigod," but his was the only speech.

One man was obviously the surgeon, since he was the one doing most of the digging around in the patient's abdomen, but there were several others who from time to time did some poking about. All were gowned and masked and bloody and looked alike, and my principal impression was of several pairs of disembodied eyes flying here and there like bats in a dark red cave. When the first pair of eyes happened to glance up at the window, they expanded in disbelief. It might have been Step'n Fetchit in a graveyard. Surely the last complication to be anticipated in an operation is an audience of dirt-and-rust-covered men gaping in at a window that had recently given onto nothing but blue sky. Several gowns bumped into others, and heads were jerked in signal toward the window. When the surgeon looked up, his eyes grew widest of all.

"What in hell," called a sudden angry voice from below and behind us, "is going on up there?" Most of us turned around, but no one spoke. Jack was standing on the plank floor, his hands on his hips and his legs spread wide, the way he always stood when he was sore. Shoetz, wearing his white hat but without his name tag, was standing beside him.

"If you pricks aren't back to work in one minute," said Jack, "you're all fired. Jesus!" He strode off, Shoetz gleefully tripping along after him. Everybody sighed and went back to work except Eddie, who said he didn't feel well at all and was going home. Somebody else filled in for him, and as soon as we'd set two more pieces, we were through in that area and were unable to watch any more of the operation.

"I think," Coley said over a beer that afternoon, "we may have killed that guy."

"How so?" I asked.

"Those medical people seemed pretty shook up," said Patrick. Various of our group nodded agreement.

144

Eddie was back at work the next day, but didn't care to discuss the incident.

There were a number of delays on the hospital job, including two major ones, so that we were the better part of a year getting it up. One corner of the lot didn't have the bedrock beneath it that was supposed to be there, and it took almost three months to sink a pile down deep enough for it to anchor properly. That wasn't our work, so some of us were let go outright, while a few others were farmed out to smaller jobs during that time. Patrick and I went to the fabricator's yard and shook out steel for the entire period.

At the very end of the job new drawings with a whole slew of alterations were sent in, and we spent two months after the topping-out moving, deleting, and adding small pieces. By the time everything was done, we were all sick of both the job and the town.

Timmy stayed dry all the way through, and his shaking gradually stopped. He got along well with Coley, and even Patrick's hostility abated. Timmy's wife divorced him, and although he hadn't seen her in several months, he was clearly unhappy about it. He mentioned it just once, however, and then quietly. Coley and I rather expected him to fall apart, and watched him closely for the first few weeks after he got the papers, but he stuck to his ginger ale.

The day we were paid off, Jack took me aside and suggested that Patrick and I should stick together, that he would call for us as soon as the next job came through.

However, he never called. Things, as we learned as soon as we were back in the hall, were very slow indeed. The chairs were all filled, and there were men spilling outside, huddled in patches of December sunshine, or sitting in small forlorn groups in their cars. The gossip and rumors were uniformly depressing.

"I was talkin' to my cousin t'e ot'er day. He's outta Four-Oh-Four (Utica), and he says t'ey ain't got nuttin'."

"I heard t'ere was a powerhouse goin' up in Plattsburg."

"Yeah, but it's t'e only job t'ey got, and who wants to work in Plattsburg, anyway? You'll freeze your balls off."

"Walter Cronkite says we may have a major recession."

"Screw Walter Cronkite."

145

"I understand t'ere's transmission towers goin' up in Nam."

"So what? T'e work ain't tough enough you got to improve it by gettin' shot at?"

I listened to most of this without participating. These were book men talking, and it was clear that if they weren't being sent out, the other permit men and I had no chance at all.

Patrick and Coley went off fishing in Tennessee, a trip I declined to join because fishing bores me to tears. I signed up for unemployment insurance, and took to returning to my room around ten every morning, after the ritual trip to the hall, to read. What bothered me most was not the lack of income, but that this joblessness was happening right when I was beginning to feel that I was entitled to be proud of what I could do.

But if Cronkite's fears of a major recession were overlarge, there was nevertheless very little ironworking going on. December and Christmas shot past, and January, and most of February. I quit going every morning to the hall, putting in only one or two appearances a week. And that was merely for show; no permit men were going out.

In O'Rourke's one evening, however, I'll-Drink-To-That asked why I didn't go down to New York City. "You got no family," he said, "and I hear t'ey got work."

"You know I'm only on permit," I said. "Why should they give me anything?"

"Maybe t'ey won't," he answered, "but you ain't got anyt'in' here now, have you?"

"Without a book," I protested, "I can't even show I can do the work."

"Crap," said the little man, obviously weary of talking, "take your old assessment receipts and wrap 'em in bullshit."

He was right, I admitted to myself. And it wasn't even a new suggestion. I'd heard it several times before, but had rejected it out of hand because I felt like I'd had New York. I had no desire to live there again, or even to visit.

Still, I'd been a long time out of work, and it didn't look as though there were much chance of things soon improving, and I told I'll-Drink-To-That that maybe I just would, and the next morning I threw my longjohns and tool belt into the car and drove to the city.

PART 3

A BUILDING ON SIXTH AVENUE

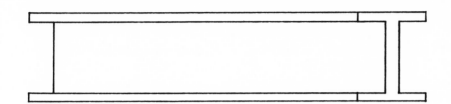

ON that February morning drive down the length of Manhattan the anxiety that I'd thought was conquered came running back at me all over again. The buildings that for years had been so familiar I suddenly saw in an entirely different and wholly disturbing light. I might as well have been a countryboy gaping in disbelief at the height of everything. The city had never struck me as so *tall* before. I tried to jolly myself out of my agitation by playing games: "Migawsh, Rufus," I said to the passenger's seat, "you surely could put a lot of feed in *them* siloes!"

It didn't help. I drove past several buildings that were nearing completion, twice pulling over to the curb to stare at them, developing a slight case of the shakes as I realized that the twenty- and twenty-three-story jobs I'd been on were, by comparison, merely carriage houses. I remembered conversations with nonironworkers in which they asked if I didn't get nervous working so far above the ground, to which I'd replied, "Of course not; after the first thirty feet or so it doesn't matter how far you fall," and I tried now to make myself believe it. I had *believed* that I believed it before, and was now shocked to discover how weak was my faith. By the time I parked the car, I was almost ready to give up the whole project.

In the years since that morning I've sometimes wondered why I went on into the hall (it's the kind of demon that jumps out at one in the dark of a sweaty night), and I have come to the conclusion that I acted out of cowardice. I knew I couldn't give anybody upstate an acceptable explanation; I was pretty sure that I couldn't even give myself one.

So I put a dime in the meter, told myself that they weren't likely to put an out-of-town permit man to work, anyway, and went inside.

At that time the hiring hall of Local Forty was a large room (plus a small office) in the old Broadway Central Hotel, a New York City monument to decay that in 1973 sloughed off three-quarters of a century's cosmetic alterations and, like the Deacon's wonderful one-hoss shay, disintegrated in one fell swoop. By the time of the collapse, however, the local, one jump ahead of the pensioners, welfare families, and prostitutes, had moved farther down the island. Looking at newspaper pictures of the rubble, several of us remarked that we had known all along it was bound to fall down, and I suppose that for once a claim to foreknowledge was supportable. The place had been a creaking pastiche of lopsided, cracked plaster walls, multilayered linoleum, and cockroaches as far back as anyone could remember. The whole building was heavily perfumed with disinfectant and mold. "What in hell," I recall thinking on that first trip in the elevator that couldn't stop within four inches of any given floor, "is the most prestigious local in the country doing housed in *this* place?" *

There were perhaps twenty men in the room, gathered in small groups on folding chairs. Some of them glanced up in mild curiosity as I entered; most didn't even notice me. I walked to the nearest group and said good morning. One man answered, for which I was grateful. There was such a heavy air of apathy in the room that I was almost surprised that he bothered.

"Is there any work?" I asked.

"Where you from?" he countered.

"Upstate," I said. "We got nothin'."

"Ain't nothin' here, either," he said, turning back to his coffee klatch. "You might as well go on home."

"Well, shit," I answered, not able to think of anything else, and

* The hiring hall, it should be pointed out, is that part of a union's activity with the lowest profile. Affairs more visible to the outside world are conducted from the Business and Welfare Offices. Local Forty's are a very handsome series of suites on Park Avenue South. I do not mean to suggest anything out of order in this; a business which in fiscal 1972 held a balance of $9.5 million after disbursements of $15.7 million is entitled to a decent facade.

secretly ashamed to realize that I was in some measure relieved, "I heard there was work." The man shook his head.

"Long as you're here," he said, still facing away, "you can sign the sheet, but there ain't no work." He pointed to a table at the front of the room, upon which there was a sheet of paper. I nodded my thanks, signed the sheet, picked out a chair toward the rear of the room, and sat down. Lack of work, I decided, would account for the men's apathy. I resolved, not altogether unhappily, to sit there an hour before driving home. There was a two-day-old Daily News in the next chair, and I began reading the sportswriters' erroneous picks for yesterday's games.

When I was halfway through my second cigarette, a frosted-glass window behind the table opened long enough for a hand to reach through and take in the list. When this happened, there were little flurries of life among the men, and the guy who'd spoken to me before came over and tapped me on the shoulder with his fist. "I was only kiddin'," he said, "there's plenty work. Stick around." As he went back to his group, they all began to laugh. Having little choice, I laughed with them.

A face appeared at the window and began calling names. In short order mine was called, and I went up.

"Why are you here?" asked the face.

"No work up home," I replied, "since before Christmas."

"How long can you stay?"

"Indefinitely." The face examined me briefly.

"We got plenty of work," he said, writing an address on a slip of paper. "Go here."

On the way out, I waved to my nameless acquaintance, who called out after me, "Didn't I tell you?" He was wearing a silly grin.

It was some weeks before I became aware enough of the situation in the city to be able to understand why there had been so much apathy in the hall. It wasn't that there was no work, but that there was so much that the men I'd seen in the hall had been, for the most part, the losers: the men who didn't really want to work and the men who (through instability, alcoholism, or incompetence) were largely unemployable. The "good guys," as Jack would have called them, were all out on jobs.

151

During what remained of the winter I carried plank. In boredom it is a job second only to carrying rods, and is tolerable at all only in cold weather, when by regulating his pace a man may avoid both heat stroke and freezing. I worked with many different partners, but I have distinct memories of just two.

The first was named Costello. There are whole bunches of Costellos who work out of Forty—I've been on jobs with at least three of them—and in spite of the Italian-sounding name they are Newfies. This one impressed me by his fascination with the local streetwalkers. When I began carrying plank with him, we were only eight floors up, which was low enough to see the people on the ground as people. The job was in north Times Square, in which there is at least one whore in every doorway on every cross street. He couldn't keep his eyes off them, although to the best of my knowledge it was a purely clinical interest. A dozen times a day I'd pick up the front end of a plank, turn around upon realizing that the other end wasn't being lifted, and discover Costello a hundred feet away leaning over the side of the building.

"Hey! Sometime today, huh?" I'd shout at him, to which he'd respond by urgently waving me over.

"You see t'at black one down t'e block wit' t'e blonde wig?" he'd ask when I drew alongside. I always said I did, although much of the time the girl in question was too far away for me to be sure I had the right one. Costello had eyes like an eagle. "Her room's in t'at hotel across t'e street," he'd say, his pointing finger shifting a few degrees. "She's been up t'ere wit' guys seven different times since lunch. If she charges twenty bucks a shot she must gross more'n t'ree hunnerd a day. Sacred Mary, t'at's over two t'ousand a week!" I was tempted to explain about pimps and payoffs, but knew that if I let a conversation about whores get started, there'd be no stopping it. He was absolutely fascinated by the economics of prostitution.

The other person was a young black whose work life was miserable on at least three counts: The men resented him because the NAACP forced him on the job; he was congenitally unable to concentrate on what he was supposed to be doing; he was utterly terrified of the iron. His situation wasn't helped by his body, which was a great mound of muscleless fat atop a pair of gigantic feet that pointed in opposite directions. Being slue-footed may not be a terrible handicap on the ground, but it seriously complicates trying to walk along a narrow beam. This fellow's feet were so big and so unalterably opposed that even the largest headers presented real danger.

Spreading plank begins with the landing in a new bay of one or more "loads." A load is ordinarily a double stack of boards fifteen pieces high.* The derrick swings the load into the bay, and the connectors land it so that each end of the bundle rests on a beam. After the choker has been cut loose, the plank carriers first flip the top two or three boards off and shove them up tight to the load, thereby giving themselves something to stand on. Once those first few boards are in place, there is nothing particularly hazardous about the job.

Slue-foot, however, would have nothing to do with this initial stage. He refused to participate in any way until I had not only laid out the first planks alone—which is a pain in the ass because they weigh, depending upon how green they are, anywhere from 60 to 120 pounds—but built him a two-wide bridge from the load to wherever he was. I forgave him this difficulty, grudgingly, remembering my own fear. What I could not forgive him was his penchant for watching his own miserable feet so continuously that I had repeatedly to drop my own end or be walked into the hole. ("Hole" is a generic term denoting any opening into which a man might fall, whether an open bay, an elevator shaft, or the original excavation.) If I was at the front end of a plank, I would walk along the previously laid plank to its end, then bend down and put the new one alongside. With Slue-foot at the other end, however, the plank as often as not never stopped coming, forcing me either to drop the damned thing or go right off the end. Time after time I'd let the north end go at the last moment, wheel around to discover him standing there in his east and west feet, saying in genuine surprise, "Whut's amatter, Pres?"

---

* This is by rule, although in some circumstances stacks twenty planks high are made up. The reason for the limit is that if piles much higher were made, the strain on the lower planks (since the bundle is lifted by a single centered choker) would soon exceed their strength.

I saw a gang pick a load thirty boards high, once. Nothing happened until the bundle was inadvertently jerked, when the lower planks split in two and fell away. The upper ones, suddenly freed of the choking effect, slipped out. The result was a sidewalk that looked like a collapsed sawmill. There were a number of injuries to passersby (two or three fairly serious), and one fired pusher.

Giving him the front was even worse, since when he got to within five or six feet of the edge his rate of travel wound down to zero.

He never did get used to the height, and after a few months simply disappeared. I still think he might have made out, eventually, if somebody'd been able to get his feet to point frontward.

In the spring I went on a bullwheel, replacing a cousin of Costello's who'd been hurt in a peculiar accident: The derrick had been used to pick decking from the street, lifting the bundles up and swinging them around to finished bays on the new floor. The fellow had put on the brake (which prevents lateral movement of the boom, when it works) while the load was coming up from the street. Preparatory to swinging the boom around when the load was up, he cut the brake loose, not realizing that the bundle was already swinging a little of its own accord. Bundles of decking can be fairly heavy—this one was around twelve tons—and when the brake was released, the swung-out load whipped the boom several feet to the side, which of course spun the wheel violently. The handle caught him squarely in the balls. His howls carried clearly over all the other job noises. The raising gang put him in a scale box and lowered him over the side to the ground, where the nurse, much to his embarrassment, packed his balls in ice before he was whisked off to the hospital. He recovered nicely, but while he was out I was shoved into service, and although upon his return I repeatedly pressed him to ask for his old job back, he declared no interest in having it.

I had never thought, watching bullwheel men at work, that it was much of a job, either in toughness or interest. (It turned out that there was rather more to it than showed, on both counts.) When the super asked me to take it over, I said sure, thinking that it would be nice to work sitting down for awhile.

For the first hour I turned the wheel with one hand, seated. The second hour I turned it with one hand, standing. By lunchtime I was using both hands—standing. By midafternoon I was convinced that both my arms were permanently ruined. When the rest of the gang saw how much trouble I was having with the wheel, they responded in standard fashion.

"*Turn* t'at t'ing, for Jesus' sake!"

"Sometime today, fella!" ("Sometime today," as you may have gathered, is standard construction argot for "hurry up.")

"Your sister gets around faster'n t'at!"

The ribbing continued all day and moved with me into the shanty after work. I would have smacked somebody, but it was all I could do just to button my shirt.

By the end of the first week I had recovered well enough to be able under most circumstances to swing the wheel one-armed and seated, which demonstrates something about conditioning that most of us who do physical work for a living know in a more meaningful way than do our white-collar neighbors: A muscle not regularly used weakens with astonishing rapidity and is brought back to acceptable tone only through painful and consistent exercise—of which there is no one kind that will keep even a majority of the body's practically uncountable numbers functioning at high efficiency. Carrying plank employs many muscles, notably the biceps, triceps, deltoids, and forearm flexors, but nonetheless fails to provide much exercise for the latissimus dorsi and pectoralis major muscles utilized by the man on the bullwheel. The fellow who sticks and tightens "soft" bolts all day (soft bolts are tightened by wrench rather than gun) will have handsome pronator teres and flexor carpi development—which is useless to him if he is suddenly told to go plumbing-up. Of course, all ironworkers climb stairs interminably, so that even the most dilapidated among us seldom suffer from cramps of the gastrocnemius, soleus, or quadriceps. Connectors tend to be the best-conditioned ironworkers, but even they will have some aches upon returning to work after a week or two off, although most of them wouldn't dream of admitting it.

It amuses me, thinking of the protests my own muscles set up after any layoff of more than a very few days, to watch my middle-aged suburban neighbors mount their Saturday attacks upon the tennis courts, imagining that they are "getting into shape." All they get for their once-weekly exercise is three days of soreness. By the time a man is forty there is no way he can stay ahead of the leakage by bailing once a week.

The notion I'd had that the bullwheel would be boring vanished as soon as I realized that inattention could all too easily result in a connector's being knocked over the side. An hour into my first day on the wheel, while we were setting iron in a corner bay, I failed to swing the boom fast enough for the piece being hoisted to clear a header on the intermediate floor. The beam, a light sixteen-footer, flipped end over end, striking the standing iron so hard that the connector atop the corner column got a hell of a shaking up. It was at least partly the fault of the bell man, who should not have given a "fast" bell with an inexperienced man on the bullwheel, but he drew no criticism. It was all directed, eloquently, at me. I had to duck one hard hat and several very accurately thrown bolts.

I celebrated the first warm day of spring that year by getting myself dangled over the side of a job on 47th Street, thirty-two floors above the traffic.

I was taglining. The piece being set was a heavy outside machine-floor header which had to be snaked up through a congested area (there was a great mass of small stuff on the machine-floor), requiring me to pull down on my line with all my modest weight. To get a better grip on the line, I took a half hitch (an upside-down loop) around my palm. That was the mistake. A half hitch can't be cast off a line when there is a strain on the load end—which I knew but wasn't thinking about. The bell man came up with the header slowly until its opposite end cleared the adjacent iron, at which point he "got up on" * the piece in a hurry, and I was lifted from the plank floor like a fish on a hook. The bullwheel man, either ignorant of my plight or deliberately malicious, began swinging the header toward its intended position between the two columns. Without a grounded tagline man pulling to keep the piece on its intended axis, however (in midair *I* was of no use), it slowly turned ninety degrees, coming to a standstill midway between the two columns but at right angles to them, with me dangling from the outer end. Because my weight was upsetting the

---

* The phrase is a double misnomer, but is standard usage. Actually, no one "got up on" anything; the piece was lifted from the floor. Further, the bell man doesn't get up on the piece: He pushes a button which causes the operating engineer to engage the drum which shortens the load cable, which results in the piece being raised. However, because all commands dealing with derrick movement (other than lateral movement, which is the province of the bullwheel man) are relayed through the bell man, he is treated, at least syntactically, as the doer. It simplifies speech.

balance of the thing, it hung with its outer end—my end—considerably depressed. I was, in fact, scarcely above the level of the plank floor, since the header was well over thirty feet long and was tipped down at something approaching a sixty-degree angle. My attention was directed initially to the choker: If its grip upon the piece slipped, I was gone. As soon as I began worrying about that, I began also wondering how well I'd tied the rolling hitch I'd used to connect the tagline to the header. Once I'd realized that there were two connections to worry about, I couldn't settle upon a choice of anxieties and gave the whole business up; there wasn't a thing I could do about either one of them, anyway.

At thirty-two floors times about twelve feet each, I was nearly four hundred feet above the ground, hanging by a thin piece of manila line. I was frightened, but not to the point of panic, and suddenly realized that while familiarity had bred *some* contempt for the height, the principal moderating factor was my knowledge that the situation was (I can't bring myself to pass up this figure of speech) out of my hands.

While I was dangling there thinking—and I *was* having this seemingly extended group of thoughts, although in fact I cannot have been suspended for more than a couple of minutes—the rest of the gang merely gaped where they stood. Into this idiotic tableau walked the super.

"What in the name of the Holy Mother," said he, "are you doin' out *there?*"

"Gettin' gangrene of the hand," I replied. Derision, I noticed, has a way of making off with a man's fears.

"Boom him back, Tommy," said the super. The bell man boomed up and came down on the load simultaneously, depositing me back on the plank. "Lots of assholes," the super said to me, realizing exactly how the mishap had come about, "have tied half hitches in taglines and gone for little rides, but I think you now hold the altitude record."

I answered with some sort of inanity and he walked away. We went back to work. I didn't have any physical reaction to the experience until evening, when over the eighth or ninth beer I had a short but impressive case of the shakes.

In July, I spent some time as the only white man in an Indian gang, which is not a desirable state of affairs. It does give a man a micro-insight into what it must be like to be a member of a minority, however. Exclusivity games were constant.

I was connecting; the bell man would yell to the other connector, while pointing at me, something that sounded like, "Haii, kana-maka-kaii!" * The fellow would reply in similar vein, also pointing at me, and the two of them would collapse in laughter. The bullwheel man would then join in, nodding his head vigorously and making mysterious gestures. Charlie, the elderly hooker-on, would then grab a piece of keel (crayon), draw some sort of crude symbol on the plank, and proceed to dance around it in a parody of a Hollywood parody of a rain dance—or a fertility rite, or a harvest charm, or a whatever. What they sought from me was any sort of outsider's response, and I sometimes, in a show of polite curiosity, played along with them by asking, "What the hell is all that supposed to mean?"

"Ahaah," the pusher breathed triumphantly, "white-eye not *know!* White-eye not know of Great Red Power! White-eye watch!" He then stood before a header that was hooked-on and ready for lifting, making standard Mandrake The Magician levitating gestures at it. With the bell man's cooperation the beam lifted slowly from the floor. When it had risen a few feet, he reversed the gestures and the piece settled slowly back down. He then bowed to me while I clapped in appropriate mystification; he bowed to his gang while they also clapped; work began again.

This sort of playing was all very well and good, but the language exclusion wasn't always a joke. Often, when a piece was giving problems or when any sort of difficult decision had to be made, consultations were conducted in their own tongue. It left me looking the fool, and frequently wore me out with trying to do something at my end of a piece that my partner was perverting by his opposing efforts at the other end. I was always assumed to be at fault when

---

* Don't take this literally; it is in no way intended as more than the faintest kind of imitation. I've never managed to pick up any of the language (languages, more accurately, as a number of subgroups seem to be represented). The one sound I know is "upa hii," which means, prosaically enough, something very close to "up high." Depending upon inflection, it suggests variously "lift this piece," "lift this piece a little (or a lot)," or "lift this piece quickly." Rather a disappointment, isn't it?

something wouldn't go right—which is the way it is, generally, for whoever has the short end of the stick. I got stuck with the hard end of every piece and the hard part of every job. I told an Irishman from one of the other gangs one night that I was beginning to wonder if I was paranoid, and he said, "Well, hell, man, even paranoids have enemies."

One afternoon when we were having a particularly bad time with a piece that didn't want to fit, everybody's temper grew short. As we argued more and more heatedly about how to make the connection, more and more of the talk was in Indian, until finally there was no English at all. I couldn't very well participate if I couldn't understand the suggestions being made and said so. When the gang ignored my remark I shouted, "Speak English, God damn it, or get the goddam work done by yourselves!" They stopped momentarily, looked at me, and went right back to their babble. I took off my tool belt and threw it down to the plank floor, making a half-serious attempt to hit the hooker-on with it. Then I slid down the column, announced that I'd be back when they were through playing games, and walked off the job.

I was halfway through my second beer at the White Rose down the block when the super, Crockett, came in. He ordered a beer and sat next to me. Crockett is four years younger than I am, but he's been in the business since he was seventeen and therefore treats me with a curious blend of respect and paternalism.

"How's the gang working out?" he asked, as though it were the most innocent of after-dinner questions.

"I feel like an endangered species," I answered. He laughed.

"I told you you wouldn't like it," he said. I reminded him that I'd gone into the gang because I wanted to go connecting and it was the only spot open. He gave a knowing nod. "You do understand what they're tryin' to do, don't you?" he asked. I looked at him. "They're tryin' to run you out of the gang."

"Oh, I don't know," I speculated. "Most of the time it's friendly enough."

"Well," said Crockett, "I never said they weren't pretty good fellows, but they'd rather have one of their own fillin' up the last place, which is understandable." I allowed that it was.

We talked idly for a few more minutes. Then he stood up, said that if I didn't want to get fired, I'd better get back to the job sometime soon, and left. It was unusually decent treatment; he could have let me go for trying to bash the hooker-on, let alone for leaving work.

I went back to the gang for the rest of the week. On Monday morning Crockett came into the shanty as I was about to get dressed and said, "Don't change clothes. Get your gear together and come with me."

"Where're we goin'?" I asked.

"Don't ask questions," he said. "All you need to know is that I'm saving you"—he made a sweeping gesture toward the Indians, who all dressed in one area of the shanty—"from these redskins." There followed two sets of groans, one from the Indians, one from Crockett. He left the door open behind him; I gathered my gear and started for it.

"White-eye follow like sheep," said a voice from the rear.*

The job to which Crockett took me (and four others) was a big hole in the ground on Sixth Avenue. I remained there for eleven and a half months, until the job was completed, and I still rather enjoy, when walking past that building, that sense of continuity which having seen a thing through from beginning to end produces. That feeling—the "I made this" syndrome—is, to me, the most rewarding part of the work. It's an over-grand attitude, obviously, since the labors of thousands of men are enclosed in any building, but the illusion persists. I doubt that assembly line workers, after putting identical handles on identical

---

* Let me here try to avoid giving the wrong impression and to straighten out three common misapprehensions about Indian ironworkers:

The wrong impression would be to imagine that this Sam Peckinpah dialogue represents a limit of their mastery of English. It doesn't; their English is perfectly satisfactory, when they want it to be.

The misapprehensions, which seem to be universally held by nonconstruction workers, are that (1) all men employed in the erection of steel buildings and bridges are Indians; (2) who all live in some sort of enclave deep in the bowels of Brooklyn; (3) and who all have a special sense of balance ideally suiting them for this work.

The facts are (1) a small minority of ironworkers (microscopic away from New York and the Canadian border states) are Indians; (2) some live in Brooklyn, but most commute on weekends to their homes on reservations in the Montreal area; and (3) there is no data to support any "balance theory." They take falls no more or less often than anybody else.

doors of identical cars through identical workdays, feel like saying "I made that," as some Floating-Power Knee-Action Silk-Upholstered Six comes coughing down the street. Ironworkers, looking at buildings, do. Further, the compulsion to look is by no means confined to one's own work. An ironworker can no more walk past a construction site without pausing than a pilot can ignore a plane taking off. For all the difference in their rate of climb, planes and buildings share a struggle to ascend, and the men who work in them unavoidably appraise the labors of their fellows. Part of it is competitive; part of it is simple fascination with the process itself.

It was early July 1971 when we started, in a hole in the ground that was three stories deep, two-thirds of a block long from east to west and a full block long from north to south. I was laid off 44 floors and 528 feet later, in late June 1972. There were varying numbers of ironworkers employed at varying stages: six of us at the beginning, nearly sixty at peak need, about eight of us at the end. I would guess that at any given moment the average would have been around forty. There were some twenty local bookmen, with the rest divided among apprentices, out-of-town books, and permit men. The number of people who came in from out of town was larger than usual because the construction economy was bent out of shape. There was very little work in most of the northeast, while New York City was still riding the tail end of a boom. (This imbalance was relieved across the first six months of 1972, when, as the last major buildings of the boom slowly neared completion, the lengthening unemployment lines and the ever more crowded union halls were proof enough that nothing new was happening.)

Patrick came down to work with me in September, and a few weeks later came Coley and Timmy. It was the job from which Timmy fell, and that is another thing I think of when I walk by.

A hole in the ground in New York City is the most expensive kind of hole there is. The Empire State Building sits on a two-acre plot that cost, in 1929, $17.5 million, which works out to a little over $200 a square foot. It was a bargain, compared to other local prices: A parcel of land at Fifth Avenue and 43rd Street was sold at about the same time for $340 per square foot; the 40 Wall Street site was purchased for $624 per square foot; Number One Wall street brought between $700 and $800 per square foot.

When land is that expensive, the skyscraper is the only kind of investment that can produce an adequate return. The value of the land requires such an investment. This can be made to sound a little weird—although clearly true—by saying simply that you can't build a skyscraper unless the place you want to put it is already crowded.

Obviously no builder can afford to approach land acquisition casually. If he were rich enough to say to some subordinate, movie-fashion, "Get me that block and hang the cost," he wouldn't have to erect buildings at all. And he can scarcely announce to the financial community that he intends to buy such-and-such a city block, since the announcement itself would skyrocket the prices. Instead, he moves surreptitiously, buying the principal front lots first, then the secondary properties, intending to keep the holders of the rear lots unaware of his scheme until their lands, cut off from access to street and requisite sunlight, are heavily devalued. This is how it was done at 40 Wall Street, by G. L. Ohrstrom & Co.:

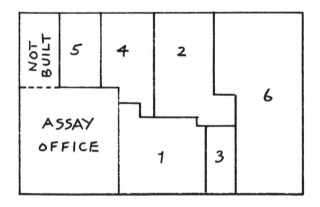

The drawing represents a city block. At the beginning the Ohrstrom group already held a ninety-three-year lease on the first lot (1), which was owned by the Iselin Estate. The second lot (2) was secured without much trouble, since it faced a back street and therefore hadn't great value except in conjunction with the first lot. Marshall

Field, the owner of the third lot (3), was willing to part with his lot, but insisted on sale rather than lease, which forced the Ohrstrom people to buy it outright. Now came a question of order: The fourth (4) and fifth (5) lots were both desired by the group, but it should be clear that if they had secured the fifth lot first, the owner of the fourth would be in excellent position to demand a premium price. Therefore, the fourth lot was secured first, and the fifth lot, now without hope of increasing in value through eventual access to the front, followed.

The Ohrstrom group intended to build on these five lots, since the Assay Office, a low building, would not cut off a significant amount of light. When it was learned that the building was for sale, however, the group was forced to buy it; ownership by anyone who might plan a taller building would endanger their plan. The Manhattan Company, owners of the sixth lot (6), eventually threw in with the group, so that in the end the composite plot was considerably larger than originally planned.

Land purchase, of course, is just the beginning. While it is too far beyond my competence for me to risk trying to produce an overview of the planning and erection of a major building, there are two architectural-engineering considerations that I will mention, since it seems to me they hold interest even to the layman:

1. It takes a hell of a lot of space to make a space. A building is rather more than the sum of the floors upon which its lessees walk. It includes boiler plants, elevator overruns, stairways, machinery, pipes, lofts, storage space, roofs, and more. In the Empire State Building (a model of efficiency for the time) there are 16.11 cubic feet of total volume for each square foot of rentable area.

2. You can't put up a really big structure unless you've something to stand it on: If you moved Chicago's Sears Building to New Orleans, it would soon sink out of sight. Everybody seems to know that Manhattan's unique skyline is made possible because of the rock beneath the island, but they have misconceptions about where it is. At 33rd Street you can get to it with a garden hoe; it's forty-two feet above high water. But at the lower end of the island the situation is quite different; the rock is 150 feet *below* high water—which happens to be 183 feet below curb level. When the foundation rock is much

more inaccessible than that, building becomes prohibitively expensive.

A hole in the ground in Manhattan in July, cut off from surface breezes and framed in sun-reflecting concrete, is a very hot place. It hadn't rained in what seemed like weeks, and every step raised little clouds of dust. The day we put the crane together I drank so many cokes, trying to cool off, that I threw up twice.

There was no room to assemble the crane in the hole—there never is—so we had to work in the street. It's not particularly difficult work (in fact, it's fun to see how fast it can be done; generally you have a finished product in an hour or so), but the insatiable curiosity of the New Yorker does tend to complicate things. Onlookers, particularly cab drivers, never understand how easily they might be accidentally hurt, and they get regularly underfoot, gaping at us in blissful ignorance of very real hazards. (My children are forbidden to walk on the same side of the street as a construction job, and I'd prefer them to stay farther away than that.) I've pushed more than one overly interested pedestrian out of the way of a maneuvering truck or a lowering boom, and will again, and will again get more vilification than gratitude.

The main reason that there aren't more crushed taxis and smashed storefronts is that the operating engineers (who run the cranes) are a pretty skillful bunch. A crane is assembled "boomed out flat," that is, parallel to the ground, and it should be evident that even the smallest movements of the cab will be greatly amplified at the end of the boom. Depending upon differing job requirements, differing boom lengths are employed; to illustrate just how quickly movement is exaggerated, however, even a short one will do: Our crane on that job had 150 feet of "stick." When swung through a scant five degrees (one-eighteenth of what it takes to get your car around a corner), the end of the boom traveled thirteen feet. If a crane is on twenty-foot "cats" (tank treads), and one cat is moved one foot forward or aft of the other, the end of the boom will travel approximately twenty-four feet. Imagine now the delicacy involved in handling a larger rig. Twice the length produces twice the swing, and when a rig is fully assembled, there is a weight ball hanging from the end of the stick, weighing as much as half a ton and perfectly capable of going through the nearest brick wall.

(And while I'm trying to impress upon you the wisdom of not getting near this street-level work, I might also point out that walking under the "bridges" that line urban construction jobs isn't overly bright, either. "Bridges" are those corridors of pipe-framing with planks placed on top. Although pedestrians love them on rainy days, they're intended to protect not from water but from falling small objects. They do an acceptable job of that; the trouble is that the things that fall off a job aren't always small. By "small" I mean things that weigh less than ten or fifteen pounds.) *

The engineer and his oiler had driven the irreducible core of their machine (the truck, crane cab, and tail section of the boom) to the job site early in the morning, because one is not allowed to move such rigs about on the streets once the rush hour has begun. Since the tail section was forty feet long, even this disassembled transportation was categorically cumbersome. Trucks arrived bearing the two forty-foot body sections and the thirty-foot head section, and we pinned these in place. When the structural assembly was finished, we ran out the load cable and attached the weight ball and hook. With the crane now completed, we boomed up nearly vertical, moved taxis and unwanted advisors aside, and started down the ramp into the hole. It was a slow trip. The oiler, Beane, who did the driving, was in no hurry, leaning out of his truck window every five feet to report another hazard, real or imagined. In order to keep him happy, we were forced to clear so many small things out of his path that Crockett finally grabbed a broom from a shopkeeper who was sweeping out his store and ran down the ramp in front of the rig, furiously brushing clouds of dust to

---

* I won't go into detail here, as some of these incidents come up again later on, but a partial list of "larger" things that I know of which have fallen in New York in the last few years includes an oxygen bottle whose improper lashing had worked loose; a welding machine, pushed over the side by a disgruntled decker; the improper load of plank mentioned earlier in these pages; a nine-ton load of pipe which drove the engine of the car upon which it landed clear through the car's frame; and a derrick weight ball which went to the street when the derrick buckled, pureeing an elevator operator who had picked that moment to go for coffee.

Periodically there are things that are merely absurd, such as the several dozen sheets of plywood that blew off the top of a job in New Haven and landed literally all over the city, some of them over a mile away.

either side. At the bottom of the ramp he bowed in ceremonious invitation. Beane seemed not to think this was funny, nor did he drive any faster. He did get to the bottom eventually, and by noon the crane was in working position.

Most oilers are nearly invisible, fueling and lubricating their rigs before the day begins for the rest of us, vanishing to God knows where during the bulk of the day, reappearing at 4:00 to preside over putting the rig to bed. Beane, however, was not of that stripe. He fussed over the crane like a stage mother, constantly wiping away puddles of oil or grease, touching up scratches with fresh paint, agonizing loudly whenever a load banged into the stick. The rig was rented from Gerosa, which provides a likely clue to Beane's behavior. The founder and continuing nabob of that company is reputed to begin each day wandering through his acres of machinery with a rag, searching out smudges.

After lunch we began taking in iron. The trucks had been standing in the sunshine all day, and the billet plates (five- to seven-ton foundation blocks) they carried were so hot that we couldn't touch them without wearing gloves, which were in turn so soaked with sweat that they kept trying to slide off. Whenever there was a free minute, I'd run over to the Sabrett cart on the corner for a coke, which I'd drain in one gulp. My partner, a scrawny-looking but apparently heat-tempered Newfie named Tommy, kept shaking his head and telling me that I oughtn't do this, but I was too dried out to listen. The first time I threw up nobody saw me, but the second time we were all sitting down on our break, and thus divorced from any immediate connection to heavy labor, it triggered numerous dirty cracks. I recovered enough to stagger through the balance of the afternoon, but found, on ordering a cold beer in an air conditioned bar after work, that I was still too woozy to drink it.

Most of my memories of that first month in the hole center on the heat. Whenever it got near a hundred, we knocked off, whether Crockett tried to shame us into staying or not. Beyond ninety-six degrees an ironworker cannot be required to work. The laborers stayed on, mucking about with their wheelbarrows, but they're crazy.

The first afternoon that we were actually setting iron, I passed out on a header just as I was grabbing the choker to cut it loose. I dropped to the piece and recall thinking as the darkness descended that it didn't matter much if I lost my grip, because it was only twelve feet down to the dirt. I did manage to hang on, but was for some minutes unable to get up. One noon the beer Tommy was trying to drink in McAnn's came instantly back out through his nose, and he took the rest of the day off. Big-Big, our gigantic tagline man, still claims he lost thirty-five pounds before the first of August. It was his habit to demonstrate to Crockett in the shanty how severely he was being overworked by holding forward the waistband of his newly overlarge pants and dropping a boot down the gap. I kept reminding myself that all my life I'd insisted that I'd rather be too hot than too cold, but this failed to comfort me.

Crockett stopped before us one day as we lay during a break sprawled on the ground like so many dogs in a Juarez street, put his hands on his hips, and snorted, "Jay-*esus!* In six months you'll be cryin' for weather like this. You'll be pissin' and moanin' and prayin' for the good ol' summertime, just like you do every year, you memory-less bastards."

Big-Big managed to prop himself up on one elbow. "Piss off," he said, "before I sit on you."

Our building was to be a plumb-rise tower. That is, like many "modern" middle-sized structures, it would have no "setbacks," but would rise from street to roof in a single edge. Setbacks are simply indentations resembling giant steps. A building has them if it rises a few floors, then jumps back several feet, starts up again, jumps back another time, and so on to the top.*

To a considerable extent this rather ugly configuration results from the architects' efforts to maximize the available space. New York City building codes project an imaginary cone over a building lot, through which no structure may thrust. Without this provision the tops of city buildings would be as close together as their bottoms, and the streets would receive sunlight only for a few minutes either side of noon, and

---

* The Empire State is a good example of this type. It has its first setback at the sixth floor, wing setbacks at the twenty-first and twenty-fifth, and a final wingback at the thirtieth. The indentations begin again at eighty-one and eighty-five, from where everything pinches down rather suddenly toward the observatory tower.

then only in summer. Today's typical sheer tower avoids stair-stepping by not building on every legal square inch at ground level. Compensating for the loss of volume are gains in ease of fabrication (it's much less trouble to produce 5000 identical beams than that many different ones), a concomitant ease of erection, and improved public relations (Look at the beautiful plaza we built you! Come, eat your lunch on the lovely stone benches by our beautiful fountain!).

Our building was also what is known as a "core" job. A core job is, in effect, two buildings, one within the other. In the center of a core structure is built a small (in this case, about fifty feet square) inner building housing the elevators, stairwells, and all principal electrical, plumbing, and steam lines. Many ironworkers avoid working on core jobs when times are good enough to afford them choices. Because such jobs necessarily involve fitting the inner and outer buildings together, and because it's axiomatic that an increase in the number of things that have to fit together is an increase in the number of things that don't, core jobs go up more slowly and create correlative frustrations.

It is also a pain in the neck to wait around for the core to catch up, which is common and happens this way: The core, because it contains the elevator shafts, must be as close to the true vertical as possible. It is therefore mandatory that the concrete that will encase any completed portion of it be poured before the outer building has risen so much above the core that the natural flexing of the skeleton pulls the core out of true. Standard procedure requires that the outer frame not be at any stage more than eight floors above the core, and if this maximum distance is in danger of being exceeded, the ironworkers are laid off until the core has caught up. It is not a situation that we like, but it is one we can't control, because the men who finish the core belong to a different union, and their concerns aren't always the same as ours.

In most parts of the country, wire lathers belong to the same locals, called "mixed" locals. In New York City, however, the wire lathers have their own union. We can't touch their work and they can't touch ours. I'm not allowed to tie rods—or even, in theory, to pick one up—and the rod men can't touch my iron. Although we generally cooperate with each other, there are times when this formal separation leads to complexities. If, on a core job, the wire lathers get sore about something and go out on strike, or the concrete workers go out, the result is that we do, too. This interconnectedness is a basic fact of life in the construction industry; there are seventeen principal building trades, and a strike of any length by any one will result in the laying off of most of the others. Still, we aren't usually placed in such close working proximity to the lathers and concrete men as when we are on a core job. On other types of structures we don't really give a damn whether the rods are put in or the concrete poured; we can go ahead and complete the skeleton, and they can do their work as much later as they please.

Beyond these two particularizations—that the building was essentially a simple box and that its life-support systems were housed in a central core—the only "special" aspect remaining was the plaza, and the only thing special about that is that a hell of a lot of work and one unforeseen event were involved in producing what must to the passerby look like a concrete flatland illogically supporting a half-dozen puny trees. You might, looking at it, wonder what sort of high-minded philanthropist could have considered funding a cement park in the middle of Manhattan. Yet, you'd do better to remember the building code's imaginary cone, and to feel, standing in that park, the vibrations in your shoes—underneath you is a garage. A brief glance at parking fees will disencumber you of any thoughts of philanthropy.

The cause of the plaza's being "a hell of a lot of work" was that absolutely nothing fit. This resulted not from any of the problems with the building core (which was at the other end of the lot and not structurally connected to the plaza), but from continuous problems with the "pockets." The east end of the plaza was to abut two existing buildings: a twelve-story brick structure and a ramshackle six-story brownstone. They stood back to back and together made up the block-long north-south dimension of the lot. The hole, about thirty-five feet deep, ran right up to the western walls of these two buildings, so that they seemed to be perching at the edge of a cliff. The concrete retaining wall that formed the hole's perimeter contained "pockets" (foot-deep by header-high indentations) to receive and support the horizontal plaza iron. None of them seemed deep enough, for if we lined up the western ends of the pieces, there wasn't enough room to fit the eastern ends into their pockets, while if we began by making the eastern ends, the bolt holes in the western ends couldn't be made to line up with their mates in the columns.

We got it done, finally, after a great deal of shoving and swearing, but the plumber-ups (a gang from the hall, none of whom I yet knew) began pulling their hair because the columns supporting the western ends had been shoved an unacceptable distance out of plumb. White-hatted architects and engineers, Crockett, and a variety of unidentifiable potentates held counter-condemnatory arguments one after another, long past the day that we squeezed the last local iron into place and moved the rig around to go to work on the tower. The upshot of those conferences was that it was concluded that everything was too far west and that the entire plaza was to be moved five inches east. Bringing that off was no mean feat. The street-level headers alone (eighteen in number) ran from fourteen to twenty-five tons apiece; the whole shebang was already bolted up; and the rig was in use elsewhere. Laborers with pneumatic hammers did what they could to deepen the pockets, but their work was greatly complicated by the fact that the iron was already in place. While they were about this, the plumbing-up gang was busy jacking up the headers wherever they rested on the tops of columns.*

The idea was to jack up the iron, slip "drift pins" (six-inch-long pieces of bar stock, seven-eighths of an inch in diameter and tapered like a sharpened pencil at each end) between each piece and its supporting columns to act as rollers, then to use the same jacks horizontally to shove the entire plaza the required five inches east.

With six men pumping six jacks simultaneously, the result was the aforesaid unforeseen event: The little brownstone, unable to withstand the lateral pressure, fell down. I should restrict the use of the word "unforeseen" to "by the workers," however. I'm not at all

---

* These jacks are hand-pumped hydraulics, called "portapowers." They consist of two parts: a pumping unit, which is merely a cylinder with a handle on top (resembling one type of tire pump), and the jacking unit, which is simply a telescoping tube. The units are connected by a four-foot length of hydraulic hose.

The smallest of these devices will exert a force of ten tons; the largest in common use are rated at thirty tons. Thirty tons is a lot of pressure. Multiplied by six (the number of jacks used in this operation), the power becomes truly impressive, as you will see.

convinced that it was unforeseen by the general contractors. The collapse may well have been hoped for, unofficially, by them. They were sore at the owner of the little building for not selling to them at their price, and may have felt they could do better in a courtroom adjudication.* Fall down it did, though, and now, after appropriate plan adjustments and revisions, an elevator to the lower garage stands in its place. The only occupants of the building at the time were a fortune-teller and a luggage company. The day it happened the luggage company was closed. (I still think, since it was usually closed, that it was some sort of "front" operation; I once tried to buy an overnight bag there, but the only salesman in the place couldn't be bothered to show me one.) The Gypsy lady, although present, was unhurt. She tried to get even by putting a curse on Crockett, but none of us could understand many of the words she used, and so far he seems okay.

The raising gang pusher was a sixtyish, balding, magnificently bellied Scotch-Irishman named Jiggs. I don't suppose that was really his name, but it was the only one by which I ever heard him addressed. He looked exactly as though he'd just stepped from the pages of the old comic strip, and certainly that must have been the source of his nickname. Do you remember a comic strip called *Bringing Up Father?* I haven't seen it since childhood, but it may still, for all I know, appear in some newspaper somewhere. Father's name was Jiggs, and he was an ironworker. He was always stepping from the end of a dangling beam through the window into his girlfriend's apartment. She was Maggie, a society dame (first generation) of ample

---

* Holding out for top dollar when approached by the planners of a major building is a delicate procedure. At its lowest level, some people, upon getting wind of a city plan to erect new housing under Title One, make a practice of renting dilapidated storefronts in the area to be affected. They put a few cans of insecticide or similar low-investment merchandise in the window, making themselves eligible for the substantial business relocation sums the city hands out. On a more grandiose level, owners of modest buildings in the way of major new private projects often refuse to sell out until what they believe to be the ultimate moment. Their dilemma lies in trying to determine, without access to the pertinent data, just how badly the builders need their land. Some owners have received astounding prices; others have found that they have been "designed around" and thus own property which (since the group is no longer interested) is scarcely worth its tax assessment.

bosom and a congenital lustiness that her cultural pursuits never quite successfully concealed. She and Jiggs eventually married, and their life together was a continuing war between his corned-beef-and-cabbage tastes and her atonal infatuation with the art song. She was forever practicing her singing at the piano; he was forever fleeing to a gin mill called Dinty's. When he came home late, she was waiting at the door, armed with a large rolling pin. (My impression is that this was the prototype of all female-wielded comic-strip rolling pins.)

Maggie and Jiggs' relationship could, if one wanted to attempt sociological weight, be offered as an example of the uneasy upward thrust of the blue-collar class—struggling manual worker moves (in this case, marries) into the world of the educated but retains some of the values (old friends at Dinty's) of his own, thereby achieving synthesis. But who believes in sociology? Certainly not the Jiggs who was our pusher. That one spent most of his time trying to shove under his belt enough of his free-form stomach to keep his pants wedged in place.

Like his namesake, Jiggs was a jolly type and not inclined to become excited. The day I dropped the choker on the pedestrian was typical. The crane was in the hole; most of the first three floors of the job had been set. Tommy and I were offloading the last of the day's trucks, jumping back and forth between the truck and the bridge we'd built over the cross street sidewalk to keep people from seeing the loads they were walking under as the iron was swung from the trucks to the hole. We kept our "street" chokers (inch-thick twenty-two footers used to wrap up large—up to half a truckload—bundles of iron) on top of the bridge when not in use. I threw one down on the planks, and the last few feet of it slithered over the end, hitting a pedestrian a glancing blow to the nose. He immediately flung himself to the sidewalk amid much yelling and moaning, and even managed, with diligence and his handkerchief, to locate a few drops of blood. It was a mighty small scratch for such carrying-on, but he was obviously of the opinion that he was on to a good thing, and you could have sold tickets to the show he gave. He rolled around on the sidewalk, further muddying his already bedraggled suit, declaiming to the world that his nose was broken, and probably his neck, and that he was going to sue the pants off somebody. Tommy, who stuttered whenever he got excited, came running over to see what the matter was.

"W-w-what's t-t'e ma-matter wit' him?" he cried.

"Choker hit him and broke his neck," I answered, not feeling extreme sympathy. Hearing the note in my voice, Tommy glanced briefly at me.

"N-n-no s-shit?" he said, now leaning over the end of the bridge to get a closer look at the fellow. The man staggered to his feet and leaned against the pipe-framing of the bridge, holding his nose with one hand and the back of his neck with the other. "H-hey, m-man," Tommy called to him, "y-you broke your n-n-neck?"

"I think so," the man answered, nodding his head atop his broken neck in confirmation. "And I've got whiplash, too, and you careless bastards are going to pay for this!"

"G-gee," said Tommy, "that's tough." He reached into his pocket. "Why-ncha g-getcher self a b-beer, man?" he suggested, tossing down a quarter. He went back to his end of the truck, I to mine, and we resumed unloading.

The injured man, nothing daunted, staggered to the phone booth and called the police. When they arrived, we were just finishing up the truck. The cops conferred with the man for a few moments before one of them came over to talk to me.

"Boss around?" he asked, pleasantly.

"No," I replied, "I'm afraid not. He's been drinkin' all this week and we haven't seen much of him. I don't know when he'll show up."

"He's a l-l-lush," called Tommy from the other end of the truck.

"I see," said the cop, rubbing his chin. About this time Jiggs came sauntering down the street, happy with the world and in his work. He paused when he saw the police car, the man sitting on the curb with his head in his hands, and me talking to a cop. "Hey, Jiggs!" I called. "You seen the boss lately?" Jiggs resumed walking toward us, albeit a little slower.

"Naw," he said, examining the cop as he drew alongside. "What's a' matter?"

"We got a guy here," answered the cop, pointing across the street to the injured man, "who alleges to have been struck by an object dropped by this fellow," he pointed at me, "and he wishes to file a complaint."

"I," I said to Jiggs, "am the alleged perpetrator."

"Nemmine t'at shit," Jiggs said, as transparently the boss as could be, "wha'd you hit him wit'?"

"Nothin'. I've no idea what happened." Jiggs gave me a queer look but addressed himself to the cop.

"Lemme talk to him," he requested. The cop said sure, and Jiggs went across the street, sat down on the curb beside the fellow, and began to talk. We couldn't hear what was being said, and having finished the truck, we went back to the hole.

When we went to the shanty to change at the end of the day, Jiggs was leaning back in his chair, his feet propped up on Crockett's desk, drinking a can of beer that was sheathed in a paper bag. I asked him how it had come out.

"How'd what come out?" he asked.

"That business with the man with the broken neck."

"Oh, t'at," he said, lightly, enjoying my curiosity. I'd done some worrying since the incident, however, and pressed for an explanation. "Well," he said, finally, "I don't t'ink t'ere's anyt'in' to worry about—he decided not to sue, and t'e cops gave 'im a ride home."

"How did you arrange that?" I asked.

"Oh, I explained t'at you'd get a bad rep if you was named as a party in a lawsuit, and t'at your brot'ers in t'e union would prob'ly get angry and figure t'at as long as a broken neck was already under consid'ration t'ey might as well t'row in a couple broken legs, and maybe some ot'er t'ings, and he began to see t'e error of his ways and decided t'at what he really wanted was a ride home. T'at's all t'ere was to it." Jiggs lit a cigarette, gave a Cheshire smile in dismissal, and the incident was closed.

August, and with it the worst of the hot weather, slowly passed. By Labor Day we'd finished with the crane, tripped the derricks, and were ready to begin moving at speed. The work in the hole had gone slowly, and we were all looking forward to being able to go a little faster.

The first part of a job is always the slowest and therefore the most frustrating. In the hole everything is being done for the first time; nobody is yet able to look at a piece and know where it goes without searching it out on the drawings. Mud obscures the numbers painted on the beams; caked mud on the ends of pieces makes them hard to fit in place; mud on the surfaces of the headers makes them difficult to walk along. Cross members don't want to fit because the columns are newly risen from the billet plates and not yet properly trued up; the different gangs are at each others' throats because they are in each others' way; and the plumber-ups dispute among themselves because they haven't yet grown accustomed to the tolerances that are going to be allowed on this particular job by this particular group of engineers. The ironwork always includes a number of pieces that can be made up only by going at them in a particular way, and the connectors argue with each other because they haven't yet worked out the best methods for dealing with these difficult pieces. The iron at any one level in the hole is likely to be quite different from the iron at any other, and while it is interesting to work with and to try to solve these differences, it is also slow.

The greatest annoyance results from the constant applicability of that principle you'll remember from high school physics which states that you can't put two different things in the same place at the same time: The connectors are trying to make pieces that have to go right where the plumber-ups are trying to pull a column over to the vertical; somebody is sticking soft bolts in the same place (and his continued existence requires shouted warnings every time a new piece swings over his head); and while we are all gathered in the area yelling for priority, two more men show up dragging a float, air hose, and gun, demanding room to run up the hard bolts.

No one can hear very well on any job because of the machinery noises, but this is at its worst in the early stages, because there is no place to go to get away from them. You are on the ground, the compressors are on the ground, the trucks are on the ground, the excavators may still be using back-hoes and bulldozers in an un-finished part of the hole, and unmuffled gas-powered welding machines are all over the place.

Every time you turn sideways you bump into a carpenter building forms for the concrete, or you have to jump to avoid being impaled on the rods being humped across the lot by the lathers' laborers, or you trip over the cables being strung out by the electricians.

If you're in a hole in springtime, when there is a lot of rain, you'll lose more time than your friends who are on jobs that are higher up. They will be able to spend some time on rainy days on detail work on lower floors, keeping dry because there are poured floors above them. You lose on both counts: There isn't yet a backlog of detail work, and there are no finished floors beneath which you can stay dry.*

All in all, it's nice to get out of a hole. I was sorry to say good-bye to Beane, having gotten rather fond of his fussing about, and it was now not possible to skip across the street for a coke at whim, but it was nice to get out of the hole. Once a job has risen thirty feet or more above the ground, there are breezes to help dissipate late summer heat, and there are fewer gnats and mosquitoes. There is none of the mud that gets between the treads of a man's boots to compromise his footing. The other trades are left below (except, on a core job, for those core-finishing lathers, carpenters, and concrete workers who are unavoidably omnipresent). The air is cleaner.** A fellow begins to feel less like an ordinary laborer doing the same things that every other ordinary laborer is doing, and more like an ironworker. (If that

---

* Every time of year has its special disadvantages. Spring and fall are too wet, summer is too hot, and winter is impossible. I'd rather be up high freezing my tail off than on the ground trying with a shovel to locate a snow-buried beam. In one winter hole I lost all the skin off the palm of one hand (admittedly through my own foolishness, but it was a mistake I could not have made at another time of year). We were setting the first columns, which rest on the billet plates. The plates were in depressions in the ground which had filled with rainwater and frozen over. I broke up the surface ice with my spud wrench and directed the rig-hanging column to its approximate spot. Using the wrench to line up the holes beneath the water, I felt around with my bare hand until I was able to stick the four bolts. Finished, I leaned on the column with that hand while waiting for my partner to run the nuts up tight from his side. My wet hand froze to the column so that when I tried to pull away the skin remained behind. For the next three months I was employed as New York's only known one-handed coffee-and-bolt punk.

** I do not have tongue in cheek. The air *is* cleaner, comparatively speaking. Solid-particle pollutants tend to form suspensions, rather than colloids, and the larger seek the lower, denser altitudes. The higher winds of higher altitudes—mean velocities thirty-five feet above ground level are 30 percent higher—help push colloidinous pollutants along. It's true that, sailing along beside Execution Rock in Long Island Sound (twenty miles from the city center) on a sunny afternoon, you can see a huge gray dome squatting cancerously over the city, but it is grayest and ugliest at the bottom.

sounds prideful and elitist, be assured that it is.) But best of all, things finally begin to move a little faster, and one's sense of accomplishment is thereby expanded.

Thursdays were paydays, which meant (although some guys stopped in every night) that on that day most of us stopped in McAnn's for a few drinks after work. "Hey," someone from one of the several other jobs in the area would ask, "how you comin' along over t'ere?"

"Settin' fourteen," Big-Big or Jiggs or Tommy or I would answer. The next week the question would come again, and we could reply, happily, "Settin' sixteen."

In the shanty one Friday afternoon, while I was packing my dirty clothes to go to a laundromat over the weekend, Crockett called me into his office. (His "office" was one end of the shanty, which was a trailer, separated from the rest of it and us by a plywood partition with a rickety door. Some weeks later, when there were too many men to fit into the little trailer, a large house was built for us on the second floor of the job, and another one was put up for Crockett and his pushers.)

"Hey, Mike," he said, when I had closed the door, "you go upstate on weekends?"

"Sometimes," I answered.

"Anybody good out of work up there?"

"Bunches."

"You'd better bring somebody down to go connectin' with you, then," he said, "because there's nobody down at the hall but scum, and Tommy's draggin' up."

"He didn't say anything about it to me," I said, surprised. "When did he decide to leave?"

"What do I know about it?" countered Crockett. "He came in here a couple of minutes ago and said he wanted to take a month off, and I told him I couldn't promise him his job back if he was gone that long, and he said to hell with it, then, lay him off, and I obliged. Now, what I'm tellin' you is that if you got a pal upstate you want for a partner, bring him down. Only, have him here Monday, because I can't wait around for somebody." Crockett had a way, when he was sore at somebody, of seeming to be sore at everybody. I told him I'd bring back a partner on Monday, and although I hadn't intended driving up that weekend, immediately took off for Elmira to find Patrick.

By the beginning of the second week of October we were on the twelfth floor (setting thirteen and fourteen), and most of the local gin mills had gotten used to Patrick's "Quittin' time!" shouts. New York is dotted with chain bars (like chain groceries) which cater essentially to a transient crowd, and in these places—the McAnn'ses, Blarney Stones, White Roses, Shamrocks—one seldom gets very well acquainted with the bartenders, many of whom are as much will-o'-the-wisps as their customers. Patrick, however, soon got to know the names and characters of numbers of them. He knew who would cash our checks,* who would (counter to official chain bar policy) put Wednesday's drinks on a tab, who would let a man have an eye-opener before 8:00 (the hour that begins both normal construction jobs and the legal serving of drinks).

This is not to suggest that Patrick was drinking particularly heavily—he wasn't. But he had no special girl, nor did he know many people with houses or apartments, and he's opposed to sitting in his room alone. When queried about going home he's likely to respond, as Jack Warden did in *The Bachelor Party*, "What for? I already read the papers."

I had a place in the city, then, but it was a scruffy hole on the lower East Side, a neighborhood which I knew well from previous years but in which Patrick was not comfortable. He was happier drinking with Big-Big and Jiggs (who is said, although no one's even known him to go straight home after work, to have a wife and kids someplace in Queens). Sometimes, especially if the evening was to begin at The Carnival or some other of the myriad nearby topless joints, Peter The Putrid Punk would successfully beg to be included.

Peter The Putrid Punk was a red-haired, nineteen-year-old college drop-out who picked at his acne. His father was a respected local man

---

* It was convenient to be able to avoid the long lines at the bank, but conversely a shame to miss the weekly dumb show: the uncomprehending, often half-frightened stares of Chase Manhattan's more typical customers as the Thursday hoards of construction workers—variously oily, muddy, or dusty and all irrepressibly and vulgarly gregarious—poured in.

who had foolishly listened to his son's pleas to be given a summer job. (It is an unhappy and all too common sequence: Dad busts his balls all his life trying to tuck away enough money to make sure that his children won't be forced, because of the same lack of education, to bust theirs. The male child goes off to school, returns home in the summer, and points out that he would have a lot more money in the fall if Dad would get him a permit to go ironworking—not at any dangerous job, maybe just planking or punking. Dad, who knows the usefulness of a buck, agrees, only to discover, come September, that the child has become addicted to his $300 to $400 a week. There is no way that Dad can talk him into returning to school. The child is too busy reading new car brochures to hear his father point out that an ironworker's average annual income isn't anything to brag about. Reminders that summer is the easy time accomplish about as much as shoveling shit against the tide.)

"Hey, guys," Peter The Putrid Punk was wont to say as we were changing clothes on a Friday afternoon, "let's us go have a beer at The Carnival." This produced moans.

"Who's *us?*" someone would demand.

"You want I should sit on him, Jiggs?" Big-Big would ask. His stock offer for every problem was to sit on it, which, in view of his great bulk, was very often an excellent resolution.

"Naw," Jiggs would answer, "if his zits pop you'll ruin your pants." More groans; some laughter.

"Peter Putrid," called Patrick. "Would you like to get into that Gloria?"

There was general derision as Peter inevitably said, "Boy, would I!"

Gloria was a haggard, prestretched topless dancer whose act consisted primarily of squatting on the cash register at the front of the dancers' runway, writhing about in simulated masturbatory ecstasy. This profoundly affected young Peter, who could keep neither silent nor still when he saw her. "Oh, please," Peter yelled, squirming on his stool in seeming imitation, "take my money and put it in your box!" This he thought immensely clever, and he looked around for appreciation.

"My God," said Patrick, throwing a couple of dollars on the bar for a tip, "I've got to get out of here."

179

I sometimes joined this group for the first few drinks, but generally by six o'clock I headed downtown.

Coley and Timmy joined us in October, after Patrick delivered Crockett's call for bolter-ups. Timmy moved in with me in my one and a half room apartment on 10th Street; Coley soon found and talked Patrick into sharing with him a rather expensive place on 65th Street off First Avenue. This is at the lower end of an area of the sort referred to in Middle America's steamy innuendo as a "swinging singles" neighborhood. In New York it's called "the meat market." As soon as Patrick mastered the local etiquette, he abandoned the chain bars.

Timmy was still on the wagon, but he'd settled into a social apathy that was in many ways as frightening. He went directly to the apartment after work, venturing out only to go to the grocery or the laundromat. His behavior was too close to my own when I'd first gone upstate, and it was depressing to be long around him. I took to spending even less time in the place than before he moved in.

The weather worsened as November began. It rained and kept on raining, and when the temperature dropped it turned to sleet and freezing rain and kept right on coming down. We began to lose time in clumps, some weeks managing to get in only two or two and a half days. When we were able to work, it was miserable. No material but leather is worth a damn for work gloves, and leather gloves soak up water like sponges and stay wet indefinitely. The shanty soon resembled a laundry room. Lengths of cord were strung from side to side above the two propane heaters, and a never diminishing collection of sweatshirts, underwear, overalls, jackets, and gloves hung steaming from them. It's possible to dry leather gloves directly atop the grill of a propane heater, but tricky: Left a little too long the leather hardens into steel. Most men chose instead to use several pairs in rotation.*

"It smells," said Crockett, on a visit to these quarters "like a whore's drawers."

---

* Elmer Weeks, now retired, grew famous through his gloves. He scavenged discards, cutting from them whichever fingers were still usable. From a glove with a serviceable body he cut away the worn fingers, then slipped the newer fingers through the holes. He wore a veritable Joseph's cloak of gloves, and never parted with a dime.

Mention of that winter (1971–1972) will draw forth expressions of disgust from any ironworker who was then in the city, unless he was on "straight time." (Straight time people—pushers, stewards, some connectors for some outfits—are paid for rainy days and are the only ironworkers who smile in January.) I lost forty-three days. The men who worked for Bethlehem and American Bridge, outfits that knock off when they see a cloud on the horizon, lost even more.

By the middle of November we were up around eighteen, at which height elevator waiting time losses began to show. Except under special circumstances (which must be cleared by the hall), the men cannot be required to climb that many flights of stairs, although up to about that height they will anyway. But by eighteen there are more refusals than consents. At 12:30, therefore, when lunch is over, long lines collect in front of the elevator doors. Many of the other trades also return at that time. There are never many functional elevators available during construction for even the partial trips possible, so these lines (that's too charitable—it's more like a mob) take a long time thinning out. The less devoted workers have a habit of falling back a few feet from their places when a car arrives, so that it may be 1:00 or even later before every ironworker is back at work. The raising gangs are made up, by and large, of competitive types (and whether a derrick is in use or not is immediately apparent to any street-side official who bothers to look up), and these men generally fight their way onto early cars, but this is by no means true of everybody.

We had just one car at that point, and you could die of boredom waiting for the damned thing. Some of us said to hell with it and walked up; some men carried lunch pails and never came down. On high jobs in warm weather I've been able, by not coming down for lunch, to eat a home-made sandwich, drink a can of beer earlier stowed in the water-cooler, and take a forty-five minute nap—all during the thirty-minute lunch break.

Contractors pull out their hair over this kind of delay. Sometimes erection plans include temporary outside elevators, although most of the ones you see (moving platforms in screened pipe-frames) are meant for concrete and materials, rather than men. The variety of legal safety requirements surrounding elevator construction renders the outside elevator a less perfect solution than it might seem. On some jobs the coffee punks are assigned to bring lunch to the men. If there are forty or fifty men on the job, taking these orders and bringing back the food will take the punks all morning, but if the men will then stay up top at noon, the additional time they'll work will take care of the punks' pay several times over. Occasionally a super will come up with a solution of his own. Frenchy Bassey, on the McGraw-Hill Building, managed for a time to make the elevator operators and others believe that he had a special deal with the general contractor to have the ironworkers taken up first. It was nice, from the erectors' point of view, while it lasted.*

Elevators have, in the past 100 years, become extremely sophisticated devices. Stepping into the elevator lobby of a modern building is almost like stepping into a computer display: Everywhere are panels showing the present locations of all the cars; signs explaining which cars go to which floors read like the information board at Grand Central Station; doors contain photosensitive cells connected through time-delay switches to the door-closing apparatus; the car into which you step may be preprogrammed or have heat-sensitive punch buttons; house telephones and intercoms may be installed.

This sophistication has come about gradually. Speeds of 1200 feet per minute were common by 1930. Most of today's elevators move only 200 feet per minute faster. The Otis Company was awarded the elevator construction contract for the Empire State with a bid of $3 million. They fully expected to lose some money, which they wrote off as research by using the job to develop a number of devices, including one which prevents several cars from arriving at any one floor simultaneously. Safety devices were, of course, in development from the beginning. By 1930 there were clamps, automatic cutoffs, brakes, and buffers. These systems largely replaced the mainstay of earlier installations: the column of air beneath the car (perfectly serviceable, unless someone leaves an inspection port in the basement unlatched).

The next time you're in an elevator in a high-rise tower, fretting because you're not getting to your floor quickly enough, pause to

---

* At the Manhattan Company Building the climbing time for all trades reached two hours per man per day. That added $7,500 weekly to the builders' costs. Not a fortune, but a bit more than pin money.

appreciate that at least you're not in the one car of the old Fifth Avenue Hotel. (Although perhaps in 1859, when it was installed, you might not have been in such a hurry.) That was the first regularly operating car in America. It was built by Otis Tufts, and traveled, believe it or not, up and down on a long screw driven by a steam engine. It could not have gone very fast.*

There was, that fall and winter, a large turnover of personnel. Men dragged up and new men arrived almost daily. The weather was the principal cause of this; everybody was disgusted with it, and some of the men who had money in the bank decided that traveling into midtown only to be sent home three days out of five just wasn't worth it.** Some guys found "inside" jobs (out of the weather); some of the Indians decided that they weren't making enough money to justify the long trips back and forth to Canada and that they'd stay home and go snowmobiling (many of them are snowmobile fanatics); some men just didn't like Crockett.

A casual dislike of the boss is probably not a central factor in a white-collar worker's decision to leave his job, but it is often the sole issue in whether or not a construction worker stays on. If the boss wants a thing done one way which the worker thinks should be done another, or if the worker thinks the boss has spoken to him in an unacceptable tone of voice, or if the man simply disapproves of the way the captain runs the ship, he is likely to make a Shove It Up Your Ass speech and leave. His loyalties are to the *type* of work he does, not to the specific project. He has little control over which company he works for, and therefore is unlikely to wave that flag. And it profits him little to play yes man, because his boss is his boss for that one job only. He may or may not ever work for him again.

With people coming and going in wholesale lots, those who remained were frequently switched around. Coley bolted up for two weeks and then moved over to the plumber-ups. Timmy went on the

---

* Actually, a primitive elevator was demonstrated in 1850 at the Crystal Palace Exposition, on the site of the New York Public Library, by Elisha Graves Otis. However, it was more in the nature of an exhibition than for useful service.

** In most parts of the country, as explained earlier, a man must be paid two hours' money for showing up, even if he is sent immediately home. This is not true in New York City.

bullwheel in the middle raising gang, and later shifted to taglining. Patrick and I stayed together, and Jiggs remained pushing, but almost the whole rest of our gang changed beneath us.

Shortly after we got a fellow called Albert for our bell man, I decided that I wanted out myself. Not out of the job, but out of the raising gang.

"I don't think," I told Patrick and Coley over a quiet drink in Maxwell's Plum one night, "that I want to be in the same gang with Albert. He's crazy."

"Yes," agreed Coley. "I have been studyin' on him, and he has got a definite rip in his seabag." Coley could afford the detached smile he was wearing; he wasn't in the gang and consequently didn't give a damn whether Albert was crazy or not.

"What're you particularly sore about today?" Patrick asked.

"I'm sore about him damn near takin' my head off by comin' down with the spreader hooks while I was bent over a piece when we were shakin' out; that's what I'm sore about at the moment," I said.

"It happens," said Patrick.

"It happens too goddam much to suit me," I replied.

"Well, don't get sore at me about it," Patrick answered, responding to the anger in my voice. "I agree with you. The man is unsafe."

"Well then," I said. "There you are. You want to keep workin' with him?"

"Not especially," he answered slowly, thinking as he spoke. "But on the other hand I don't feel like goin' on bolts or carryin' plank."

"Good job in winter," put in Coley. "And I do believe that winter's on the way."

"I just think he's goin' to hurt somebody," I insisted.

"Keep yourself safe," said Patrick, ritually.

"I'm not worried about anythin' *I* have any control over, damn it. I'm just never sure what Albert's goin' to do."

"Good plank on this job," Coley interjected. "Not that bunch of fat green trees that American Bridge uses."

"Shut up with your goddam plank, Coley," I said. "I'm too old to carry plank."

"Ahh," cooed Patrick. "Now I see what the problem is." He put his arm around Coley's shoulder, pointed at me, and began to whisper.

"You see what's happenin', don't you, my lad?" Coley shook his head elaborately. "It's very simple. You and I are *young*, but he is *old*. He's old, and his life has begun to pass before his eyes. He's afraid that crazy Albert, who doesn't really do anything wrong but get up on the load without bein' told to, or come down with the hooks when nobody's lookin', or who prefers to take his bell box so far away from where we're settin' that Superman with his X-ray vision couldn't see what he's doin', is goin' to get him squashed underneath a header or flipped over the side—before he's finished relivin' it. Now, if *we* were as old as *he* is, maybe we'd understand. But of course you and I are in the prime of youth."

"Prime of youth?" I interrupted. "What the hell is prime of youth?"

"Prime of youth, as I was saying," he resumed, "and we don't really know in our guts what it must be like to get up every mornin', wonderin' if we're goin' to make it to the end of the day." He stopped long enough to give me a solicitous tap on the head and a theatrically patronizing smile. "Did you see him," he went on, turning again to Coley, "tryin' to make up his end of that header this mornin'? Seventeen degrees cool, it was, and the wind blowin' twenty-five refreshin' miles an hour down his neck—ideal conditions—and there he was, sweatin' boilin' water."

"Poor man," said Coley, dolorously.

"Yes, indeed," agreed Patrick. "You see before you a man on his last legs who's afraid that crazy Albert is goin' to chop them off before they have a chance to fall off by themselves." He and Coley both leaned over to pat me on the head. Coley called to the barmaid.

"Give my father a drink," he said.

"Actually," Patrick added, after we'd all had sips from fresh beers, "he's right. Sooner or later Albert is goin' to hurt somebody."

It was sooner, and it was relatively minor, and it didn't cost Albert his job, because it was not his fault alone.

Patrick took a day off, and Crockett sent a beginner in his place. The boy was about nineteen and had been on bullwheels and taglines but had never been connecting. He probably wouldn't have been allowed to go up, but we had only an hour or so of connecting to do

185

(the rest of the day we were taking iron from the street and shaking out), and he begged persuasively, and Crockett and Jiggs let him have his way.

He did everything wrong, of course. A new man categorically does everything wrong. Nobody got sore at him for doing the wrong thing trying to get the iron in place, but everybody got sore at him for doing the wrong things with his body. He was forever on the wrong side of the pieces, and it still amazes me that he wasn't knocked over the side. He hurried too much and, in his eagerness to look good, took foolish chances. Jiggs continually screamed at him to be careful. Several times I pulled and held pieces away from him and told him I wasn't going to let him have his end until he stopped bouncing around.

When a beam with a flange on each end (designed to make up between two headers) is reluctant to go where it belongs, various approaches to getting it there present themselves. All begin with one connector making up his end with a single bolt, loosely. The other connector tries to wedge his end over laterally by prying it with his wrench. If this doesn't give him enough leverage, he uses his connecting bar (a steel rod about two and a half feet long with a point at one end and a chisel tip at the other) for the same purpose. If it is so tight that it can't be brought in with the bar, someone throws him a sledgehammer and he stands on the header and proceeds to try to beat the thing in. If an ordinary sledge won't move it, he'll ask for a Monday. "Mondays" are overgrown sledges, weighing sixteen to twenty-two pounds, and yes, the weight yields the name: Swing one, and you feel like it's Monday. With such a heavy beater a man can strike a hell of a blow, if he can hit what he's aiming at. Incompetence isn't automatically a valid charge when a man misses his target. Remember that he may be standing on a beam five inches wide, encumbered by heavy clothing, leaning into a gusty wind, aiming at a target six inches below his feet which he knows is going to shake violently at the moment of impact.

I once watched a man trying to open up a seat lug on a column. He stood on the upper lug, hanging onto the column with one hand, swinging the Monday with the other. He missed the lug entirely, and as the hammer swooshed past the target and continued on around, he was forced to let it go—if he had tried to hold onto it, he would surely have been carried off the column. It sailed out perhaps a hundred feet and down twenty-four floors and landed in the seat of a bulldozer. Had the driver been in his machine, cleaning him up would have been a hose job. As it was, the seat and all adjacent sheet metal were destroyed. Operators, and everyone else whose jobs are on the ground near a rising tower, develop a protective fatalism. Things are constantly falling near them.

Sometimes, however, the iron has been so badly bent in shipment or handling, or the pieces are so poorly fabricated, that even repeated mighty swats won't move the piece into place. When that is the case, the connectors ask for the ball (the weight ball that hangs at the end of the derrick load cable just above the hook). It is swung over so that it hangs next to the offending piece. The two men wrestle it a few feet away, then run with it along the header to push it into the beam. A one-ton or even half-ton ball does not have to be moving very fast to develop considerable force, and the piece generally yields.

It behooves anybody involved in this sort of maneuver to be extremely careful of his hands. Jiggs yelled at the kid to be careful; I yelled at him to be careful; everybody cautioned him not to put his hands on the cable from which the ball was hanging.

We gave the piece two good raps with the ball, and it slid over. I dropped to the beam to wrench the holes around to their places and was sticking the second bolt when I heard the ball start up and the kid yell. Or the kid yelled and I realized the ball was going up. It was too much all at once to decipher which I was aware of first.

In any case, the kid had apparently been bracing himself with a hand on the load cable while watching me make up the piece, and Albert had got up on the load. The sheave, running up the cable as it rose, sheared off the boy's thumb with surgical neatness.

Albert's defense was threefold: He said that since we had finished with the ball, we were categorically aware that it would be taken away; he further insisted that he had yelled beforehand that he was getting up on the load; he rightly contended that only a horse's ass would stand with his hand on the cable. My response was that yes, we knew the ball should be moved away, but that neither of us had given him a signal. The kid should have given one (instead of standing around watching me), but hadn't. There was no resolution to the matter of a yelled warning; the fact that no one recalled hearing one wasn't proof that none had been given. Albert's greatest delight was in ringing his bells from as far away from the work area as he could get, presumably thereby demonstrating his visual acuity and depth perception. (A bell box is connected to a great length of cable, allowing its user to move around to any necessary place.) He may have yelled; from fifty feet away he could well have yelled unheard. And it was true that only a horse's ass would stand with his hand on the cable, but it was also true that the kid was a known horse's ass, and that because this was known, Albert should have made allowances.

I went to the hospital with the boy (the partner of an injured man traditionally accompanies him), returned to the job to report to Crockett how it had happened, spent the night brooding, and the following morning told Crockett that when there was another man available to take my place, I wanted out of the gang.

Patrick asked why I was taking a relatively minor accident so seriously, and I couldn't give him a reasonable answer. He asked if I were scared, and I said no, but that Albert's peculiar ways and his inability to imagine that he could ever make a mistake worried me enough to take away my pleasure. He said I wasn't being paid to enjoy myself. I said bullshit—the pleasure was the only justification for busting your balls all day, and the money was exactly the same bolting up or carrying plank. And I reminded him that he'd had indefinable misgivings about that industrial park job upstate and had wanted out, and I told him I had similar feelings about that particular raising gang.

I got lucky, winding up in a situation that permitted some variety: A week after I'd asked out, a new man took my place, and I went plumbing-up with Coley's gang (Coley was pushing by then). Yet, when any of the connectors was out, I was sent in his place, thus keeping my hand in while not daily destroying my rapidly aging body trying to keep up with kids and animals. ("Animal" is standard argot for a guy whose strength—and use thereof—exceeds his good sense, like King Kong or the Creature That Ate The Monster.)

When we knocked off for Christmas, the derricks stood on twenty. We had by then lost time to a number of problems besides the weather, and the job was far behind schedule. The truck drivers had walked out for a couple of days, and we'd been unable to do any erecting because we'd run out of material.* The elevator constructors had shut down for three days in some sort of dispute. The lathers had done the same thing at a different time, holding up work on the core. Sixteen weeks had passed since we'd tripped the first derrick, and under ideal circumstances we would have been nearer to thirty-five than twenty. (When things went properly, we jumped—that is, set all the iron for and moved the derrick up two floors—every four to four and a half days.)

Christmas Eve day there were snow flurries. They might have been heavy enough for us to shut down on another day, but not on that one, since it is regarded as a "tit" day. (December 24th and 31st are the only two such days in the year.) The job shuts down at noon, but everyone is paid for the entire day. Even the morning hours are relatively painless; everybody is full of holiday spirit and there is more conversation than labor.

At noon we all trooped over to McAnn's. Coley bought a round, announced that he had to catch a train at one o'clock, and left. Jiggs, who hadn't been seen near the derrick but once all morning, was drunk when we got there. Crockett came in, set the house up twice, and made a speech about "anybody who don't show up the day after tomorrow can consider himself fired" before leaving. Timmy sat down with Patrick and Big-Big and me and had a beer. He bristled when I asked him when he'd started drinking again.

"Who's drinkin'?" he said. "This's beer, not whiskey."

"Suit yourself," I said, shrugging.

"I will," he answered, scowling defensively at everybody at the table. "I damn well will." Nobody said anything.

However, he had only two beers before suddenly jumping up, wishing everyone a Merry Christmas, and walking out. Big-Big sighed.

"Chris'mas," he said, "is harder on some guys t'an ot'ers."

"You s'pose he's goin' down to the apartment?" asked Patrick.

"I don't know," I answered, "but on the chance that he might be, I don't think I will. It's the wrong time of year for heavy things, man; let's just sit here and let it happen slowly."

* In the city you cannot skirt this problem by predelivering the iron; there isn't any place to put it. The lack of storage room is part and parcel of the urban real estate economics discussed earlier.

"Yes," said Patrick, "let's just do that."

"T"at's fine wit' me," Big-Big offered, nodding his great head in ponderously thoughtful agreement.

"I'll get us a drink, I will," said Jiggs, knocking over his chair as he got up and cursing at it cheerfully.

We drank and told lies about childhood Christmases until late afternoon. Then we all got up to leave simultaneously, wishing the stay-behinds from other gangs a happy holiday. This produced a few rejoinders and a lot of silence.

"Your sister," Jiggs declared to the bar at large, apparently offended at the lack of response, "jumps on me for half a buck. Whaddaya t'ink about t'at?"

"'At's awright," called a voice from the rear, "she's not really my sis'er anyhow."

"Maybe I should sit on 'im," Big-Big wondered.

Outside we turned the corner and stopped to look up at the job. The iron from twenty down to fourteen stood black and naked against the gravel sky. Below fourteen were six floors girdled in canvas tarpaulins. From there to the street the outer sheath was more or less in place. (I say more or less, because there was not yet any glass, and there were many open places in the siding through which, at some future point, with the aid of a Chicago boom, materials would be taken in.)

"How much you figure we got up there, Jiggs?" I asked.

"Oh, I dunno," he said, working with his little finger at some wax in his ear, "sixteen, eighteen t'ousand tons, I guess."

We all nodded in reflection. It wasn't exactly an impressive figure, but it did have a certain ring to it.

"I've spent whole years in the sticks without hangin' that much iron," said Patrick.

"Well," Jiggs offered, "it's bigger'n a breadbox."

We shook hands all around and wished each other Merry Christmas. Jiggs headed off east; Big-Big lumbered away west. "What do you think, Patrick?" I asked. "Is it quittin' time yet?" After a moment he shook his head.

"I don't think so," he answered. "Let's go up to the Recovery Room and have the last one."

When we got on the Sixth Avenue bus, Patrick stood next to a pretty girl in a suede coat who was struggling to maintain control of a large collection of packages. "Ho Ho Ho!" Patrick bellowed in an imitation basso profundo while sticking out his stomach and patting it with both hands, "Merry Christmas! Carry your bundles, lady?"

"What the hell's the matter with you, buster?" she snarled. "You some kind of a nut?"

One Friday afternoon early in February, Coley invented the fire truck.

The middle derrick's twenty-fifth and twenty-sixth floor iron had been shaken out and stood in neat parallel rows on the plank floor. Half a dozen of us (the plumber-ups and a couple of plankies) were sitting on these beams drinking our coffee, when Coley, who was sidesaddle on the innermost piece in the group, suddenly grabbed at an empty fifty-gallon drum that stood nearby. He tipped it over toward himself at an angle, so that its rim resembled a steering wheel.

"Gimme a spud wrench," he called over his shoulder. I handed him mine, and he slammed the pointed end into the rusty side of the drum, creating a gear shift.

"Clang, clang, clang!" he called out. "Hurry up! Hurry up! All aboard!" A couple of the old bolter-ups looked at him like he was crazy, but the rest of us, realizing that the iron had become some sort of vehicle, swung round to face in the same direction that he was. "Eee-yoooww," he wailed, sirenish. Then, "mmrroom, mmrrrooom-oom," as he shifted gears. When we were tearing along at a pretty good clip, he spun the wheel to the left and leaned over with it while making screeching tire noises between his teeth. We heeled over with him. Somebody toward the rear took over the siren noises, enabling Coley to concentrate on the gear shifting mmrrooms and cornering squeals. Patrick, who was having his coffee on a header not far away, called over to ask where we were going.

"Fire on Seventh Avenue!" hollered Coley, between his various sound effects.

"Stop the truck!" I yelled. "Stop the goddam truck!"

"Eeeecchh!" screamed Coley, braking violently. We all pitched forward at the suddenness of the stop. "Whattsa matter?" he shouted.

"We forgot the ladders, for Chrissake," I yelled back. "Can't get up to the fire without ladders."

"Right on!" replied Coley. "We forgot the ladders. Harrison! Peter Putrid! Get the ladders!" Harrison, a normally quiet, middle-aged fellow who was the nearest thing we had to an animal in the plumbing-up gang and who therefore did most of the cable carrying and all of the turnbuckle turning, went off rather bemusedly looking for a ladder. Peter Putrid stood up and asked unhappily why Coley wanted ladders.

"Why?" Coley yelled at him. "Why? Because there may be women and children trapped and burnin' and about to die in the flames, you asshole! Get a ladder, God damn you!"

When Harrison and Peter Putrid returned with a pair of the short one-story ladders that the bolter-ups use, we arranged them one to each side of the truck, several men holding on to each. Coley shifted through the gears, the man in back again took up the siren, and we resumed our run, tearing through the streets at breakneck speed, screeching and leaning as one man around corners, pitching forward en masse at sudden slowdowns, tipping backward with the acceleration of rapid starts. Everybody on the floor broke off conversations to watch our progress. Crazy Albert tore the bottom out of his coffee container and used it, standing in front of us like a traffic cop, as a megaphone.

"This way!" he called, his voice through the styrofoam cup taking on an officious timbre. "Bring her forward, now!"

"You get the hell out of there, Albert!" I shouted at him. "The cornice's all charred and's liable to fall on you!" I never had managed to get to like Albert, and half wished it *would* fall on him.

The truck slid to a stop and Coley jumped out shouting, "Where away, man? Where away?"

" 'Where away'?"I yelled. "What the hell's on fire? A fuckin' ship?" Nobody got it.

"I see it!" shouted the man who had been the siren. "Up there!" He pointed to the east derrick's iron, some of which had been set, and on one intermediate-floor beam of which a short and skinny bolter-up sat munching on a Danish. The bolter-up, roused by the shouting from some private reverie, paused in full-mouthed confusion.

"Get t'at old lady outta t'at kitchen before she croaks wit' smoke ineration!" foghorned Burgess, the bolt-up pusher.

"I got'er!" responded Big-Big, who hadn't been in the fire truck at all but who had no intention of being left out, "I got'er!" He snatched one of the ladders and put it up to the header next to the bolter-up, who still sat with his mouth full. Harrison ran to help hold the foot of the ladder in place.

"You, there," came Coley's command in my general direction, "get a hose on this blaze, and be quick about it!" I grabbed the nearest air hose and disconnected the gun from its end. It popped loose with a great rush of air. (The hoses are inch and a half and the air pressure some eighty pounds.) Two other guys grabbed it at five- or six-foot intervals behind me, and we worked our way cautiously into the fire, spraying everything in sight. Fallen bolts and washers clattered away before the air jet, and residual patches of packed snow turned into clouds of icy dust. Big-Big shot up the ladder and grabbed the hapless bolter-up around the waist. He tossed the man over his shoulder like a sack of potatoes and came back down the ladder to the thunderous applause of all. When they were within three or four feet of the plank floor, Coley yelled, "My God, the poor old thing's on fire!" whereupon my hose gang and I ran over to spray our compressed air over victim and rescuer alike. Big-Big put the fellow down, and he ran off spewing profanities and pastry crumbs.

As the applause died away, Coley sat down on a pile of plank, giggling tearfully. Peter Putrid, also laughing in imitation hysteria, sank down beside him.

"Get away from me, numbnuts," said Coley. "The men don't fraternize with the chief!"

As Peter stood up looking hurt, Burgess could be heard in the distance, yelling after his vanishing bolter-up, "Get back here, you miserable miscarriage; I got a goddam building to put up!"

Jiggs's voice drifted in from the other end of the building. "Albert! Getcher ass down here, we got trucks ina street!"

So, the flames were out, but the fire still smoldered: Coley's game became an irregular feature of the job. Three or four more times during the course of the job, on slow afternoons, some disembodied voice would be heard calling, "Clang clang clang!" and the firehouse gang would come running from wherever they were, jump in the truck, and race off heroically.

Peter Putrid, whose sense of humor was but marginally developed anyway, quit playing with us when he finally realized that Coley was never going to let him drive the truck. We straightened him out in the spring, when on a harmlessly balmy Friday we decided that it was he who was on fire, and Big-Big saved him by pouring over him the entire contents of a ten-gallon water cooler.

As winter slowly plodded past, Timmy became more and more the man who was not there. He came to work most days, and was civil and sociable enough, but at the end of the day he vanished. Many nights he didn't come home, and when he did it was always so late that I was in bed. We often rode up to work together, but they were silent trips. I watched him on the job to see if he was shaking or sneaking nips, but learned nothing except that he didn't seem to be drinking. He did his work, answered when spoken to, and started no conversations. The only time I remember him offering a statement from Christmas through the next six weeks was the afternoon that two men were killed on the Grant Plaza. It happened in full view of our job and was seen by several of our men. At that time the Grant job was up and the ironworkers were gone, but finishing work was still underway. A window-washing scaffold hung on cables down six or eight floors from a pair of track-mounted davits on the roof. There was a man at work in the scaffold when the friction on one cable released, tipping the platform down ninety degrees and spilling the man out. When he fell to the roof of the eighth-floor setback, he landed atop a workman who was spreading tar. Both must have died instantly. Burgess and one of his bolter-ups were among the witnesses.

"T'at," said Burgess, "is why you can't pay me enough to be a window-washer—or a stone-derrickman, eit'er, for t'at matter. T'em dumb fucks, trustin' t'emselves to cables like t'at. You gotta be out of your mind." *

* This feeling, which revolves about self-reliance and partnership-reliance, is a general one. Burgess' statement about not being willing to trust his safety to a cable is altogether typical. An ironworker *does* trust himself, and he *must* trust his partner. He avoids, as much as possible, putting his trust in mechanical devices. I am quite willing

"What made the cable part?" asked someone.

"It didn't part," answered the other witness. "Look at it; it's still hangin' there."

"Then what happened?"

"Friction let loose," came another voice. A general discussion followed on how the friction (a drum brake) might have loosened. At the height of this babble Timmy made his lone remark.

"Friction doesn't 'let loose,' " he said, in an uncharacteristically loud voice. "It has to be released. Somebody on top had to cut it loose. Probably, since the man was alone in the scaffold, it was his own partner. Whoever it was did it without looking, and they should throw him over the side."

The vehemence with which Timmy said this brought the conversation to a halt. He walked away, but even after he had gone, no one resumed talking. We never did learn how it had actually happened.

By the middle of February we were on the thirtieth floor. One of the connectors on the east derrick got his leg caught in a bundle of iron while shaking out and broke it, and Timmy went up in his place. Crockett, who had seen Timmy handle himself all right on this building but who knew nothing of Timmy's drinking years, gave him the job as soon as he asked for it.

Watching him work, which inevitably triggered memories of his mornings on the bridge job ("But it's *my* iced tea!"), was an amazing experience. I couldn't escape the feeling that I was looking at somebody I'd never seen before. He was up this column and down that one, flitting across this header and back on the next, tiptoeing across needle beams so lightly that they didn't wiggle, even with sixty

---

to cling to a column with one arm and one leg while wrestling a header into place. I know from experience (and the use of this word indicates that there was a time when I did *not* know this) that I can. Because I know I can, I enjoy it. But I am not willing, any more than Burgess or Patrick or Coley or a lot of other people I know are, to trust my life to a cable whose upper end I can't even see.

Jobs in the city frequently go up in sight of other jobs, and the workmen watch each other. We watch, among others, the stone-derrickmen (who hang the limestone or marble slabs that face many buildings), and they watch us. They think we're a bit strange, but we know perfectly well that they are mad.

And what is one to make of coincidence? *The New York Times* reported, two weeks ago as I write this, a near-duplicate accident: A window-repairman working on 82nd Street fell because his harness broke. He landed on a coworker.

pounds of tools and bolts strapped to his body. He so successfully anticipated every move, going always to the right spot before each new piece came up, that I realized that he'd all along been watching every piece that went in on every floor.

"Who the hell is that?" Coley said, coming to stand beside me as I watched. He sounded as surprised as I was. "That's not our old shaky Timmy—it can't be."

"I don't know," I answered. "I never saw him in a raisin' gang before. The first time I met him he couldn't stand erect on a four-lane highway without the aid of a handrail."

"I know, I know," said Coley, softly.

The other connector's name was Henry. He was a local man, about Timmy's age, and had been on the job since that derrick was tripped. He expected, since he'd been there all along and since Timmy was a new man and from out of town, to be the lead connector. He knew where all the iron went, knew everybody in the gang, and by all rights he *should* have been the lead connector. But these positions have a way of solving themselves, and the two men hadn't worked together an hour before it was clear to both of them that Timmy should call the shots. Timmy beat Henry to the choker after every piece, regardless of who made up first; he trotted down the next header, laying out all the bolts that would be required for the intermediate pieces while Henry was still running up the nuts on the last piece in the previous bay. He did not do these things as though a contest were taking place; he just did them. His normal pace was faster than the other man's. Timmy didn't yell, but he did point out, here and there, easier and faster ways to make given connections, and Henry yielded to Timmy's expertise.

I hope I can avoid being misunderstood here. I am not saying that Timmy suddenly stood revealed as the world's greatest connector. He was no more than very good, and I've seen a number who were much better. (I daren't name names, since whoever I leave out will undoubtedly come looking for me with blood in his eye.) All I'm saying is that he was good and that I was surprised. I'd have been impressed even if he'd been just barely able to get through one day, because the man I'd thought he was would have failed.

At the end of the day Timmy was dressed and gone as quickly and as silently as ever. Patrick and Coley and I went uptown for a beer. We talked about nothing in particular, until Coley said, "Hey, Patrick. You notice Timmy's gone connecting?"

"I noticed," said Patrick.

"Does nice work," Coley continued, bent on paying Timmy a compliment irrespective of Patrick's obvious lack of enthusiasm.

"Glad to hear it," Patrick replied. I opened my mouth to do a little pushing, tired of the mystery of Patrick's hostility and wanting the thing out of the way once and for all, but the blandness of his voice told me that I wouldn't get anywhere, and I shut it again. Before I fully convinced myself to leave the subject alone, I opened and closed my mouth several more times, looking, I suppose, rather like a goldfish in an airless bowl. Coley, too, seemed to conclude that it was a subject best dropped, and we went on to other things.

On April 4th the center derrick was jumped to the thirty-eighth floor. It was the third from last jump, and on the basis of the old saw about three strikes being out in any ball game, we all began to sense that the end was coming. Actually, it would be six weeks more before we topped out, and another seven weeks beyond that before the job was wholly completed (as far as the ironworkers' part in it was concerned); yet, as John Kenneth Galbraith said about something else entirely, "the end had come, but it was not yet in sight."

It had come in the sense that what remained to be built was more an extension of what had been built than it was anything new. We were so used to putting up floors exactly like other floors that a kind of somnambulance had set in, and without the artificial injection of a finishing point, we might have gone on forever simply adding more iron. There was no longer the sense of rising from the ground; we were so far above the street that changes were hard to see. Pedestrians were mere dots, and even large trucks appeared so tiny that they all looked alike and even seemed to be the same color. The horizon, which earlier had expanded significantly with every jump, had some floors ago taken on a static quality. I was sorry when this happened; on the lower floors it had been exciting to see how much more of the world could be seen with each jump. (Is it too sloppy a sentiment to compare the rising of the building to a child's growth? There is something of that in it. When we had first begun everything towered above us; we could see barely to the knees of the adult buildings. But with each jump we gained on them, and were within a few months looking down on the roofs of the lesser buildings. When nearly everything was shorter than we were, the excitement of growing was over.)

Early in January the horizon extended far enough for us to see the Hudson; a month later the East River came into view. As the weeks passed, the Jersey shoreline and Queens appeared, and finally the Triboro Bridge and on clear days the Throg's Neck and Whitestone bridges. Near us the only buildings that blocked the view were those in Rockefeller Center, the McGraw-Hill Building and the office tower just south of it, the new buildings on the east side of Sixth Avenue, and the Telephone Building on 42nd Street. The Empire State, whose considerable magnificence is enhanced by its position as the only really tall structure in its neighborhood, blocked from view all but one edge of the World Trade Center towers three miles to the south.

In the dead of winter, arriving for breakfast at the local coffee shop well before dawn, I always stopped before entering for a moment to stare up at the dark top of our building. But by the time it reached up thirty stories and more, there was no longer any point in looking: Changes and new heights were too far above to be seen.

By the middle of April an anxious note had begun to enter into the men's conversations: The hall was rumored to be getting crowded and work was said to be slowing down. Word spread that Atlas had nothing on their books and that Dreier was getting out of the erection business altogether. American Bridge and Bethlehem Steel, the two giants, were said to be pulling out of New York.*

"Tuck your money in t'e bank, boys," said Jiggs. "It's gonna be slow for a year or more."

"How do you know how long it's gonna be?" asked Peter Putrid.

"Ain't no holes in t'e ground, dummy," answered Jiggs. "And when t'ere ain't no holes, t'ere ain't no work."

* This proved untrue, but rumors exist to communicate fear, not truth. Hyperbole is the soul of rumor.

"There's holes all over the place," argued Peter.

"Not for us t'ere ain't. Little holes don't count. Little holes are for t'e lathers and t'eir goddam concrete jobs. You just tuck some money away, boy, 'cause you're liable to be outta work for a long time."

Peter Putrid walked off looking worried. He was engaged, and held only an apprentice book, and rightly wondered if it was a good time to be getting married.

Crockett came to Patrick and me with the same advice that Jiggs had given his gang. "I'll keep you two and Coley and Timmy on as long as I can," he said, "but things are gettin' tight. This company's got nothin' else planned, and I don't even know where I'm goin' myself, so there's nothin' I can do for you guys from out of town. Hang on to your money, because you won't be gettin' anything out of the hall. The Indians are goin' to be paid off pretty soon after we top out, and then you guys. If I were you, I'd run up home some weekend soon to put my name in the pot."

When he'd left, Patrick asked me what I was going to do. I said I didn't know, but that I guessed I'd make out one way or another, and besides, a slowdown couldn't last forever.

"True," agreed Patrick. "It'll pick up, sooner or later. I got a friend runs a little snake outfit; we'll give him a call when this job's done." (A "snake" outfit is one that is nonunion.) He made a fist and hit me a playful jab on the shoulder. "Hey," he said (and somehow I knew that what was coming next would be the universal ritual speech of an ironworker who's just been laid off or fired), "what of it? I was lookin' for a job when I found this one, right?"

The weather warmed and the rains diminished. There were now, in May, more men on the job than ever. We still had our full complement of ironworkers on top, and the other trades were operating at full speed everywhere else. In addition to the lathers and rough carpenters, plumbers, steamfitters, electricians, and so forth, there were now added finishing carpenters, tin-knockers, tile workers, sprinkler installers, door buckers, glaziers, marble cutters, asbestos workers, mail chute installers, pipe fitters, boiler makers, and more. There were white-hatted bosses for all these men, and inspectors for every trade. In and out of the job moved timekeepers, accountants, real estate brokers, zoning experts, arthitects, and mechanical and structural engineers. Getting up to the top through this host of people became more and more difficult; the elevators were in constant demand, and the stairwells were jammed with the clutter of the plasterers' sawhorses and planks.

A Chicago boom was rigged for hoisting other trades' materials. The lower floors, as the boom's lifts were completed, were glassed in. The plaza that we'd had to shove sideways the summer before was now a cement field covered with concrete trucks offloading at the hoists and rod trucks dumping loads of re-bar for the lathers. Finished marble walls appeared in the lobby. Suddenly, instead of merely walking onto the site and heading for the elevators from anyplace, the street-level glass went in, and it became necessary to look for a doorway.

Spring is the best time of year to finish a job. The realization that the cold and wet of winter are once more past calls forth an extra enthusiasm, regardless of how far along a job is, and when to this is added the adrenalin that flows when the end of a job is in sight, the total exceeds the sum of the parts.

Coley became more finicky about truing up the iron. Before, if a column had been lying a half-inch out, he had usually said to hell with it. He now demanded that we hang a guy and suck it over plumb. "We're too near the top to let these things go, anymore," he pointed out. "We got to be dead on the money on forty-four, and we have to make sure now that we aren't goin' to be too far out to get back." So we hung more cables than usual, and took more pains than usual, and Harrison worked his animal butt off turning the buckles tighter than ever, and somehow all this got done in less than usual time.

Albert finally managed to get on Patrick's nerves to the point where Patrick lost his temper. I was sitting on a header, holding the plumb line, when Patrick shot by me, jumped from the header to one of the derrick guys, and went sliding down. He grabbed Albert by the throat, shoved him up against a four-foot-high bundle of iron, and told him that if he ever again did *anything* with the friggin' hook without being told by him personally to do it, he was going to throw him over the side. Albert tried to get out of Patrick's grip, but wasn't nearly strong enough to succeed, and every time he began squirming, Patrick bounced him into the iron, until at one especially hard bounce the load fell over and Patrick and Albert landed on top. Jiggs jumped into the dispute and there was a three-way shouting match, but the coffee boy appeared then with Jiggs' six pack, and after Jiggs handed Albert and Patrick each a can, they all sat on the fallen iron to drink it, and things were gradually smoothed over.

"Must be a full moon or somethin'," Patrick said, after work in McAnn's. "I very seldom lose my temper."

"Nah," said Jiggs. "It's spring and t'e end of t'e job. T'ings get bent out of shape near t'e end, t'at's all."

"Lissen," put in Big-Big, "he gives you any more trouble, you tell me, and I'll sit on 'im."

We topped out on May 15th. It was a beautifully clear, warm spring day, which added appreciably to the number of dignitaries attending the ceremonies. Jiggs' derrick got the honor, not so much because they were naturally ahead of the other derricks as because the company's public relations department wanted the flag column to be the most visible. The most visible part of the job was its Sixth Avenue face.

In the middle of the morning a truck arrived bearing just one column. Both the truck and its load were clean, and when the driver of the truck jumped out, he, too, was clean. I learned this not from looking (we were much too high to see such detail), but from Patrick, who'd gone to the street to hook the column to the load cable.*

"You won't believe this," he gasped, out of breath from running up the last ten flights of stairs in an effort to beat the column to the floor, "but Filthy Fred is drivin' the truck, and he's wearin' new clothes." Filthy Fred is justifiably famous for the amount of dirt he carries around on his person. "The company must have bought 'em for him."

The column came up with its giant American flag attached, and Patrick and his partner wrestled it into its splice plates. When they

---

* This was a special procedure used for this one column only. Ordinarily, a truck brings up to nine columns, and as many as three are wrapped up at a time. They are lifted to the plank floor and offloaded for tripping later. For show, the flag column was hooked up in the street with the setting shackles, permitting it to be picked and set in one operation. It was also the only time anyone ever saw a clean truck and a clean driver.

finished, various luminaries took turns standing beside it in what they imagined to be laboring poses, while lesser functionaries took their pictures. Jiggs managed to talk one portly gentleman into striking a stance in which he appeared to be installing the column with the aid of a three-pound beater. We had a terrible time keeping our faces straight while this was being recorded for posterity. A three-pound beater is a little hammer with a six-inch handle. You might be able to club your mother-in-law to death with one, if you hit her often enough.

After the back patting was over and the chairmen and vice-presidents disappeared, we went back to work, although not very seriously. Coley said we had some work to do lower down, and we dutifully followed him to the fifteenth floor. As we got out of the elevator, it was immediately obvious that it was a finished floor, completely glassed in.

"What is this shit, Coley?" asked Harrison. "We ain't got any work here."

"When I tell you we got work to do," Coley intoned, "we got work to do. Just shut up and follow me." We followed him through a maze of insulation bundles and unidentifiable boxes until he stopped in an area whose perimeter was piled so high with these materials that it was effectively isolated from the rest of the floor. "This," said Coley proudly, "is my office, and this," he reached into a small recess between two bundles and withdrew a large brown paper bag, "is our work." From the bag he produced four bottles of champagne.

"Ahh," said everybody, and we sat down cross-legged on the floor.

At three o'clock, when we were changing clothes to get ready for the party, Patrick said, "Where were you guys at lunch, for Chrissake? I looked all over for you."

"Busy, busy, busy," I answered. "Got no time to fool around with mere lunch." Then I gave it away by hiccuping.

I don't remember a whole lot about the party. It was held in the banquet room of a nearby restaurant and featured good food and what the men admiringly referred to as "top shelf" liquor, and there were rumors that in order to have it so handsomely staged, Crockett and the other pushers had footed a piece of the bill. None of them has ever admitted to this, however, so we still don't know.

I sat in a corner most of the evening, suffering from complicated reflections about the past ten months—about how it was that I'd been so worried about being able to handle the work at one time but had since been dangled over the side of a building and had several times tripped while walking along beams, with only brief and rather casual thoughts of dying. I remember that I meant to talk to Patrick about such things, but that when I tried to, he said something like, "No, man, alcohol and philosophy are like oil and water." And I remember that I told him to piss off and went down to a bar called Allen's on 14th Street and drank away the rest of the night. And that I had a hell of a time getting to work the next day.

Plenty of iron remained to be set. The topping-out column is the *first* piece on the highest elevation, not the last. Standing it up doesn't, in spite of the ceremonies, mark the end of anything, but it does mark the beginning of the reduction of the labor force: As each operation is performed for the last time, the man who performed it is let go. On that job all of the column splices were bolted first, then welded. As these welds were finished, the welding gang shrank. Within a week about a third of the bolter-ups were gone. In the same week the plank gang was cut in half, and by the end of the second week it was gone altogether. What little plank carrying remained was taken over by the holdovers from other depleted gangs.

Timmy's derrick was the last to get all its iron up. He died before it was all in place. He and Henry had spread a few planks in a completed bay for the welders to sit on while working. Somehow, Timmy, in hurrying from one side of the bay to the other, managed to put his inside foot down an inch to the right of where he should have, and the plank, which had a slight warp in it, rocked. At least, that's Henry's analysis. I didn't see that part of it. Coley and I were on the plank floor two stories beneath the connectors, and saw nothing until we looked up when we heard Henry yell, "Watch out!" The yell was instinctive and of course a waste of breath, since there was nothing to yell about until it was too late. Timmy tumbled over the side, passing by us almost close enough to touch. He fell in silence, and no sound from the impact of his body on the concrete plaza reached up to us. For awhile the only sounds that registered on me were Henry's repeated cries of "Oh Jesus! Oh Jesus!" Then, as what had happened dawned on the others in his gang, there were random shouts and calls and finally the scuffling noises of men rushing to the building's edge. Coley and I just sat down where we were. I turned my head the opposite way, looking toward the western end of the job, and saw that Patrick was the only man there. He was standing on the top, on a header, his arms hanging loosely at his sides. He was too far away for me to see the expression on his face.

Eventually I got up, put my tools away, climbed down, changed clothes, and left. Most of the other men were already gone.

I'm tempted to pause here to indulge in some probably sappy philosophizing, but am resolved not to give in. The man died because he made a mistake, and that's about all there is to it. These things happen. It's true that I can't walk near that building without seeing him hurtle past me, and it's true that this sight produces a brief wave of nausea and sets me to wondering Why, but I know perfectly well that no answer will appear. It was an Accident. "Accident" is a short way of saying "Causes Permanently Concealed."

Besides, as Isak Dinesen said, "What is man, when you come to think upon him, but a minutely set, ingenious machine for turning, with infinite artfulness, the red wine of Shiraz into urine?"

Many more operations remained before our part of the job was done. After all the floors were poured, we still had eight floors of plumbing-up cables to cut loose. Minor alterations remained to be made in some of the still open cellar iron. All three derricks had to come down.* Some welding was still to be done, and there were a few

* One derrick is used (in this case the center one) to assist in the dismantling of the others. Their sections are lowered to the street with it; all heavy tools, the one-car-garage-sized tool house, and various scale boxes and other materials are also lowered. When nothing remains up top but the one derrick, it is separated into halves and temporary guys are rigged to hold it in place. The one half is used to take apart the other, the remaining half is lowered through the opening beneath it, and it is broken into sections. A Chicago boom is then used to snake these sections out over the side and lower them to the street. A temporary sheave is rigged above the Chicago boom, and the boom's load cable is passed through it. Using this cable, the boom itself is lowered, the cable cut free, and the sheave removed by hand. Once the small holes in the floors through which all these cables passed have been patched, there is no sign that anything other than the building itself was ever there.

hundred odd bolts yet to be stuck. There were a few pieces of falsework (the temporary iron within the core) still to be taken out. There were a few bent beams that had to be heated and straightened. But this was all detail work, and dull. I stayed on despite the boredom, because I didn't know how long it might be before I could find another job, but the place had become strange. The shanty was practically empty. The nails that had held so many jackets and overalls and sweatshirts were nearly all unused. Patrick had gone when the raising gang was laid off, and Coley quit the following week. The punks were gone, and twice a day we argued, the eight of us remaining, about who would go down for the coffee.

On June 24th, Crockett came over to me while I was making up a bundle of old cables and told me that it was my last day. He had to lay somebody off, he said, and the other stay-behinds were all local books. He sounded almost apologetic. He said something about being sorry that there wasn't anything he could do for me, and how it was too bad that I didn't have a local book. Then he handed me my check. This slowdown was temporary, he said, and perhaps we'd all get together again when things picked up. I told him it sure as hell wasn't his fault I didn't have the book and that I couldn't see where I had any complaints coming. I'd been employed in the city without a significant break since the first day I'd come down, local book or no, and had made pretty good money during that time. More money than enemies, anyway, I hoped.

"Well, there you are," he said, and after shaking hands, he walked off toward the stairs.

"Hey, Crockett!" I called after him. He turned. "You know, I was lookin' for a job when I found this one." He laughed.

"I don't care if you sneak out," he said, "but don't let anybody see you leavin' with all your gear."

I finished up the bundle and smoked a cigarette before going down to the shanty to gather up my things.

I have left out much. There never seemed to be a chance to tell about Melvin the Mungo Master's smoky but harmless deliberate fire, which led to a spud wrench versus fire axe standoff between the ironworkers and a half-dozen members of the New York City Fire

Department. And a funny story about a fellow who, the night of the topping-out party, leaned over so far backward on the street while trying to admire the job that he fell backward through a plate glass window, cutting himself rather spectacularly. And the time one of our men performed such a strange act at the massage parlor across the street that the madam sent word that no ironworkers would ever again be admitted.

But there are still buildings to put up, and still gin mills to tell stories in, and if you should join us in one of them some night, we'll tell you the rest of it. It's easier to tell stories than to write them, anyway.